# Glamour

## IN THE SKIES

# *Glamour*
## IN THE SKIES

## The Golden
## Age of the
## Air Stewardess

### LIBBIE ESCOLME-SCHMIDT

This book is dedicated to all the 'Stargirls', air hostesses and stewardesses in British Airways and its predecessors during those golden years of flying. Their enthusiasm, dedication and participation in the airline industry contributed to and furthered its development and vision.

To my sons, Trader and Rupert, who share my fervour and passion for aircraft and travel. As youngsters wanting a bedtime story, they often simply said: 'Tell us another BOAC story, Mum!'

First published 2009
Reprinted July 2009

The History Press
The Mill, Brimscombe Port
Stroud, Gloucestershire, GL5 2QG
www.thehistorypress.co.uk

© Libbie Escolme Schmidt, 2009

The right of Libbie Escolme Schmidt to be identified as the Author
of this work has been asserted in accordance with the
Copyrights, Designs and Patents Act 1988.

British Library Cataloguing in Publication Data.
A catalogue record for this book is available from the British Library.

ISBN 978 0 7524 4904 3

Typesetting and origination by The History Press
Printed in Great Britain

# Contents

Pat Burgess in 1958 on the aircraft steps leading to a BEA Pionair (Douglas DC3 Dakota).

# Foreword

# Frederick Forsyth CBE
## The Ladies Who Flew

I recall with great clarity the days when to make an international journey by air was an adventure and a glamorous one at that. And there were few things more glamorous than the clothes model young women whose job was to look after the often terrified passengers – the stewardesses.

It all began before the Second World War and therefore before my time. But it was still quite an experience in 1952 when I made my first air journey – from Northolt to Bielefeld, then a British base in Germany – with BEA.

I was thirteen and although I had crossed the Channel by ferry each summer for four years, this was my first time by air. I forget the aircraft, save that it had twin propeller engines and like most airliners then was a derivative of something originally designed for the Royal Air Force.

By today's standards (Heathrow was still to open) Northolt was absolutely miniscule and formalities almost zero. Check-in took a few seconds and the valise was carried away by hand. The passport was stiff, blue, glittering and brand new. Passport officers actually smiled. No one was frisked. All men smoked Players or Senior Service. It somewhat resembled my father's golf club.

And the stewardesses! The ground hostess who led the crocodile of passengers out to the airplane ('airliner' is a bit grand for this old kite) were smart enough and shapely enough but the smiling Hartnell model at the top of the steps was to die for – at least if you were thirteen.

Back then international, let alone intercontinental, air travel was for a few only. This was long before the package holiday at an all-affordable price. Benidorm was a Spanish fishing hamlet. Male passengers wore suits and ties. It was a cross between grand as in formal and tally-ho chaps – as the aircrew had all flown something in the war.

But lest we get any wrong impression, it was also much tougher in other ways on passengers and crew. The seats were much narrower – but so were backsides! One stooped to get up the aisle. Once the petrol engines roared into life, the noise was terrific. Airborne, the kites bucked and rocked through the turbulence, flying at about 10,000ft and therefore right through the storm clouds.

Through it all the young goddesses in the creaseless uniforms weaved down the aisle with trays of tea and coffee – I do not recall any food on the Germany run.

But it was BEA's sister company BOAC that did the long-hauls and hammering along from Northolt to Basra via Gibraltar must have taken the stamina of a triathlon 'gold'.

How ironic that we are back to real beds on the long-hauls; they had them in those days also, before the many years of seats-only. I recall the adverts showing one of the smiling goddesses tucking up a beaming businessman, and outside the porthole the moon wore a nightcap!

It is a long haul from there to the present Airbus with an Economy Class (sorry, World Traveller) looking in the half darkness like a snoring troopship; to the ripple-free ride at 37,000ft; to the Atlantic crossed in seven hours without disturbing Reykjavik or Gander; to the X-rays and body searches; to the presumption that you will try to hi-jack the aircraft if allowed to keep your nail-clippers; to the rainless race from seat to taxi-rank without ever emerging under an open sky; and from the catwalk model 'airline stewardess' who, despite the title, is more a waitress and coat checker.

One still flies, of course. And each visit to Heathrow means once again to be enveloped in a world of security checks, computerised booking, impersonal greetings, waxen smiles and anonymity. But not glamour. That went out with the ladies who people this book.

*Frederick Forsyth*

# Introduction

This book is about the golden girls of flying and how they made their contribution to civil aviation history. It is not about comparisons with today. Air transport must surely be one of the most dynamic industries to emerge this century. At the turn of the century travelling by air was unimaginable as a concept. Within thirty years people were travelling around the world with speed and relative comfort. Within seventy years they were doing it at twice the speed of sound.

As a young university student living in Brisbane, I used to watch the TAA aircraft fly over my grandmother's house in Clayfield. About an hour later, I would see a very glamorous TAA air hostess walk past the house to her accommodation next door. I found it incredibly exciting to think that just an hour before she had been up in the skies in that aircraft. She looked so confident, elegant and mysterious. Where had she been that day? I had no idea that many years later, I would also be up there in the skies. Civil aviation opened up to me a world of travel, education, friendship, unique experiences and a fascination for aircraft. This career developed in me skills that I did not know I possessed, all of which were later to influence my life. It provided the impetus for other careers and eventually led me to start my own company in Brisbane and run it for seventeen years. It also provided me with the incentive to write this book.

In September 2003, I was on a personal mission. I was going to the UK to do research for this book on stewardesses in British Airways and its predecessors. This meant I had to go to London, to begin to put my goal into action. Coming in to land at Heathrow, the PA system, as usual, announced our arrival time and the weather: 'This is your Captain speaking … Captain Janet Spencer.' The voice was female. There was a female captain in charge of this sturdy and impressive 747. 'This is an omen,' I thought. The sound of her voice seemed to encapsulate how things have changed and what a long way women have progressed in civil aviation. We were also coming up to the celebration of seventy-five years of stewardesses in flight, and Concorde had a female captain.

My primary sources have been the surveys, tapes, discs, letters and telephone calls which came in from all over the world. There were the interviews with the numerous contributors. When many of the survey questions elicited the same sort of reply I have condensed them as historical fact. I spent many months interviewing stewardesses, several from each decade, and discovered that there was an abundance of exciting material to use. Their contributions, including memorabilia, are marvellous material which in itself tells a story. I have used secondary sources as listed in the bibliography.

The interest in this book was worldwide. Stewardesses from Pan Am, TWA, United Airlines and Qantas all asked if they could contribute. What I did discover was the lack of historical material available about the women in civil aviation in the United Kingdom, particularly British Airways and its predecessors. There were a few autobiographies of ex-BOAC stewardesses, which I have used as a valuable resource. Stewardesses in the USA and Australia have produced several books celebrating their contribution to flying careers, and Qantas has written about their first sixty-five years on its in-flight service.

The evolution of the stewardess reflects the social and cultural changes of our times. My intention is to bring the past alive, to capture the atmosphere. It is said that history should evoke all the immediacy of the present. This book is primarily about the females, not the aircraft. There are countless experts in the technical field of aviation history and I do not claim to be one of them. Besides, a great deal has already been written about aircraft and pilots. My focus is on the women and how they have left their legacy to civil aviation history. Today and yesterday, stewardesses have contributed to the success of a flight for passengers, mainly because they are female. However, as the airline industry has evolved, so have stewardesses. In this book I hope to illustrate this historical journey. There is a story here of all who came before – the trailblazers for the career as it is now.

In discussions between the women and me, it was decided that, where possible, maiden names would be used (their flying name). Only one contributor, out of several hundred, asked to be anonymous. There were also those who asked that their comments not be attributed to them, but wished these comments to be included.

I am not claiming this is a full, detailed and historical record, as my interest has to some extent been limited to the interviews and surveys I carried out with the women. How did I find them? It was not through British Airways. Owing to the privacy policy of most corporations and organisations, including BA, I have accessed these wonderful women from their own private lists, in-house gatherings, advertisements and mainly via the bush telegraph and message stick. My aim throughout for what follows is that this history is to be fun, frank and factual!

The story starts in 1936 and ends in 1980, the years many of my colleagues and I feel represent the Golden Age of Stewardesses.

# Preface

## The Golden Age

The Golden Age is known in Classical Literature as time by which other eras of time are measured. It is usually seen as a time in history where there is an atmosphere of optimism, excitement, creativity and a feeling of boundless opportunity.

Hundreds of the stewardesses with whom I was in contact while writing this book commented on the Golden Age in civil aviation. They all agreed that the four decades from 1935 epitomised this concept. It seemed that the magnificent Jumbo Jet, after only a few years in service, changed civil aviation forever. However, this book is not a comparison with flying as we know it today.

So what did change? The passengers felt that a great deal of the personal service had disappeared and that the journeys had become too long and more arduous. For the crew members, the longer sectors with the much larger crews brought to an end the once unique camaraderie. They also considered that the passengers became more demanding. The halcyon days of flying were over for both passengers and crew.

When I asked Andy Bennett (1972–1998) if she missed flying, she summed up her thoughts, similarly held by so many of the other stewardesses, by saying, 'Well no, because that sort of flying doesn't exist anymore.'

The Golden Age was over. However, it is now fondly remembered by many in the pages to come...

*Much have I travelled in the realms of gold,*
*And many goodly states and kingdoms seen.*
*– Keats*

# Acknowledgements

*I* should like to express my warmest gratitude to various people who have helped with this book.

To all the adventurous women who flew with BSSA, your exciting recollections were an inspiration. To the BEA, BOAC and BA stewardesses who contributed so much personal documentation and memorabilia, their wish being that I completed this book. Without their information there would not be this history of the Golden Age.

To Geoff Thomas, noted aviation author and journalist, who is a mine of information about aircraft and for his additional photos and sound advice. Thank you to Trevor Nash, a former Fleet Street journalist who worked with BOAC for many years in the PR and Press Department for his editorial assistance. To the delightful, ebullient, talented and positive Oni (Ione) Wyatt for her brilliant cartoons. I first saw these when she was on one of my earliest training courses. A talented cartoonist and illustrator with an adroit sense of humour, she encapsulates so much of our airline history and experience. I thank her for her time, commitment and attention to detail, scanning hundreds of photos and documents. Her patience and continual good humour were invaluable. Additional photography by my daughter-in-law, Nikki Schmidt. Gillian Sparrow for her knowledge and interest in our uniforms over the years. To Hugh J. Yea, the noted writer on commercial and military aviation history, for confirming facts and details of those very early years so graciously and meticulously. And Alan Gallop, a mentor by default, whose vast experience in writing was shared with me through many tips. He continually offered encouragement and was always at the other end of the telephone.

BA girls such as Virginia Sheehy, Delia Creedy, Peggy Thorne, Jean Melville, Cynthia White, Theresa Kwa, Audrey Iliffe, Tess Curtin, Olive Carlisle, Elizabeth Kirby, Val Selwood, Sally Brotherton, Sheila Luke, Jeannie Sutherland, Susan Graham, Judy Beachell, Andrea Bennett, Gaynor Jones, Patricia Dickin, Dr Lesley Runnalls, Mary Warwick and Mary Colley ex-BEA. To the focus groups organised by stewardesses to gather information, and all the contributors who offered photos from their own personal collections, crew memorabilia, copies of material and those who sent tapes, cuttings from newspapers, extracts from their diaries and log books, emails and phone calls with additional information, and personal memoirs. Thank you to Joan Crane for allowing me access to your unpublished and informative memoir of your BEA days. Retired stewardesses Sylvia Kirtley and Jean Gorton who persistently researched facts. All these women shared their insights and gave exceptional support and encouragement. To my old buddy and another stern critic, author Peter Chandler. To many retired crew members like Sue and Roger Kempson and Richard Cragg, charming people who would answer my simplest queries with grace and forbearance. Friends such as the Hon. Diana Mc Gill and Trader Faulkner, Nick Day and Robin Voelcker in London who gave me accommodation, and fed the 'inner person'.

Pat Pearce MBE and her Dreamflight team for assisting me to get some of the earliest surveys out, and whose wonderful work for Dreamflight inspired this book. To the many women I interviewed and who brainstormed with me. Lyn Watts, BA Qld Manager, who enabled me to transport piles and piles of manuscripts back and forth across the world. Captains Gerry Holland, John Hutchison, Harry Hopkins, Peter Riley, Ken Emmott, John D'Arcy, Peter Royce, the late Roger Gorton and David Holloway who each contributed a piece about an aircraft from their perspective. To Captain Peter Royce for his technical advice and clarifying questions from the material sent to me. Qantas Captain Ian Flett and Engineer Officer John Douglas for input re aircraft details, and a very special mention to retired Middle East Airlines Captain Des Dieckmann for aircraft indexing.

To Celia Day, a very special woman who offered to help me from the first day I started writing and was always there for me. Celia retyped vast quantities of this book, her calming influence, continual support and contagious sense of humour meant we shared many very special and memorable moments. Wise, warm and generous throughout, I valued her steadfast support.

Six young wonder women – Caroline Cooper, Nikola Errington, Lara Squire, Lauren Insch, Courtney Douglas and Francisca Voges – absolute whizzes on the pc, uncomplaining PAs who gave untiring and stoical service to this project. Thank you to Chantal Yaldo in the UK, my emergency PA. Peter Adamson for his computer help and especially Mark Vilimaa, who rescued me countless times with my laptop dramas. The best neighbour in the world for a writer! To Rod Cobain, another computer whiz, and Rod Bencke of CASA.

Emeritus Prof Bob Milns of the Classics Dept. Uni of Qld for suggestions and style for the surveys, and academic and author Martin Stuart Fox for editing ideas, suggestions and advice. Dear friends Margery East and Chris Kerridge, always at the ready to sort and file surveys and keep the paperwork on track. Tony Cocklin, who is a walking encyclopaedia on the airline world.

Finally to an old and dear school friend, Miriam Rogers, who ruthlessly cut and pasted and edited... an English teacher for years, so who was I to argue? Enduring gratitude to her and fellow grammarian and husband Peter Rogers, who were both so generous with their time; I relished our numerous brainstorming sessions. Her candour and guidance I valued, although I don't think she thought so at the time! To Michele Hyde, whose proof reading skills were tested to extremes. My editor Amy Rigg and fellow editor Emily Locke and the friendly team at The History Press for their patience and belief in me. Finally my dearest friend Professor Nadja Alexander, University of Queensland, for editorial advice and advice on simply how to hang in there and for reminding me that writing is rewriting.

I must point out that British Airways plc has had no involvement in the editing or publishing of *Glamour in the Skies: The Golden Age of the Air Stewardess*, although it has permitted their photographs and material to be used, for which I thank them. Accordingly, none of the views expressed in this book are those of British Airways, which makes no representations or warranties about the accuracy, completeness or suitability for any purpose of the information contained within this book. The majority of the material is from the stewardesses' own private collections and their personal archives.

And finally thank you to all the wonderful and willing women who responded so painstakingly in completing the lengthy surveys. I appreciate so much your knowledge, wit, understanding and honesty. Mary Alexander, Vee Allworth, Cynthia Arpthorp, Kathleen [Kay] Bailey, Pamela Banfill, Susan Ann Bannerman, Wyn Behenna, Andrea Bennett, Diana Beresford Davis, Helen Beresford Smith, Judith Black, June Blackler, Diana Borthwick, Heather Bradley, Valerie Brand, Susane Brattle, Jane Briggs, Sally Brotherton, Susan Brown, Audrey Cartmell, Caroline Chambers, Margaret Clegg, Caroline Closs, Lisa Clifford, Mavis Clough, Veronica Collen-Smith, Linda Cowe, Audrey Crome, Mary Crosbie, Pamela Crouch, Gwen Currie, Shirley Dakin, Lorna Dand, Sybil Daniel-Tanner, Diana Davis, Kay Dempsey, Patricia Dowding, Margaret Earle, Jill Edmonds, Elisabeth Eker, Terry Erasmus, Anne Evans, Judy Farquharson, Pip Feeney, Sue Fendick, Shirley Fogg, Elissa Forbes, Sarah Forsyth, Patricia Foster Hall, Betty

E. Fox, Angela Froude, Anne Fullagar, Diana Furness, Joan Gardner, Margaret Gerke, Heather Gjertsen, Betty Goodfellow, Evelyn Goodliffe, Mary Gordon, Margaret Gordon, Helen M.S. Gough, Susan Graham, Sheila Mary Grant, Jean Haines, Gaynor Halliday, Veronica [Roni] Hardiman, Jeannette Hartley, Joan Haskett, Enid Hewitt, Kitty Howell, Mary Hughes, Barbara Hulme, Yoshi Ishikawa, Patricia Jones, Joan Kelly, Pat Kerr, Maureen Kinally, Brenda King, Kay Kircher, Theresa Kwa, Sylvia Ladley, Jeannie Lardner, Kathy Lavers, Frankie Lief, Joanne Luchian, Sheila Jean Luke, June Malcolm, Annetta Markman, Olive Marshall, June Martin, Michiko Masuda, Jennifer Maxwell, Sue McGuire, Carol McIntyre, Josephine McKay, Jean McLaren, Freda Moore, Gloria Morrison, Jean Patricia Nourse, Margaret Nutall, Terri O'Grady, Liz Orr, Cori Palomares, Mary Patterson, Patricia Pearce, Jill Peck, Celia Penney, Joan Piggott, Virginia Pontifex, Isobel Proctor, Daphne Pryce-Jones, Victoria Radcliffe, Elizabeth Renwick, Gillian Ritchie, Jenny Roberts, Marigold Roberts, Toni Robinson, Ingrid Rohr, Anne Phyllis Rossi, Virginia Sheehy, Anne Sheridan, Shirley Sherwood, Patricia Simmons, Rosamund Skinner, Ann Slymon, Nadia Smart, Brenda Smith, Katie Smith, Jane Store, Shirley Swinn, Irene Tait, Marilyn Tobitt (Lady Swann), Susan Thomas, Cynthia [Sally] Tibbits, Daphne Vyvyan, Maureen Wade, Vivien Wass, Clare Weston, Cynthia White, Carol White, Patricia White, Pam Wolfson, Jose Irving-Bell, Marilyn Cox, Marigold Roberts, Anita Homann, Hazel Faulkes, Margaret Lloyd, Shirley Sherwood, Heather Woodcock, Jo Morris, Maggie Wainwright, Margaret Nutall, Rowena Leder, Heather Hanson, Penny Tutt, Helaine Michaels, Peggy Thorne, Diana Natalie McCall, M.C.H. Wilkinson, Fiona Graham, Glen Turner, Margaret Fairlie, Joyce Ann Hogge, Kathleen Dorothy Fuller, Alix Quested, Josie Watson and Oni Wyatt.

There are not enough words to thank Oni Wyatt for her professionalism and talent in creating the design for both the cover and colour section of this book. With her considerable skills she showed infinite patience, care and attention to detail. Her contribution has been invaluable. I could not have found a more willing and capable friend to do such a lengthy and exacting task.

All the pictures unless otherwise stated have been lent by the women who feature in the book.

Throughout all of the process of writing and researching I want to remember my parents who brought me up in a household full of books where learning was valued, a most precious gift in childhood, and to my two sons, who loved, supported and believed in me.

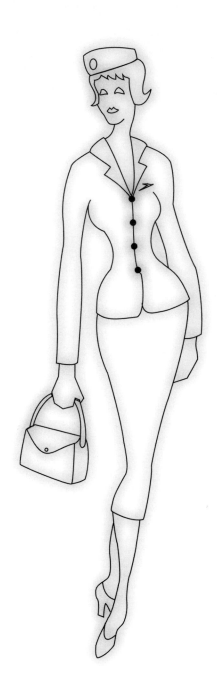

**CHAPTER 1**

# The Allure of the Air Hostess

## *A*N ANALYSIS

Mention at a dinner party in the '40s, '50s and '60s that you were an air hostess and immediate cachet was yours; it was a job that gave you instant worldliness. The top job categories which many young women aspired to in the '60s were to be a stewardess, model or an actress. By the mid-1930s stewardesses, particularly in America, had become popular icons. There were movies like *Air Hostess*, magazines which featured their beauty secrets, opinions and career tips, and books which extolled their bravery as they pulled passengers from blazing crashed planes. These women were admired for their beauty, heroism and professionalism. The stewardess in the '50s reflected the image of the 'perfect wife'. They were described by *Come Fly With Us* as 'part mother, part geisha', and a popular conception of them was as 'glamorous brides in waiting'.

Down the routes and in London one was invited to Naval dinners, Embassy parties, film premieres, glamorous functions, club openings, TV talk shows, radio interviews, airline launches and so forth. There was the tendency for some of the stewardesses to believe their own publicity, but what they did not forget was that there were hundreds of girls out there just as suitable for this career, all waiting for their chance to join the airline.

Stewardesses were the supermodels of their day. According to Keith Lovegrove in his book *AIRLINE: Identity and Culture*, 'Air stewardesses were seen as almost equal to models or rock stars in the glamour stakes. The stewardess was now clearly recognised and implemented as an intrinsic part of the corporate identity by most of the international airlines.' Glamour, charm and allure were marketing tools for the airlines. The aura of romance hovered around these slender, young and single women chosen for their scrutinized respectability, conversational skills, style and the indefinable quality which became the mystique that would identify with this career for years to come.

Jean Haines, a stewardess from 1966–72, adds another dimension when she says: 'Since the sixties were before mass travel, we were ambassadors for the UK, treated like royalty overseas, staying in the best hotels, invited to all the diplomatic functions, meeting the locals, seeing the world – a great life.'

The opinion of a fusty old gent, Malcolm Muggeridge, in BBC TV documentary *Suburbs in the Sky* (1986), is a very unusual and indeed ridiculous one. He said he would like to kill

**Left:** Betty Goodfellow, 1950–56. Betty's photograph evokes pleasant efficiency – there is a slightly military flavour. **Centre:** Sheila Luke, 1953–63. An even more relaxed look which gives a hint of the glamour to come! She later had a long career on the ground until 1983. **Right:** Patricia Jones, 1955–57. Patricia is allowed to look more relaxed and the uniform lacks a tie.

a stewardess and called this murder the 'reverse of the crime passionnel'. The BBC *Wingspan* program in 1972 followed the training, development and life of a stewardess and was the least sexist and the most accurate of all the television programs produced at this time.

Elegance, beauty and intelligence were just some of the qualities captured in the publicity photographs. The style of beauty in the faces of the stewardesses was changing. The women employed in the early '50s were fresh-faced, sensible, and with very little makeup. There was a healthy, common-sense approach to the profession. Many had an understated elegance. There was also the gradual change from the military-style uniform to a softer and more classical look. The 'passenger smile' emerged, which was later to be used in so much publicity for the airline. The image culminated later with Virginia Sheehy's life-size cardboard cut-out greeting passengers in every BOAC office around the world. Every day and every night for four years, thousands of passengers also saw her face in their Flight Companion booklet, the 'Welcome Aboard' compendium at the back of the seat pocket.

Virginia Sheehy's face was seen by more people at that time than most movie stars. The stewardess became the public face of the airline. Her appearance was a priority and her contact with the public sold seats. And the majority of passengers were men.

The seeds of the perfect air stewardess were sown in the 1930s. Personality and character were added to the criteria. Swissair employed their first stewardesses in 1934, KLM in 1935 and Lufthansa in 1938. The experiment in KLM was short-lived. The girls received so many proposals of marriage while in the air that they were apt to remain in the job for only a few months. KLM came to the conclusion that it was all too much trouble and decided to do away with stewardesses altogether. Meanwhile Lufthansa had decided on the type of girl they were looking for – someone with the ability to give the aircraft a homely atmosphere. She also had to have beauty, education and breeding. The perfect woman! Were they thinking of a modern version of the Hetaerae of ancient Greece?

'The image of the air stewardess epitomised the excitement of travel for a whole generation of young women in the 1960s and '70s whose options had previously been to become either secretaries or shop assistants.' This generalisation from Keith Lovegrove suggests that image was all the airlines wanted. That may have been true for some airlines. British Airways and its

**Right:** Virginia Sheehy, 1960–70. Note the hairstyle: this was the era of the bouffant. Now we are into glamour, Virginia's image was used to promote the airline worldwide for many years.

**Far right:** Susan Thrush. The changing face of the stewardess. The image has evolved from the almost military commonsense of the early '50s to the glamorous efficiency of the '70s.

predecessors were primarily seeking nurses, teachers and women with hospitality experience. Previous professional training was most desirable, almost essential. At the same time, however, the recruitment process placed such emphasis on youth, marital status and appearance that it would now be considered blatantly sexist.

Most stewardesses did *not* believe their own publicity. However, the concept of exploitation and sexism has been mentioned by many of the retired stewardesses. After ten years, or aged thirty-five (whichever came first), the girls had to leave and they justifiably saw this as unfair and discriminatory. Neither could they marry and if they did they were told to leave. None of these rules applied to male stewards. Their bosses did not see the females as having management potential. All of this made flying a career with no future and no job prospects. They rightly asked, who did come up with the stereotypical trolley dolly image of the '60s and '70s? It had not been this way earlier!

Charles Reid, in an article from *World Digest* in 1952, gives this verbal snapshot:

✈    The figure is noticeably trim. The BOAC tunic, winged lions rampant on all its bright buttons, sits elegantly on her. The smile comes easily without giving her or anybody else a pain. And yet there is something impersonal about it. The charm of an air hostess, like the complimentary cocktails and glossy magazines that are handed out at the beginning of a flight, is up to a point an official treat which comes to us by courtesy of the management. The accent is genteel; correct without being intimidating to rough-diamond passengers.

This description by Reid evokes an image only akin to a flying Stepford wife.

Advertising in the '60s was virtually a paradox, a mixture of the 'Madonna/whore' syndrome so espoused and aptly described by Dr Anne Summers in the '70s. A stewardess was to be maternal and at the same time, particularly in the USA, almost a saloon girl. Naturally with an aura like this around the job, i.e. being a flying sex symbol, the career was never really going to be considered to be a serious one. Today legislation has changed all that. Also the spate of hijackings in the '70s forced security to become the main consideration. Security came before comfort and the docile charming image of the stewardess.

There was no doubt that the airlines wanted stewardesses to be slightly suggestive. The uniform was the way to do this. The image was trying to combine dichotomies: 1) 'I am in a service situation', and 2) 'I am in an authoritative situation'. Most men find very pretty women in very pretty uniforms extremely sexy. On top of all this, passengers thought that the stewardesses were sexually liberated, particularly in the '60s. This notion was assisted by the mini-skirted uniforms, which should have been, but were not, irrelevant. Sexist exploitation of the stewardess's image reached its height in the '60s. The 'Swinging '60s', the era of the mini-skirt combined with glamour, was a corporate product.

American airlines were more overt and treated their air hostesses as the greatest selling point in the competition between the airlines. It is generally considered that they sexualised the role. Jonathan Root (quoted from an article by Auberon Waugh), a journalist who undertook a survey of American air hostesses, concluded that 'sex appeal seems to be as vital to commercial aviation as the wings of an aircraft. Wings merely enable the airplane to fly, but it is the stewardesses that bring in the paying passengers'.

When stewardesses were interviewed for the job in Southwest Airlines in the early '70s, a spokesman said he 'started with their legs and worked up to their faces'. Indeed in 1958 in the *Manchester Evening News* there was an article entitled 'Look to your legs, girls, if you want to fly high'. The article continued: 'They are one of the first things air chiefs note when interviewing prospective air girls', and this was BEA (British European Airways).

In the USA in the '60s the airlines designed uniforms which created and conveyed the notion that 'sex sells seats'. The uniform which really turned heads was Braniff. The international designer, Emilio Pucci, produced two dresses in pink and plum with his inimitable Pucci pattern of squares, rectangles and circles in many shades of pink to deepest maroon. He also introduced multicoloured tights, and a matching hat and scarf. The *piece de resistance* was a Pucci-designed bubble helmet, used to keep the hairstyles and hat in place while walking to the aircraft as this was before there were air bridges. Southwest Airlines of Texas sported hot pants with knee-high white leather boots.

There was a fine line between being an air hostess and a catwalk queen. Flying seemed in the '60s to be one long beauty contest. Braniff, it seemed, almost hinted at the airline striptease as their stewardesses set about discarding endless items of their uniform before starting their meals service in their 'working' number. Braniff was definitely of the belief that you sold the airline with sex. National Airlines in the USA developed this theme further, with their 'Fly Me, I'm Jennifer' television advertisements in the early '70s. The girls' names were also painted on the fuselage. This image was further distorted with literature such as *Coffee, Tea or Me* published in 1967, which described the airline stewardess and her lifestyle as one continual promiscuous jaunt. The Swinging '60s changed the public's perception of the stewardess forever. The sedate '50s image of the typical Western woman as wife and mother was superseded by the sexual revolution of the '60s, where the pill, and singledom, reigned supreme.

This certainly gave a new meaning to the 'f' word used in flying. Needless to say these ads were intensely disliked by women. Feminists were appalled and campaigned loudly against such blatant sexism. Unfortunately, one result was an increase in the harassment which a stewardess was forced to tolerate in the interest of the job.

'For a first class route to success – become an air hostess – the rise and rise of the trolley dolly.' Such was the contribution in an article in *The Sunday Telegraph* magazine in April 1996 entitled 'To the Manor Airborne', the theory being that the high-flyers of this world, prime ministers, multi-millionaires, top sportsmen, airline and media moguls and princes marry air hostesses. The writer, Jessica Berens, suggests that high-flyers seek air hostesses as partners. 'They know that the person trained to serve a seven-course dinner in a first class compartment flying thousands of feet above Dubai will have no difficulty accomplishing the same feat in a penthouse thousands of feet above New York's Upper West Side.' She goes on to say: 'The trolley dolly wife comes complete with a first-aid certificate of great use later on to the woman who is fortunate to attract the eye of someone who is not only wealthy, but also old and ill.'

This reference was, of course, to Dimitra Papandreou, who was working for Olympic Airways when discovered by the former Prime Minister of Greece. Anita Keating was a stewardess on Alitalia when she was spotted by Paul Keating, later Prime Minister of Australia. Mariam Bell was seen as attractive by the Sultan of Brunei while working for Royal Brunei and became wife number two, living a life full of splendour beyond description. While I have listed only a few examples, the article's main point was Berens' comment that: 'The problem for the socially elevated is that they can never live down their past. The air hostess, like the nun, the au pair and the mother-in-law, will always be funny.' As we know, some stewardesses did not marry high-flyers and many went on to establish successful careers elsewhere. They would dislike Berens' comment intensely.

This perception of the stewardess is not only a media one. Julia van den Bosch was the longest-serving Concorde stewardess, a tall, blonde and elegant woman who never married. I trained Julia and she told me an interesting story: 'On one of my flights (and I had been flying by then for many years), one of my old convent school friends was a passenger. I hadn't seen her for years – probably since our school days. And I was amazed when she said to me: "You are still flying – but you were so intelligent at school".' This reaction reminds one of the commonly held concept that sexuality and intelligence are incompatible in a woman.

Television and film documentaries perpetuated the myth of the continually smiling trolley dolly, and yet what the stewardesses did after they left flying would totally contradict that fatuous image. Many returned to their previous professions, nursing being one of them. Andy Bennett took early retirement after becoming involved with Tibetan refugees on her many flights to the Himalayas. She had talked to a doctor there and decided: 'I'd have a go at nursing so I could help them. I applied and was accepted for King's College Hospital. I was over fifty at the time, but am now happily nursing at the Chelsea and Westminster Hospital'.

## $\mathscr{A}$ DIFFERENT FUTURE

Other ex-stewardesses have forged successful careers in Law, Medicine, Academia, Government, Public Service, Business, Education, Politics, the Arts and Religion. There were a few firsts. Shirley Dakin carved a career for herself in cuisine for film sets. In fact Shirley was the first freelance food stylist in the UK. She became internationally acknowledged as being one of the best in her field. The former cookery editor of a leading British magazine now concentrates on making food look appealing for the camera. Her jobs have ranged from a biscuit commercial in Sydney to arranging food for a scene in the film *White Knight*, starring Mikhail Baryshnikov, the Soviet-born ballet dancer. She worked on several movies including *Little Lord Fauntleroy*, *The Last Days of Pompeii*, and *Julia* with Fred Zimmerman, and was acknowledged through her commercial and film work as a food director.

Here's another example of how flying paved the way for other careers: 'At the end of my ten-year contract I was very lucky to have been offered the post of Trainee Staff Manageress with Marks & Spencer, having had Managing Director, Sir Edward Sieff, as a passenger,' said Clare Weston.

Flying is not the career it was. Today's independent and adventurous young woman has more than one degree under her belt and seeks international careers in IT, law, science, academia and politics. Many women obtained their private pilot's licence while with BOAC or after they left. However, until the mid-'80s, there were no women pilots in British Airways. In 2004, there were 161 women piloting planes and thirty-three of them were captains in BA. In fact, one of the Concorde's captains was Captain Barbara Harmer. Women move quickly when they get the chance. Many of the stewardesses, foreseeing their retirement, were studying while still flying, no mean feat when one remembers the exhaustion factor. So there were brains as well as beauty in abundance. The ultimate experience?

At sixty-five, Sara Ginders has had an amazing career, and for the last nine years she has been the only stewardess on a Gulf Stream 550 corporate jet. She chose her own uniform, which is a very smart grey Ann Taylor of Fifth Avenue suit, uses Kristophle cutlery, Baccarat crystal, superb china and linen, shops for her own catering, and produces cordon bleu meals for her crew, her boss and his passengers. Her boss has been known to jump off a Concorde, get a helicopter to his Gulf Stream jet, where Sara and his crew are waiting, race up the stairs, and ask: 'What's for dinner? I have been saving up for your excellent cooking.' As a corporate flight attendant,

Sara flew all over the world to some of the most exotic and interesting places. She has a great personality, is an excellent cook, has superb organising skills, a slim figure and speaks many languages. She lived an exciting and fun-filled existence in an exclusive world.

Veronica Collen-Smith did seven years on a private 727:

✈ … outfitted in pale beige leather, with the deepest carpet you can imagine. The 727 consisted of a bedroom with shower room, the taps and basin were all gold-plated, the loo and bidet covered in caramel leather. The bed was covered in gorgeous rough silk that was quite sumptuous. The main sitting room, with an office area, had an antique look with Waterford crystal lamps – all leather upholstery. There was a dining room and a proper kitchen. My role was to do the lot. It was something of a shock initially to find myself doing things that others had done for me whilst flying with BA. But I was treated so well and had carte blanche on the purchase of the silver, crystal, Doulton china, cashmere rugs, linens – all my suggestions were accepted and I bought the lot at Harrods. A true shopping fantasy. I had a fantastic boss who gave me lots of notice before flights to go to Harrods and buy up vast quantities of caviar, smoked salmon, paté de foie gras, and all the fresh flowers for every flight. My menus meant I cooked a lot of things like steak and prepared my sweets, like chocolate mousse and crème caramel at home. When I was abroad I used to order fabulous food direct from the restaurant to the aircraft. I had the best lifestyle, housed in wonderful hotels during our stopovers, some of which could last for weeks. It was a totally committed time, in that we would never know where we would be, but a wonderful experience.

## ALLURE AS MARKETING

BOAC was unable to resist using the allure of the stewardess to attract customers. Her appearance was emphasised and the BOAC Family Day included a Miss Speedbird competition. In 1972 Miss Speedbird was Sue Thrush. Interestingly, in 1974 the title Miss Speedbird gave way to Miss Personality. A BOAC press release from October 1966 begins: 'World wide BOAC uses world wide glamour to take good care of its passengers in many lands.'

In fact there was even an entrant in the Miss World beauty contest. This was stewardess Betty Ann Lindo, who was 'Miss Jamaica' in 1970. The theme of using attractive stewardesses to promote the airline began in the mid-'50s, when Anne Price, competing against other stewardesses from airlines all over the world, was chosen as 'Queen of the Air'. In May 1955 Sir Miles Thomas, the then chairman of BOAC, said: 'Your success is a great tribute to British girlhood. BOAC is indeed proud of its "Queen of the Air".' Fifty years ago a remark like this might not have seemed patronising. Where were you Germaine Greer? Anne was judged on good looks, charm and personality. BOAC were not averse to using 'their girls' in beauty competitions.

The theme of BA's promotional campaign around the world was 'We are a warm, friendly and helpful airline, more than capable of taking more care of you. We want you to feel more welcome'. In the late '70s British Airways were changing their slogan from 'We take good care of you' to 'It's nice to have you with us'. This was certainly an improvement on 'Fly Me', which the American airline, National Airlines, used to great effect. The very pretty Roz Hanby became BA's ambassador and David Bailey, famous in the world of fashion photography, gave her a new look.

Roz Hanby helps to sell the airline in the '70s.
The implicit message of her look was very important.

'It's nice to have you with us.

That same warm welcome awaits you on every Superflight.
Whenever you fly British Airways you can be sure of our ever-willing care - from the moment you arrive at the airport until you collect your cases at your destination.
And remember, if you're flying to London we offer you a direct Super VC10 every Sunday from Addis.
Ask your travel agent. He'll tell you.'

**British airways**
We'll take more care of you.

Are we now able to say that the image of the stewardess and the trolley dolly is no longer exploited? I very much doubt this, as in 2005 an airline was taken to court for discriminating against women because of their age and looks. In an extract from the *Courier Mail*, October 2005, Alex Murdoch, reacting to this case, asks passengers what they really think about the age of flight attendants: 'She was always young, immaculately groomed and impossibly glamorous with perfect teeth flashing a mega watt smile.'

Men fantasised about her, while women wanted to be her, dreaming of an exotic lifestyle in romantic locations. The original air hostess – as she was known then – was always a woman, often seen more as a fashion plate than as a real person with needs and wants of her own. She would glide up and down the aisle like a supermodel on a catwalk, the epitome of feminine perfection.

Until, that is, she grew older. Once a hostess passed her prime she was quickly moved away from the public eye or told to find employment elsewhere.

Most people believe those times have changed, blown away by the wrath of feminism and equal opportunity movements. But have they really? Are we able to say that the image of the stewardess and the trolley dolly is no longer exploited? I doubt this, as Murdoch's article above clearly indicated. The airline in question was taken to court for discriminating against women because of their age and looks.

The career of an air stewardess is a subtle blend of many professions: public relations, hostess, nanny, waitress, and, for some, less of a career than more of a finishing school. 'Docile, domestic and decorative' is another description often used for the stewardess, an anodyne for the tired businessman in flight, every man's dream. The romantic view of the air stewardess saw them as smart and sexy, living the life of romantic fiction, sporting a year-round tan and wearing mink off-duty. If flying was considered sexy – and to many it was seen as very sexy – it was the air hostess who injected the sex appeal.

In fact she was viewed as the tired businessman's entitlement. As Anthea Hall writes in 1994: 'To many a stressed businessman, the adrenalin that flows through eye contact with a pretty female member of the cabin crew is one of the saving graces of air travel'. So in 2005, with the 75th anniversary of flying, the stewardess had become one of the defining icons of the age, and the fascination of the life and times of the airline stewardess continues to have an intriguing hold on the imagination of those on the ground.

# ℛECRUITMENT

Personal allure was closely linked to recruitment, although in the very early years luck also played a part. Rumours abounded – that Daddy had to be a Harley Street surgeon or a High Court Judge, that only twenty-eight of 40,000 applicants were accepted and so on. Clare Weston said she thought her employment was luck: 'BOAC were recruiting stewardesses to replace the stewards sacked in "the gold rush"', a reference to the gold smuggling in the '50s.

'Do your parents know you have applied for this work and do they object?' Can you imagine young women tolerating this question today? They did in the early years of commercial airlines. Hundreds of would-be stewardesses fronted interview panels to answer such questions. Thousands only got as far as an application form.

The work obviously had enormous appeal as something different and exciting, especially for women who had been in the forces during the war. Pay was not astronomical but was comparable with the wages of work available to many women at the time. In 1952 you began on £5 a week with an additional £2 when allocated to a flying roster. Fifteen shillings was paid for each day away from the UK. By the late '60s the annual salary was £1,154 with an away allowance of fifteen shillings a day. In April 1964, my first month's pay was £27 10 shillings.

Advertisements for the work gave limited information but one I have found from 1947 is interesting, published with approval of the Ministry of Labour and National Service under the Control of

Engagement Order. Age requirement is listed as between twenty-one and thirty-five years. Later this varied slightly but in the '60s and early '70s stringent age limits were still in place.

Application forms reveal more than the advertisements. In the '50s and early '60s a would-be stewardess had to provide details of educational institutions attended, examination results, previous employment and nationality. Apart from such routine information a recent photograph was demanded along with measurements of height, weight, bust, waist and hip! Wording changed little over the years and always emphasised appearance: 'Should have a neatly proportioned figure and be of pleasing appearance.' In real terms of being effective on an aircraft, other qualities were more important. A '50s application form asks for 'A high standard of physical fitness, a reasonable relationship between height and weight and good eyesight'. Ultimately, however, the photograph was the great decider.

Reasons for some of the discrimination are obvious but one must question the attitude to marital status and age. In the 1958 application sheet, under the heading Important Notes, there was a stipulation that married women would not be recruited as air stewardesses. Was it not fair to a man or his children if his wife were away flying? Were older women not attractive? Also, according to Alexander McRobbie, 'the unstated idea was: what male could dare show fear in the presence of these mere slips of girls who flew every day without concern?' Right to the present day this thinking makes most airlines stick to having women at least as some of their cabin attendants. And most of the customers were men! This discrimination lasted until 1975 when the UK's equal opportunity legislation came into force.

By 1960 civil aviation was expanding worldwide. Everyone was on the move, aircraft were larger, and with the introduction of the Boeing 707 in the early '60s there were over 100 seats. By the '80s some Jumbo's held more than 400. Safety regulations, let alone comfort, stipulated one cabin crew member to about thirty passengers. The recruitment net could be more widespread than in the '40s and '50s when nurses were favoured. Languages were an asset, though French might limit you to constant flights to Montreal. Needless to say the limitations placed on marital status, age and appearance stood the test of time.

## The Interview

The interview ranged from quite informal chats in some early cases to a formal process with a panel of up to four interrogators. Nadia Smart, who started flying at twenty-one with British South American Airways (BSAA) in 1946, remembers: 'My father took Air Vice Marshal Bennet to lunch at the Dorchester Hotel in London. He gave me a job on the spot because he knew my father was also AVM and I had been nursing in the RAF during the war.'

Later came the panel, usually with a captain, an experienced senior stewardess, one of the training school lecturers and sometimes a representative from Elizabeth Arden. They used a battery of questions such as the following, just a few from the original list Audrey Cartmell used when interviewing:

+ Could you address some fifty to sixty people?
+ Do you read books? What kind of books?
+ Are you amenable to discipline?
+ Do you drink intoxicating beverages?
+ Have you any objection to waiting upon coloured people?
+ Would you object to a different hairstyle?
+ Have you waited at table?
+ Could you attend to people suffering air-sickness, and other unpleasant duties?
+ What is the essential requirement when preparing food on a plate?

To cap it all off, the interviewee was asked to parade the length of the room. Some stewardesses told me they felt like prize cows at an agricultural show. It was a nerve-racking and demeaning experience that they hoped never to repeat. I will allow these women to speak for themselves:

**DELIA GREEN:** 'I was asked if my hair was natural but was requested to kneel at the feet of the female questioner so she might examine it more closely.'

**JANE STORE:** 'I was asked what my hair would look like if the plane crashed! I replied that I didn't think that would be my first concern.'

**JANE BRIGGS:** 'One man asked me what I would do if the Captain knocked on my door at night. I said it would depend on the Captain. I think he was trying to make me cross.'

**MARGARET GERKE:** 'I spent all the money I had on a smart navy blue suit and white blouse – to look like a stewardess.'

**ANDY BENNETT (1972):** '"If we don't offer you the job will you apply to other airlines?" they asked. With a twinkle in my eye and tongue firmly in cheek, I said: "If I can't fly for the best airline in the world, I don't want to fly with anyone". The reply – "When can you start?"'

**SHIRLEY FOGG (1955):** 'I was asked how I would cope being alone with seven men for three weeks at a time. I said I wouldn't know until it happened. I think they liked the honesty. I was short, plump and jolly and surprised that the tall beautiful blondes with me failed, perhaps giving the impression that they would be too busy preening themselves to pay attention to the passengers.'

**KATHY LAVERS (1956–59):** 'The panel asked me if I had ever flown before. I said: "No, but I once had a 10 shilling flight at Chobham airfield." I remember them all laughing.'

**JENNY MAXWELL:** 'I remember Captain Stacey saying "You are stranded on a desert island with a handsome Second Officer. He makes a pass at you. What would you do?" I replied, "In those circumstances, sir, I would be disappointed if he didn't."'

**DAPHNE PRYCE-JONES ('50S):** 'I was asked what I would do if an amorous Captain tried to seduce me under romantic tropical skies. I replied "Much the same as I would do back in the UK!"'

**SYLVIA LADLEY:** 'When I applied to return to flying in 1998 when I was fifty-three, the interview was very, very similar.'

It is refreshing to note that some panels appreciated a sense of humour, but most applicants were far too nervous to be cheeky. What really counted in the interview? The typical successful applicant shows what counted. Many women would have been wasting their time applying in the first place – those who were over thirty-six, married, too short, too plump, black or unattractive according to the tastes of the time. The preferred woman, it seems, was unmarried, young, attractive, preferably European, and from the sort of background that meant she did not speak with a pronounced regional accent .Of course, poise, personality, refinement and tact was a given. All this reflects the social mores of the times.

However, although the interview was not all sweetness and light, BOAC always attracted plenty of applicants, some going to great lengths to get an interview.

Vivacious Alix Hallowell Jones told me that:

✈    In 1964 I was working as a ground hostess for Qantas in Hong Kong. Eager to return to the UK to apply to BOAC I heard through the grapevine of an air charter company which flew Chinese seamen to Rotterdam and was known to let one hitch a lift. A friend at Kai Tak Airport pointed out the captain of the charter plane, and I approached him for a lift. He told me to meet him at the departure desk on Thursday – this was Monday – he put me on the manifest as supernumerary crew, adding it would help if I wore my uniform. I duly unpicked my Qantas insignia, reported at the said time, and five days later in an old DC3, which kept breaking down, I landed at Gatwick. Safely back in London and still with Qantas, now managing the Qantas desk in Australia House in the Strand, I applied to BOAC, and was called for two interviews. Then a letter landed on my desk. It was addressed to the Manager, Qantas Desk, Australia house. It was from BOAC asking for a reference for a Miss Alix Hallowell Jones. In those days you had to almost be a Duke's daughter to get in – seizing the moment I filled out the reference, ticking the boxes and giving myself one 'excellent' and the rest very good, and guess what, I was successful!

# TRAINING

In June 1970 there were 1,038 stewardesses with BOAC. When training started for BSAA in 1943, there were just six and training for the stewardesses was a rather ad hoc affair. Some had little training at all. Many of the Stargirls learnt their job on the go, as it were, under another Stargirl, and as AVM Bennett ran his airline like Bomber Command, those not flying worked in other areas, so 'hands on' training was a continual process.

BOAC and BEA on the other hand took a more serious and regimented view. Courses ranged from six to eight weeks – initially some courses were twelve weeks – with copious notes taken in large blue exercise books. Training was very much a chalk and talk situation; there were weekly tests and the requirement was to achieve 100 per cent or fail!

Although fine tuning in training changed over the years, certain basics are always important; Air/Sea Rescue, First Aid, Posture and Deportment (this lecture delivered by a man), Silver Service, Galley Routines, Doctrinal Foods, Jungle, Desert and Arctic Survival, Insect-Borne Diseases, Hygiene, Theory of Flight, Passenger Comfort in Flight and of course Fire Protection, which meant days spent learning how to use fire extinguishers and crawling through a smoke-filled tunnel on our hands and knees.

BOAC, BEA and then BA also made sure that their cabin crews appreciated cultural differences. Jewish passengers were presented with their own Kosher food blessed by the Rabbi and carefully sealed by the Beth Din kitchens. This was the only food that the traditional Jewish passengers would eat – apart from the barley sugars (not Kosher) which stewardesses offered to passengers on descent. These passengers took handfuls!

In fact it was all a condensed catering course without the cooking, which was done by the steward. It certainly assisted you when you went fine dining. One felt quite knowledgeable. Many people did appreciate this aspect of the course as they later became rather smart dinner party cooks in their own right. Many cabin staff went into hospitality when they left the airline. All of this fine cuisine followed the cocktail service and everyone knew how to mix a Bronx, a Gibson, a John Collins and to this day the best G & T we mix at home is the British Airways recipe! 'Great emphasis was placed on knowledge of cocktails, ingredients and presentation' said Sue McGuire, 'but during my twenty-five years of flying I was never once asked for a negroni.'

In the early '70s I was allocated most of the promotional training for first class meal services. Stewardesses who had been flying for a few years needed this to upgrade to stewardess A, as it was called. We practised a very long, and for many, incredibly tedious, seven-course routine in a very small and cramped room alongside the economy mock-up in the huge training hall at Cranebank. This tiny room became the first class cabin and the trainees acted in turn as First Steward, Stewardesses A and the passengers. The limited space and mass of equipment meant it was quite a shambles really, but I really enjoyed training the A girls. A few years down the routes had given them all kinds of experiences. There

In the late '60s the national stewardesses practise cabin service in the mock up.

was lots of laughter and it could seem as if the training was not taken seriously! It was, but a sense of humour was needed to survive the tedium of this long meal service.

These seven courses were introduced to the 'passengers' on a gold trolley with various shelves and a bar cage and a revolving display top for hors d'oeuvres. After the first course the top ended up in the one space available, behind the only door, and so on with the other courses. Anyone opening the door created our wonderful diversionary tactic; all the trolley bits went crashing across the room. As a result, the Chief Instructor Len Smee on his daily checking up rounds usually bypassed our training room. In the event that he did pop in, the noise of the scattering metal pieces was a wonderful cover for hiding the wines the girls had smuggled in. We passed many a happy lunchtime. Of course no one failed, and their wine appreciation skills improved out of sight!

British Airways trained all sorts of nationalities in the '60s and language could be a problem for them. Sue Brown recalls training Nigerian stewardesses for Nigerian Airways; she had described the ancillaries required for Consomme, which were cheese straws. After a longer than usual time for her students to prepare this soup course, Sue went to the galley and found her students trying to suck up the soup through the cheese straws. It was expecting far too much from these young Nigerian women, who had no idea what first class service entailed.

## Grooming Disaster

It's always certain training days that stand out in our memories. There were many accounts of the day we attended grooming and deportment featuring Elizabeth Arden consultants. Hazel Faulkes said, 'BOAC wanted us to look like Elizabeth Arden ladies, and we all looked the same afterwards; blue eyes, pink lips and cheeks!'

My favourite Elizabeth Arden recollection was from my own course. Weeks after we had our Wings, I rang a friend of mine who was on my course for a gossip. She had really taken on

Training stewardesses Libbie Escolme, Ann Watt, Francine Carville, Judy de Jong and Phyllis Hall learn how to teach deportment at the Cherry Marshall Modelling Academy in Bond Street in 1969.

board the Elizabeth Arden philosophy which was 'If you continually waxed your legs, several months later you would find them becoming increasingly hairless' – a dream for a stewardess, who was always on show and where strict attention to grooming became an intrinsic part of life. She had just waxed her legs when I phoned her. We chatted for at least half an hour, and a few minutes after we had put the phone down, she rang back in an enormous panic, 'I can't uncross my legs! I am stuck together! I can't walk! I am hobbled! What will I do?' Utter anguish from the other end of the telephone. There wasn't much one could do except say keep calm through smiling teeth. Elizabeth Arden came to the rescue and she was 'unlocked'. The rest of our group were put off waxing for ever.

## Trainers

In the early '50s the training was in a draughty old convent building, St Mary's on Hayes Road in Southall. This establishment was always freezing cold. It was also known as 'Joe's Academy', named after Joe Lawrence who ran the place.

Joe Lawrence was a stocky, bombastic fellow with a rolling gait and a loud and severe countenance. He seemed to take up a lot of space and an aura of aggressiveness surrounded him; many of the stewardesses had not met anyone like him in their lives. It was difficult to know how to react. Most of us simply tried to keep out of his way!

But Joe Lawrence will always be remembered for his obsession with 'dish and plate appeal'. The meat and veg or whatever it was had to look good! Where the vegetables were placed on the plate and the colour were serious training exercises. He would draw a plate of food on the blackboard and everyone would watch with great concentration as the carrots (used for maximum colour) and the beans, plus mashed potatoes were carefully drawn onto the plate. A work of art, and if there was a tomato on the menu there was such excitement as that really made his day. There are few stewardesses who were trained by Joe Lawrence who do not, when serving up the carrots and peas at home today, think about 'dish and plate appeal'.

Marjorie Tong quotes him as saying, 'To appeal to the stummick, a dish has gotter appeal to the eye'. He would continue, 'You got your meat on the right, you got your veg on the left. You got your soft veg at the top, hard veg at the bottom. This is dish and plate appeal, and I don't want it set out different' – and we didn't! Josephine McKay remembers Joe Lawrence 'because everything had to be garnished with parsley' and that she had to memorise 170 French menu definitions.

Of course the trainees always remembered the bloopers you may have made while giving the lectures. I am told that in the '60s, whilst I was teaching PA announcements to be made to passengers in the event of turbulence, I reputedly told my trainees to make sure they did *not* say, 'hold on to your drinks and nuts'.

Peggy Thorne, who joined in 1950, said: 'The trainers were mostly ex-services NCO types, short on a sense of humour! They used Army 'discipline' which still lingered in the '50s.'

Many of the trainees commented on the harshness of the lecturers and in fact the term bullying was used. Audrey Cartmell mentions: 'Towards the end of the course we were told that this was so that they could study our reaction to awkward passengers.'

Lorna Dand described the trainers as: 'Down to earth and taking some of the glamour out of our heady imaginations.' Lorna also jokes about Mr Belcher presenting deportment instruction wearing a stewardess's hat and strutting up and down the aisle of the mock up!

When Jane Store was asked if she enjoyed the training, her succinct reply was: 'Yes and no. We were rather bullied. I think many of us emerged gibbering wrecks.'

June Malcolm said it was: 'Frightening, we were all terrified we would fail and quite a few girls did.'

Glen Turner felt that the instructors knew that trainees had previously held responsible jobs and had a certain amount of self-confidence. 'Training instructors, we felt, set about knocking all that out of us and making us feel inadequate.'

Joe Lawrence explaining his colour-coded 'dish and plate appeal' to his 1950s pupils at the convent, 'chalk and talk' for the air.

Delia Green's exam results in 1957 – she was astonished to find her sandwiches were below average!

| SYLLABUS | Proficiency Attained |
|---|---|
| 1. B.O.A.C. Air Catering Standards—U.K. and Overseas | Average |
| 2. Food uplifts and stations | Average |
| 3. General knowledge of the methods of Pax, Reception, Care and Escort | Above Average |
| (a) Seating | Above Average |
| (b) Unregistered Baggage | Above Average |
| (c) Salutations | Above Average |
| (d) Dressing of Cabin | Above Average |
| (e) Dressing of Powder Rooms | Above Average |
| (f) Use of Amenities | Above Average |
| (g) Carrycots and Skycots | Average |
| (h) Babies Bottles and Foods | Average |
| (i) Rug and Linen Checks | Above Average |
| 4. Unaccompanied Children | Above Average |
| 5. Invalid Foods | Average |
| 6. Children's Foods | Average |
| 7. Preparation of sandwiches | Below Average |
| 8. Aircraft Meal Services | Above Average |
| 9. Cleanliness of aircraft interior and aircraft furnishings | Above Average |
| 10. Proficiency in Briefings and Public Address System | Above Average |
| 11. Off Schedule and Transit Duties | Average |
| 12. Bar dispensation including wine service, cocktails and currencies | Average |
| 13. Passenger Psychology including care of invalids, children and aged passengers | Above Average |
| 14. Special services for Dietetics, Doctrinal and Invalid Passengers | Average |
| 15. Catering and Official documentation | Above Average |
| 16. Mandatory Checks | Above Average |

Although Joe Lawrence terrified everyone, the girls felt able to sing to him new words to an old tune, 'The Very Thought of You'. Rosamund Skinner remembers they said they were novices at the convent:

> The very thought of you and we forget to do
> The ordinary little things that you taught us to do.
> The pommes and the zests and every garnish,
> And words we never knew – The very thought of you

As a trainer for BOAC/BA for many years I believed that discipline should be a way of life for stewardesses (now called flight attendants), similar to that of the defence forces. Many of the women substantiated this belief by saying they had absorbed the training school lectures and for the most part accepted the discipline. They speak of their automatic response to an emergency situation and mention their own surprise at how much information came into their minds when they needed it.

## Safety – Air, Sea and Jungle Rescue

The essentials of safety and emergency procedures were, and still are, taken very seriously by stewardesses, however light-hearted some of their comments about the training may seem: 'The air/sea rescue lectures were given by someone affectionately known as "Polly Parrot",' said Joan Piggott, 'so called I suppose because he told us how to survive if we crashed in the jungle.' On one occasion during air/sea rescue training he alerted the entire Airport Emergency Services by sending an SOS from the training dinghy on the Staines reservoir near London Airport.

Barbara Hume did her air/sea rescue, jungle, arctic and desert survival courses in 1953 at Meadowbank: 'The survival books were full of practical suggestions and I can still quote "In the desert, dried camel dung makes a good energy fuel, burning with a smoky yellow flame". I suspect my grasp of desert survival dictated my posting to the North Atlantic where there was rather a lot of ocean and absolutely no desert to get excited about.'

Jill Edmonds felt that: 'The emergency drills were quite scary – having to put out a raging wall of fire in a channel of fuel and finding our way through the smoke-filled building to the exit.'

Many of the girls recalled from their old training notebooks that: 'In the event of ditching, do not allow the passengers to sing hymns.' This was considered too depressing, and remember to wear your hat!

Enid Hewitt recounts: 'So in the Hounslow baths, whilst being hauled into a life raft, I nearly gave up the ghost there and then, let alone having to remember not to let the passengers sing hymns, should we ever find ourselves in a life raft for real.'

Sheila Luke trained in 1953 and was told that in shark-infested waters you must scream underwater, an excellent shark deterrent.

When Peggy Thorne did her air/sea rescue training in 1950, jungle and artic survival played a big part.

✈  We were taught to strap the dinghy radio to our knees, set to Automatic and crank the handle to send our distress signals once safely aboard the life rafts in the heaving seas – only in our case we were on the calmer waters of Staines reservoir. Our classroom was a Nissen hut with temperatures varying from sub-zero to near boiling point in the proximity to the iron stove. What was that about 'spending a penny' when marooned on an ice floe? We were told always do it in groups – the freezing cold might cause a permanent attachment whilst in midstream, as it were.

In the tropics and always supposing there was a jungle clearing at hand on which to land safely, the survivors were briefed on how to tackle a tiger on a forest pathway. Cut a stick and with a steady hand point it straight between the eyes and for crocodiles, another stick was needed to gouge out an eye. It seemed doubly dangerous to approach habitation where one could encounter perhaps some 'natives'. The handbook said to offer the native chief or headman a small gift.

In our hearts we secretly doubted the practicality of our ability to survive in the jungle and hoped we never had the opportunity to face these situations.

However, this training almost became a reality in 1964. James Nightingale was the first officer on a Comet IV airliner with sixty-two passengers aboard which touched down in a Nairobi Game Reserve. Nairobi Airport was nine miles away! Some pretty quick thinking on the part of the pilot meant that the passengers felt only a jolt as he took the plane up into the air again. The Aviation Ministry and BOAC officials at the time flew to Africa to investigate what was being called the most fantastic air escape for years. There were many theories about the cause of this Comet touching down in the Nairobi Game Park, one being that the aircraft was lower than it should have been on its approach, because of a misreading of an altimeter. The Comet had two altimeters, one showing the height above sea level and another which had to be set according to the height of the runway being used.

Neither were the rigours of a forced landing in the desert forgotten. One had to start filling life jackets with water after some sort of hasty conversion job was done beforehand. Even the bar box had to be padlocked with a key. All this at such a busy time as we descended!

There was also a place for training cabin crew on the basics of childbirth, caring for both mother and baby. 'We had to learn how to deliver a baby,' remembers Margaret Nuttall (BEA). 'We were shown a film in glorious Technicolor. At least two stewards fainted! We were told we must collect the afterbirth in a teapot if necessary. We all laughed when the doctor remarked that they say that too much flying makes you sterile – but don't bank on it!'

Linda Crowe recalls her group also had to revive a steward who fainted during the childbirth film. Was this another test?

## Getting Our Wings – Allure or Not?

The title *ab initio* was used for trainees and you were called this until you passed all your exams and actually got your Wings. Your brevet was presented to you in a little box and it was a very significant moment for many to be able at last to sew this onto your uniform! For everyone it was a huge milestone and without a doubt everybody secretly was as proud as punch and so excited. To achieve these 'Wings' seemed a long, tedious and anxious time.

Apart from the weekly exams, one had to take whatever was dished out, and you were aware that a bad reaction would have had you off the course immediately. In the '70s there was a prize for the top of the class – a 'golden' ashtray. This changed to a silver tray, the kind that you would use for your calling cards, a more politically correct prize for the top of the class.

But what happened then? So many women told me that when they reported to their cabin service officer the first thing they were told was to forget everything they had learnt at school! 'The niceties of Majestic service etc. were of no use once on board,' recalls Patricia Jones. 'The Chief Steward had his own ideas anyway. Emphasis was on cabin announcements, dealing with passenger problems and obeying the Chief Steward at all times!'

Gaps in training showed up when the reality of flying hit stewardesses. Virginia Pontifex would have valued a few tips in training on how to handle the Queen's Messenger. The QM had the task of sitting beside the bag of Royal Mail in first class and never letting it out of his sight. The boredom of these repeated journeys was often only relieved by consuming massive amounts of Nuits St George and cognac. This led to some tricky situations both during the flight and at the end.

Susan Brattle says it will always be a mystery to her that 'You assumed you had been selected for your individuality but immediately you started training you were expected to be peas in a pod – typified by our end of course photograph.' Susan would also have liked some advice about jetlag!

Some training was not relevant at the time. Jane Store never made maître d'hotel butter while in the air. Audrey Cartmell agrees, 'On board we never had the foodstuff for the recipes we were inundated with during training.'

As Margaret Lloyd recalls:

✈    During our training, it was emphasised that we females must not expect to be treated any differently just because we were women. Doors would not be held open for us, we must pay our share at the bar and accept the fact that crew conversation was usually about flying, second-hand cars and sex in that order. So always anxious to 'stand my corner' I would try to buy a round of drinks when the crew got together for a drink after a flight. I never succeeded!

She continues:

✈    The briefing was done without a microphone in those days. I was glad to note that the wording of the life-jacket briefing has been changed. It was an exercise in self-control to say

Some of the first 747 stewardesses of the early '70s in an end of course photograph, 'peas in a pod', posed at Cranebank. The mock-up of the Boeing 747, the aircraft which forever changed the way we flew for passengers and stewardesses alike, is in the background. Bottom row fifth from right is Maggie Davies, seated next to Libbie Escolme.

'pull the red knob smartly downwards' with one of the stewards in the front row pulling faces and making rude gestures.

Training might have better prepared June Blackler for being the only girl with nine men on a flight. 'We were all rather innocent in those days. It was a challenge. I went to Montreal in June '52, flew into the midnight sun and was overwhelmed by the shops, food and clothes. The UK was still on rations. I remember going to a restaurant where we all ate a mountain of spare ribs from a huge platter.'

As Margaret Lloyd said:

✈ Training was a cross between finishing school and boot camp! Exams every Friday, and off the course if you failed. Duties of a stewardess? Must have strong arms and legs and an agreeable disposition at all times. Service must be modelled on that given by servants in exclusive residential clubs in London. You must know how to address the Queen and lesser dignitaries and how to deliver a baby in the aircraft aisle.

Keeping the loos at a 'single satisfactory standard' was not easy. Some passengers had never seen one before. Using the ice-buckets near the galley was often the easy option. Training had not prepared us for that!

'For passengers and crew alike, glamour and flying have always been synonymous. Hollywood scriptwriters and bestselling blockbuster authors continually used the skies as an arena for staging glamorous histrionics. The airline industry is a catwalk for the image makers and the image takers'. (*Airline Identity, Design & Culture*) For the young woman of the '40s, '50s and '60s this was the career of a lifetime, flying off to exotic places, meeting and caring for the world's elite. It was the ultimate finishing school in the skies.

## Fine Tuning

Trainers in the late '60s and '70s were dealing with women from a wider socio-economic background. Besides, many aspects of everyday life were changing and trainers found that many successful applicants had never been exposed to discipline in their lives. Problems were compounded by shorter training. Time in the training school decreased from eight to six weeks and soon to only twenty days. Then it was on board without a supernumerary trip – all of which can work well if one is motivated and intelligent. This was not always the case, and often caused quite a problem on a full aircraft.

This was the era of youthful rebellion against authority. Many stewardesses demanded explanations for the rules and discipline. The ideas of hats, gloves and short hair seemed archaic to these new stewardesses. They no longer bothered to hide or tie engagement rings around their necks, wore earrings and wanted to just tie their hair back. They wanted change and the Air Hostess Association encouraged them to seek it out.

Such sensitivities caused chagrin and controversy, particularly when a week-long course named 'Social Skills' was introduced in the late '60s. I was involved in the training of thousands of cabin crew on this course. The trainees, anxious to get their Wings, for the most part threw themselves into the situation studies and managed to get through the week. However, crews who were already flying and who didn't know anything about the curriculum really took umbrage at the title, believing the course to be about how to eat with the right knife and fork! It was the first course of its kind to introduce basic passenger psychology as part of cabin crew training. It continued for many months until Management felt the results were beginning to show. Complaints from passengers dropped and it was decided that its impact had achieved the end product. Interestingly enough, in the early '80s the subject was reintroduced and other airlines then began to look into similar schemes. TWA employed BA instructors to give 'behavioural analysis courses' for their own staff in America.

The term 'Social Skills' was now replaced by 'Psychology of Customer Care', a phrase that could not offend even the most sensitive of cabin crews. A great deal of emphasis has been placed on this since and it features in the BA training manual at some length. In the mid-'70s the BOAC training school was directed by Jill Parker, a former stewardess. Both verbal and non-verbal communication between crew and passengers is the core of the training. For example, explained Jill Parker, 'If you look down from a great height, it's like the nurse-patient relationship, and businessmen in particular don't like being in that kind of subservient role. The stewardess, or steward, should therefore lean forward until he or she is between 18ins and 2ft from the passenger.' That, said Mrs Parker, demonstrated 'Eagerness and a relaxed relationship'. Anywhere within 18 inches, on the other hand, was dangerous, the aerial equivalent of territorial waters. 'That means either love or war,' explained Jill Parker, 'so we tell them not to do it unless that is what they mean.'

The most far-reaching change for stewardesses, however, resulted from the Equal Opportunity Act, UK 1975. Limitation placed on age and marital status was now illegal. Newspaper stories carrying headlines such as 'Flying Grannies' were par for the course. BA declared firmly that the increasing age is a boon rather than a problem. 'The glamour element,' insisted Jill Parker, 'comes low on the list of passenger requirements, even for the middle-aged businessmen.'

That comment was made a few decades ago. Whatever changes have occurred, whether you are a middle-aged businessman or not, poise, tact, personality and looks still remain passengers' expectations of a flight attendant.

## *A* STEWARDESS FOR JUST ONE DAY

After six to eight weeks of training you evolved into a stewardess – actually it can also happen after an hour! Pip Feeney had just met a handsome man and this time, no matter what, was determined to go to a dinner party with him in London. Rosters in the '60s could be up to twenty-four days away, and this threw your social life into complete chaos. Thus she asked her sister Jane to go in her place on a short trip to New York: 'I had checked the roster and found that I was the extra crew and would return in one day, while the rest of the crew went around the world.' I asked Pip how did her sister know what to do? 'Oh,' said Pip, 'I just sat her down at the kitchen table and gave her an hour's training.' Shades of *Ab Fab*, I thought, as I needed to spend nearly six weeks turning out a stewardess, while Pip could do it in an hour. She continued:

✈  I then took her to the airport and she checked in under my name. As you can imagine this procedure has now changed! The Chief Steward, whom I met later, told me that he was surprised that there were two stewardesses by the same name! I didn't think of it any further. He did suggest to me that she should get some experience. On this flight in First Class, my sister ended up serving tea and told me afterwards that she thought BOAC should buy larger teapots, as she had to keep filling them up, not knowing that in the First Class that each passenger should have their own little teapot!

All I asked of her was that she did not answer the room telephone. She did think that this was a bit odd, but followed my instructions, and indeed the Lexington Hotel did indeed try to contact her. However, remembering my words, she did not answer the phone. Eventually their persistent ringing forced her to answer the telephone and she found her flight to London delayed. For Jane this was a most considerate notice, she now had a few more hours in bed before her flight and the new pickup time. So she had entered the USA on a false passport, under a false name and with my crew certificate. She then had a night flight on her return back to London, with a very light passenger load, so she spent most of her time on the Flight Deck chatting-up the crew.

The allure of flying captivated the imaginations of all ages. Stephanie Ponsford aged ten with stewardess Edith Potts in a late '50s publicity shot at London Airport, with a young captain to be.

I have never been so glad to see my sister in all my life and told her not to tell a single soul, especially the parents. But guess what? She sent a postcard to my parents from New York City. Jane, though, still had a huge query as to why the big 'no no' about not answering the phone, I told her, 'Ah well, you could have been called out in an emergency and ended up going around the world for twenty-four days'.

We were never found out and I planned to sell this story to the *News of the World* if we were.

It was discovered, much later, but by that time Pip was well into another career.

# CHAPTER 2

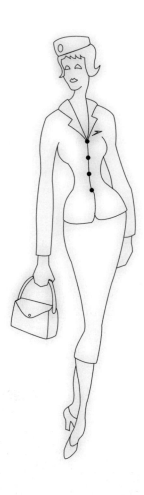

# The First Stewardesses and the Forties

he first stewardesses in the world were not British, but American. Their work in the USA began in 1930 with Boeing Air Transport, which subsequently became part of United Airlines. However, US Government legislation later forbade aircraft manufacturers to operate airlines. There were eight stewardesses at the time working for Boeing. Later, TWA adopted the idea and took on its first group of women for cabin service training in 1933. A new and exciting career began for women. This was to fire the imaginations of young women all over the world.

These first eight stewardesses, the true pioneers, were all registered nurses. This legacy of nursing being the most suitable profession for recruitment remained with all the airlines for

The Hythe-class Short S.25 Sunderland flying-boat.

many years and such a qualification is still a desirable attribute today. It was Ellen Church of Cressbill, Iowa, who came up with the idea of female stewards, which she presented to Boeing Air Transport. She contacted them just before her twenty-sixth birthday. Before that, all Boeing's flight attendants had been male. Boeing Air Transport later adopted twenty-six as the cut-off age for joining for their stewardesses. They were grounded at thirty-two. This age regulation remained with many US airlines until the mid-1960s.

As noted by Andrew Buncombe in *The Independent* in May 2005, Ellen approached Steve Stimpson, Manager of BAT of Boeing's San Francisco office, with her revolutionary idea that 'if stewards were there to keep passengers calm, what better way of achieving this than by having supposedly weak and fragile women working on the flights?'

Flying in those days was a terrifying experience. The planes had to fly below 10,000ft because there was no oxygen on board. This meant that you also experienced severe turbulence, as well as being very cold and uncomfortable. Ellen argued that the profession of nursing was an indispensable attribute to have on board an aircraft. She told him, 'Mr Stimpson, imagine women casually living in the air, choosing to work there. It would have a good psychological affect in helping rid the public of any fear.' Boeing found this difficult to resist and seven more registered nurses were then recruited to look after the passengers on their aircraft. Ellen helped recruit Alva Johnson, Margaret Arnott, Inez Keller Fuite, Cornelia Peterman, Harriet Fry Iden, Jessie Carter and Ellis Crawford. They wore a white nurse's uniform during the flight. On the ground, the uniform consisted of a dark green woollen twill suit with an A-line skirt just below the knee, a double-breasted jacket with silver buttons, and a cape and beret. As passengers' wicker seats had to be secured to the floor of the aircraft, the cape had pockets large enough to hold a screwdriver and a spanner. They also wore sensible shoes that could only be described as boarding school lace-ups or nursing shoes. This military look was later adopted by BSAA and BOAC for their stewardesses.

They earned US $125 a month for about a hundred hours of work, plus US $6 a day for meal allowances. The uniform was provided free of charge as was the cost of having it cleaned. They had to weigh no more than 115lb and be over 5ft 4in in height.

These first stewardesses worked on Boeing 80s, the latest tri-motor design. The passenger cabins were fitted out to look like a Pullman railroad car and as such could accommodate about a dozen passengers. A typical route was between Oakland and Wyoming, a distance of 950 miles. It had five stops. This was supposed to be an eighteen-hour flight; it ended up being more like twenty-four.

The passengers were served cold chicken, bread rolls and fruit salad. Some would say this seemed a cut above what one is often served today. Safety briefings were done by the stewardesses and passengers were particularly reminded not to throw their lighted cigarette butts out of the windows. Swatting flies in the cabin and mopping up leaking loos in rough weather were also part of their duties. The stewardesses preferred these chemical loos in spite of the leaks as these loos replaced the windy open-air variety. The latter lavatory was a can, set in a ring with a hole cut in the floor, so when one lifted the seat, it was an open-air model. Often the stewardesses' duties were not over until they had helped push the plane into the hangar. When there was an emergency landing in a field, the stewardesses had to assist in knocking down the farmers' fences to allow the plane to take off again.

The aircraft flew at a height of 2,000ft and much of the flight was uncomfortable. The cabins were not pressurised, the heating system was inefficient and the noise from the engines deafening. The passengers were issued with earplugs on boarding. The stewardesses' duties were very varied and included being expected to help with the five-gallon cans from which the aircraft tanks had to be refuelled and loading baggage. Caring for sick passengers in an unventilated un-pressurised plane provided a lot of in-flight illness to be dealt with.

The captain and co-pilot were always given a salute when they boarded, this being an instruction from the manual devised by Ellen and Stimpson. The priorities on an early 1930s flight were mail, passengers, stewardess in that order. If the pilot thought the aircraft was overweight, the stewardess was dumped and the flight continued without her, in spite of her salute.

# Here to Stay

Ellen Church's idea quickly started to pay dividends. Soon after the first eight began their flying career, bookings at BAT rose by 30 per cent. The concept of using stewardesses for commercial advantage had begun. Soon other airlines were rapidly emulating the idea, and the stewardesses quickly made their mark.

There was no going back now. People felt safer with a woman on board, especially one who was a nurse. The psychological effect and benefit was enormous. However, although the passengers took to stewardesses with enthusiasm, the pilots' reaction was less enthusiastic and that of their wives even less so. Reactions to female flight attendants varied from gratitude to jealousy, depending on whether or not you were a passenger.

Early stewardesses flew unlimited hours for years, but by the spring of 1946, hours were limited to eighty-five per week for US $125. There were still restrictions for the women. A stewardess had to be under twenty-six and unmarried. Other airlines had adopted Ellen Church's idea and insisted that she also had to be a trained nurse, for reasons other than her obvious medical skills. Having a nursing qualification came with the supposition that her training had given her other essential attributes. For example, she had been taught to obey orders, she had learned how to put people at ease and how to be pleasant to them, and all this with tact and consideration. So comfort would be the domain of the girls. Everything else in the airline industry was controlled by men. However, Ellen Church pioneered an industry, as Andrew Buncombe says, 'overcoming the odds in a business world dominated by men and at a time when aviation was a decidedly precarious activity.'

In England, Imperial Airways was operating with stewards and had no intention of changing. According to Captain Young, whose wife was interviewed by Imperial Airways in 1943, 'this scheme fell through due to World War II'. In 1940, when British Overseas Airways Corporation was formed (this was a merger of Imperial Airways and British Airways), many innovations were introduced. BOAC did employ stewardesses during the war according to Harald Penrose in *Wings Across the World – An Illustrated History of British Airways*, but these were few, and it was 1943. Most 'would-be' stewardesses had to wait until the war was over to begin their exciting new career. However, according to Hugh Yea 'their employment was but a wartime expedient and was never contemplated as being a prelude to the post-war recruitment of stewardesses for long-distance overseas operations.'

The first and only pre-war British air hostess had begun flying duties on 16 May 1936. Her name was Daphne Kearley and at nineteen she was recruited by Air Dispatch to serve aboard its 'Blue Plane' service between Croydon and Paris. The aircraft was a sixteen-seat Avro 642/2m G-ACVF.D. For the sum of £3 a week, Daphne had to serve salmon and caviar, type business passengers' dictation, mix cocktails and speak French. It was only a ten-month career as the one and only Avro 64 was sold by Air Dispatch at the end of 1936.

## *M*EANWHILE, DOWN UNDER

Blanche Due and Marguerite Grueber were the first Australian air hostesses to take to the air in March 1936. The airline was called Tasmanian Aerial Services, initially known as Holymans Airways. After many mergers and takeovers, it became Ansett Airlines of Australia. Blanche and Marguerite were told to fit themselves out, which they did, in uniforms costing about four Aussie pounds each. They also organised the airline's catering requirements, which consisted of carrying two thermos flasks of tea, waxed paper cups and biscuits onto the aircraft in a suitcase which was usually stowed on a spare seat. The aircraft were DH 86s, then DC2s, flying from Launceston to Melbourne and Sydney.

Crossing the Bass Strait was always a toss up for passengers as to whether to brave the all-night ship journey which battled the high seas, or take a chance on one of these new aircraft. The weather was and still is notoriously rough here, so instruction included exercises to train the air hostesses in surefootedness in turbulent weather, while carrying cups of tea or trays of food. This took the form of walking across ten 'wobble boards' that were round in shape, flat on top and rounded beneath. So it was a balancing act to help one navigate and step one's way around the course carrying liquid and food.

## Qantas

Although this book is about BA and its predecessors, one couldn't possibly write about the airline's history without mentioning Qantas. A partnership with Qantas began in December 1948 on the London to Sydney run with the Constellations, and being an Australian, I feel very proud of Qantas.

Stewardesses were able to join Qantas much later than British Airways. In Qantas' early days, cabin service had been in the hands of stewards. However, towards the end of the '40s and beginning of the '50s, Qantas saw the need to employ women when many children and officers' wives from the substantial forces in Singapore and Malaysia were travelling home. The usual height, age and weight restrictions, nursing experience, an excellent education and a second language were preferred criteria. In May 1948, Qantas had its first stewardesses, including Marjorie de Tracy, who was appointed Senior Flight Hostess and remained with Qantas for many years. Australia used the term 'air hostess' or the vernacular 'hostie' for many years.

In 1934, Qantas formed an alliance with Imperial Airways as part of their Empire Route – Australia to London. Qantas handed over its passengers at Singapore and Imperial Airways took them the rest of the way to London.

During the Second World War all her planes were taken up with war service. After the war, Qantas regained her dream of flying the Empire and began taking her passengers as far as Karachi and then handing over to BOAC crews. This was called the Kangaroo Route. In 1947 Qantas flew the journey from Australia to Britain on its own, but it was not until early 1993 that the alliance with BA started again. For those of us who flew and intermingled with the Qantas crews at the Karachi Resthouse, many fond memories remain. Qantas always brought a touch of madness, and hilarity and larrikinism to Speedbird House.

It was at Charleville, my local airport after I left BA, where the first Qantas scheduled flight began on 22 November 1922. The route was from Charleville to Longreach and was operated by a single-engine wood and fabric plane. And it was the Charleville Airport tower to whom I spoke from the 707 in the early '70s, and who passed on a message to my fiancé as we were flying over his cattle station en route from Darwin to Sydney.

<hr />

## The Great Debate – Stewardesses: To Be or Not To Be for BOAC?

An article in *The Aeroplane* of 29 November 1946 indicates that the idea of employing stewardesses was indeed controversial. BOAC boards vacillated on this notion and there was lengthy ambivalence on the subject. 'It may be all right for the Americans but British transport operators have proved that men can do a better job' was a common point of view, according to the article. A change of policy came with a new Board in 1943 and stewardesses were operating on the London to Lisbon service. Then another change of Board announced that women would be employed, but only on the ground. However, yet another policy reverted to favouring the idea and BOAC announced that thirteen girls were to be employed on the North Atlantic route. The Board's announcement defensively added that the women were chosen for their 'personality, tact, enthusiasm, physical fitness, education and that indefinable quality, "appearance".' Advertisements asked for young ladies 'with poise and an educated voice'. The article goes on to point out accompanying photographs, indicating that the airline had not gone out of its way to choose 'no nonsense plain Janes'! The application form actually said 'Glamour Girls need not apply'.

## BOAC'S First Stewardesses

It was on 10 May 1943 (the day before BOAC began a DC3 service between Britain and Portugal) that Rosamond Gilmour flew in a 200mph four-engine D.H.91 Frobisher Class Albatross from Whitchurch Airport, Bristol in Somerset to Shannon Airport, Rineanna, a shuttle service connecting the BOAC flying-boat services from Foynes. She was the first BOAC air hostess.'Discipline was strict and departure and destinations had to be kept secret for security reasons. Wartime food rationing made catering difficult ... washing up was routine, as was helping the cooks on the ground prepare the food for the flight.' As the *BOAC Review* for July 1964 said: 'This was to create a whole new profession for women.'

In November 1943, BOAC recruited five stewardesses to serve aboard its short-haul feeder services, operated by an assortment of flying-boats and land planes. These were Miss Helen Wigmore, Mrs Peggy Keyte, Miss Momkea Winter, Mrs Jeanne Cox and Miss Rosamond Gilmour. These five were soon joined by Jean Wortley and Barbara Baker (who replaced Rosamond Gilmour in 1944) to become the original seven.

The recruitment and initial training was carried out by Dudley Gibbons, BOAC's catering manager. By the summer of 1944, several of its C-47 Dakotas, and two of its stewardesses, Helen Wigmore and now Viva Barker, were based at Croydon to operate the civilian shuttle services between Croydon and Shannon Airport, Rineanna. These connected with BOAC's transatlantic flying-boats, and those of Pan American Airways and airlines which terminated in Ireland at Foynes.

The role of the stewardess was firmly established in the '50s. In their advertising, airlines cashed in on the image of elegance, confidence and professionalism that these young women projected. Some selected one of their stewardesses to be the public face of the airline, and the marketing and advertising men portrayed her in magazine after magazine and on hoardings. Air travel was taking off and the stewardess with her poise and feminine attributes was considered a prime driving force behind the growing army of air travellers.

United Airlines was one of the first to make radical changes to attract women to the job and in 1957 lowered the minimum age from twenty-five to twenty. Also, framed glasses were then permitted; up until that time only contact lenses were allowed. Then, somehow, the cut-off age for women (there never was a cut-off point for stewards) seemed to have been lost.

Records reveal that increasing numbers of female flight attendants, as they are now called, worked until thirty-five, forty and even up to the current fifty-five and fifty-eight years. Obviously the age of thirty-two as a cut-off point for women never worked for the American Airlines, even then. United Airline's oldest stewardess in the summer of 2004 was Iris Petersen Copin who 'is eighty-three years young with fifty-eight years of service'. (*Clipped Wings Quarterly*, summer 2004)

## The Formidable Forties – The Rara Avis

In the early days of the '40s the stewardess was still a rare bird. In fact the work was called 'air hostessing' by many, particularly in the USA and Australia. However, in England they were *always* known as stewardesses. According to Winston Bray in his *History of BOAC*:

✈     In 1945, BOAC had given some thought to the use of stewardesses and had decided for the time being that only the North Atlantic was a possible route. The catering branch set up a training school for entrants and the conditions laid down were strict. The age limits were twenty-three to thirty years and the girls had to pass a course of First Aid in addition to instruction on how to prepare and serve food.

The corporation was anxious to present the girls as hardworking members of the crew and not as glamour hostesses; this was the line followed in the press handouts when the first stewardesses were allocated to the Constellation flight in November 1946, dressed in what might be described as the female equivalent of the stewards' dark blue uniform.

During the war women had flown as nursing orderlies in the WAAF, and for many years the majority of the girls employed by BSAA (British South American Airways) and BOAC came from the Defence Forces. As Audrey Cartmell points out, 'Women from the Forces were seen as more suitable because we had been used to working with men.' But it had to be more than that.

## Stargirls of BSAA

Talking to many of the women who flew in the middle to late '40s is like being in a time warp. They speak of their flying time as if it were yesterday and, of course, I was very keen to talk to them before too many of them departed for the great airport in the sky.

I needed some assistance, so I plucked up the courage to ask a man who literally terrified me during my time with BOAC. I wanted him to describe the perfect stewardess to me. This man was a legend in BOAC. His name was Stan Bruce and he put the fear of God into just about everybody in Cabin Services. In spite of my fears, he could not have been more helpful. Immediately he said: 'Cynthia Arpthorp-White! You must talk to her!' Later he gave me a lot of information about himself, which I now realise made him the man he was: an authority on aircraft cabin service. So began my search for Stargirls.

So while the US had their pioneering 'First Eight' with Boeing Transport, Britain had the famous Stargirls. They flew with BSAA, the airline started up by Air Vice Marshal Don Bennett CB, CBE, DSO. Bennett had commanded the Pathfinder Group of Bomber Command during the war and had a distinguished flying career. He founded the North Atlantic Ferry organisation that was responsible for the delivery of aircraft from American factories to the United Kingdom. He had been a captain with Imperial Airways, and was renowned for doing things his way. A workaholic, he expected everyone to work as long and hard as he did.

The first Stargirl to be employed by BSSA was Mary Guthrie, a former Aircraft Transport Auxiliary pilot in 1943. Originally Mary had been with the Voluntary Aid Detachment during the war, where she gained experience in nursing. Then she joined the ATA and gained her Wings to become Third Officer Guthrie. She ferried aircraft such as the Spitfire from one RAF base to another. Her first flight out of Heathrow was in January 1946 to South America in Avro Lancastrian G-AGWG with AVM Bennett as the captain. Mary made history as this was the first official flight from Heathrow. She wore her ATA pilot's uniform as the Stargirl's uniform was yet to come.

The aircraft the Stargirls flew were converted bombers – the Avro 691 Lancastrians and Avro Yorks. All the aircraft were given names beginning with the word 'Star', which is why the stewardesses were given the affectionate 'Stargirl' name. The thirteen-seater Lancastrian operated the first services to South America in 1946, flying over the Andes. Although the aircraft was capable of flying at 25,000ft or more, it normally cruised at 10,000ft. Joan Thompson had the distinction of being the first Stargirl to cross the Andes. Joan was the first Head Stargirl and responsible for shortlisting the hundreds of applications for the Stargirl selection boards. Out of 300 applications thirty were chosen.

The Stargirl was given the task of managing the oxygen supply, as this was the only flight (from Buenos Aires to Santiago) that required the passengers and crew to wear the masks. She had to ensure that the right amount of oxygen was issued from the control panel in the galley. The captain would ring his buzzer when it was time for the passengers to put on their masks. When they were all settled the stewardess would plug in the intercom set in the galley seat where she could keep an eye on the cabin and carry out her instructions. The aircraft would start to climb to an altitude of 20,000ft, and by the time it reached 12,000ft all the passengers would be ready. At every 1,000ft after that the Stargirl raised the control dial in accordance with the captain's instructions. She waited for the go ahead from the captain for the oxygen to be switched off after the descent had begun.

One Stargirl with BSAA remembers: 'My bottle of oxygen, which I wore over my shoulder, lasted just eight minutes.' Ruth March later observed that it was 'difficult to believe … that the same light mask we were all wearing was also keeping the crew fully aware and responsible and able to fly the aeroplane.'

Sybil Daniel-Tanner remembers:

✈    On the Yorks we cooked scrambled eggs and served 'frood' – our name for the frozen food that Lyons prepared for us. My worst experience was on take off from Hong Kong Kai Tak Airport. A very large dog in a crate in the freight compartment on the flight deck broke loose in terror! Blood and froth everywhere. We had to make an immediate and very rapid landing with a full load of fuel.

Sybil provides other impressions:

✈    The noise … we handed out cotton wool to the passengers. Thinking what a small spot in the ocean Bermuda was to find. How beautiful in the sparkling sunlight were the groups of islands with the colour-washed houses with white lime-encrusted rooftops and the blue, blue sea all around.

As Sybil recalls, 'there was no PA system in Lancs and Yorks … our equipment was huge flasks, 'the thermos flasks' holding anything from soups, hot meals for plating up and fruit salads. Soda siphons and saucepans.'

On the Lancastrians, the girls were issued with a uniform, which included a divided skirt, what we today would call culottes. This was because the galley was forward of the 2ft-high main spar between the wings, which was a formidable obstacle the stewardess had to climb over every time she went out from the galley into the passenger cabin. One had to have the dexterity of a ballet dancer as food and drink had to go over the spar as well. As well as this hurdle, the cabin had eleven seats in the rear of the cabin and two just behind the galley, which was a step higher than the main part of the cabin. Anyone who sat in these two specific seats was privy to a marvellous view of glamorous pairs of legs continually hopping over it during the flight.

The Stargirls' salary was £4 a week, and they received no overseas allowances. The training was very much 'hands on', or 'on the job training'.

✈    The training consisted of one week's catering in a London airport shed, making sandwiches, followed by six trips between London and Lisbon and back with another Stargirl who was senior to you. Then you were on your own. After those six flights to Lisbon and return you became a trainer yourself and took a novice with you for her first six flights. And of course these aircraft were not pressurised and the conditions could be very bumpy. It was indeed difficult not to feel very airsick a lot of the time.

The Yorks carried two stewardesses, as they were twenty-one-seaters, so they were not always alone.

Catering was a truly amazing feat. Coffee and biscuits were served, followed by lunch. Every passenger's tray was laid individually and the frozen food was heated in very slow ovens. It sometimes took up to three hours to get the food to edible standard. The Stargirls did all the washing up on board; they cleaned the ovens, and washed the galley floor as well. On top of this they had to check and count all the equipment. As passengers were seated they were given barley sugar to suck during climb and descent, and cotton wool to protect their ears from the thundering roar of the engines.

Archie Jackson, a pilot with BSSA, tells a story about one of the Stargirls:

✈    We used a radar system called 'Eureka Rebecca' which enabled the navigator to measure the aircraft's distance from a similarly equipped airport when it was flying within a ninety-mile range. The Stargirl collecting the dirty cups and saucers from the flight deck heard the navigator complain to the captain that his set seemed to be unserviceable. 'Can't get a peep out of the bloody thing,' he grumbled, thumping the top of his receiver in disgust. 'Let me have a look,' suggested the Stargirl. A mere ten minutes later the set was in working order. 'I was a radar mechanic in the WAAF,' she explained.

## A Legend in Her Own Flying Lifetime

One of the greatest stewardesses for passengers to chat with was Sylvia Haynes. With her unique, ebullient personality, she was known to have 'passengers eating out of her hands'. Sylvia served as a Leading Wren with the Fleet Air Arm for three years before joining British South American Airways in 1947. She flew on Lancastrians and Avro Yorks to the West Coast of South America from Nassau, where she was posted. She was flying at the time when the Tudor 'Stardust' crashed into the Andes. Fifty years later, when well and truly retired, she read in the paper that the wreckage had at last been found.

Sylvia joined BOAC when the merger occurred. She was known fondly in the airline as 'Starbottom', for as well as being described as buxom, she had been one of the famous Stargirls. I caught up with Sylvia in 2002, and although I hadn't seen her for at least thirty years, she still had a complexion like alabaster and was impeccably groomed. She was in her middle to late seventies but looked at least twenty years younger. I commented on her meticulous approach to her grooming and she said: 'I would never go outside without being completely made up. I take my time now, but feel it is important to always look perfectly groomed.' Her high personal standards regarding dress meant that she carried out the wearer trials for the Hardy Amies uniform. She flew for thirty-four years.

Sylvia told me of the first time she flew to Australia. She had already flown 1,500,000 miles, but had never been to Australia. After they had left Sydney the captain, flying the Britannia, received a mercy call to land at a place called Cloncurry, which was a small outback town in central Queensland. The call was to pick up a severely injured pilot of a Royal Flying Doctor plane. The flying doctor and the pilot were searching for a stockman kicked by his horse. Later the stockman recovered sufficiently to ride seventeen miles to get help. The pilot had been seriously injured when he had hit a fence on landing. The doctor and his wife, who was the nurse, were also injured. Moreover, the 70-ton *Britannia* was bogged in the runway because of heavy rains and another aircraft from Qantas had to be called in to take the injured pilot to hospital. Townspeople and graziers came out to offer help with tractors to pull the Britannia out of the bog or just to watch. After many unsuccessful attempts, the BOAC crew had to remain in Cloncurry and wait for conditions to dry out.

The people with whom she flew reads like a Who's Who list: Prime Ministers Hume, Eden and Thatcher, Sterling Moss, Frankie Howard, Derek Nimmo, Cilla Black, Uri Geller (she still has a bent first class silver spoon to prove it), Sir David Frost, Michael Parkinson, Joan Crawford and the 1948 Arsenal Squad among many others. But it was the Queen Mother who impressed her the most. 'She was the nicest person I ever flew with,' commented Sylvia. Lying on the table, as she spoke, was one white uniform glove – the glove that shook the Queen Mother's hand, in 1957, when she took the Queen to Rhodesia (now Zimbabwe) in a Britannia.

"They don't make them like that anymore!" (CSO Sylvia Haynes retired recently after 34 year's service)

In 1977, she ended her career on 747s as a CSO, having also flown on Argonauts, 707s and VC10s. In that same year, Sylvia was the recipient of the Silver Jubilee Award, presented to her by the Queen, in recognition of her loyal services to both the company and the public. In fact this was the only award ever given to a member of British Airways cabin crew.

## Juggling Duties on the Lancastrian

Diana Chester-Masters was a Stargirl with BSSA in the late '40s. Diana felt the qualities that got her into the airline were her languages, which were French and German. She had spent four years in the Armed Forces during the war. Joining up at eighteen, when she was demobbed from the army, she had reached quite a high rank. She remembers being told when she was twenty-five that she was at the right age for becoming a Stargirl, and that she looked the part: 'So it was the spirit of adventure that drew me.'

Diana maintains the only discipline 'that was strictly kept was the eight-hour ban on drinking before flying'. She remembers how they would often joke around with the crew and recalls one such incident: 'The captain said he had accepted an offer of two camels from an Arab if he could take me off at the next stopover. I remember being quite upset as I thought he meant it! And of course we were the only girls with a crew of four and had to get used to all these tricks being played upon us.'

A typical trip lasted for a little over three weeks, which was London to Lisbon, Dakar, Natal, Rio, Buenos Aires, Monte Video, and Santiago. The Stargirls' favourite stopovers were Rio, Buenos Aires, Santiago and Bermuda. Diana recalls always staying in first class hotels wherever they landed. 'South America in the late '40s was the most glamorous of places. We didn't get allowances and were always broke. We would go to some local bar, eat peanuts and drink beer and sometimes survived on that.'

There were no Stargirls over the age of twenty-nine. Mostly they were in their mid-twenties. All the girls were expected to resign before their thirtieth birthday. The gods who managed airlines in those days had obviously decided that women had passed their 'use-by-date' on reaching thirty. As Diana says:

> ✈    Girls today would not be able to cope or put up with the long hours and low pay. There were no flight time limitations either. We once did a flight of thirty-six hours without a break but mostly it was around twelve hours. It was more of an adventure than a job!
>
> Food preparation on the Lancastrians meant handing out picnic boxes as there were no fridges. Later we went into heating prepared food in the galley ovens on the Yorks, which carried twenty-one passengers, and the Tudors thirty-two. We started to serve passengers using trays. I might add that even though the Lancastrians didn't carry many passengers, thirteen men to look after could be very demanding and of course in those days it was all one class! I took all the cash for drinks in many different currencies and had to carry the box about with me at the various fuelling stops. At destinations the money was counted up against the bottles and locked up.

Diana relates one of her best experiences. It was on 10 November 1947 and her flight on the *Star Tiger* was from Bermuda to London. She tells the story: 'We set a record. Completing the 3,500-mile flight from Bermuda to London in 11 hours and 32 minutes. The BSAA Tudor IV airliner established a new commercial record with a cruising speed of 310 miles per hour.'

And then there was the Queen's wedding: 'I was in charge of a wedding present from the British in Havana to Princess Elizabeth. It was a chest of two hundred cigars.'

But there are lows as well as highs with every job. Diana maintains that her worst experience was 'losing the Lancaster *Star Dust* over the Andes with our great crew friends. My crew were waiting in Santiago to take over. We went searching for the wreckage for hours from the air to no avail. The wreck was found forty years later.'

One of Diana's more memorable experiences was taking over the plane: 'Sometimes during long ten-hour night flights from Lisbon to Brazil, if you knew the skipper well he would let you up front to sit in his seat and "fly the plane", saying only "Don't make my passengers sick!".' Diana tells me that she had never spoken of this to the others, but when I asked another Stargirl, she said it was not uncommon to have a chance to sit in the pilot's seat.

## Catering to the Rich and Famous

Meeting Cynthia Arpthorp-White, who was now in her eighties, was like seeing an old friend. The camaraderie that existed between crews, and our memories of life down the routes, were very much alive. This petite and extremely attractive lady was still infused with vestiges of '40s glamour. We opened a bottle of red wine, and between many sips and laughter, she led me through her fabulous career.

During the war Cynthia was a Wren radar mechanic in the Fleet Air Arm where she held a highly classified position. In 1942 she worked with 'Catseye Cunningham', an RAF ace who attributed his success against German aircraft to eating lots of raw carrots: he reckoned this gave him 'good night vision'. Cynthia told me, 'I didn't wear category badges or any other insignia. However, I did a lot of flying to test radar sets and thus began my love of it'.

After the war Cynthia returned to teaching, but how she missed flying. A school friend had joined BSAA, and soon Cynthia joined her friend as a Stargirl:

> ✈   We had no training, and just simply hung around the airport doing ground staff duties, loading the aircraft, reception duties, taking the passengers to and from the aircraft. We learned what we could as we went along. We also worked in the shipping and freight department and did some administration. Air Vice-Marshall Bennett was running BSAA at the time and was the definitive martinet. No one was allowed to be idle for a minute.

Economy was paramount in Air Vice-Marshall Bennett's mind. He had strongly disapproved of BOAC, and regarded it as bloated with unproductive and thoroughly inefficient staff. He wanted no idle hands at BSAA, so between trips there were other jobs to do in the catering department, and having to scrub the floors both on the ground and in the air. Diana Chester-Masters later told me: 'We were never told beforehand that we had to scrub the galley and loo floors before each stopover.'

Cynthia continues her story: 'So in the ten days it took Debenham and Freebodys to make my uniform, I worked at the airport. And when the uniform was ready, and with no training, I was rostered out, and faced twenty-one passengers for six hours on a flight to Lisbon.'

These girls from BSAA really flew by the seat of their divided skirts. It was an exciting career for women who had had wartime experiences and stretched their imagination and their skills. There were very few jobs for women at this time that could offer such adventure and challenge.

There were no stewards with BSAA, although the possibility of recruiting male stewards had been mooted. Air Commodore Brackley, previously an air superintendent of Imperial Airways in the 1930s, met a delegation of three Stargirls who were most displeased that stewards were to be employed. They were reluctant to take orders from the newcomers not because they were men, but because the women had experience and feared that this would not be valued. There was also the question of seniority. In the short time that Brackley, who took over from AVM Bennett, was with BSAA the question was never resolved. Cynthia made it very clear: 'We were *not* stewardesses. We were *Stargirls!*'

The flights up and down the Andes under the rule of Pathfinder Bennett were both adventurous and often hazardous:

→   We flew in unpressurised Lancastrians and Yorks. Then came the Tudors, which were the first aircraft to be pressurised. However, they were somewhat unreliable. Once we were bringing back live turtles from the Bahamas, lightly crated for the Lord Mayor of London's annual ceremonial dinner, and the pressurisation went and these poor things ballooned out of their shells.

She continues:

→   BSAA introduced the first ovens, as we also were the first airline to use frozen food. BSAA were innovative in this way.
   I used to liaise with Lyons, who froze our food, about what worked and what didn't. With only one class (first), a full silver service of five courses involved laying up tables with white linen cloths and napkins, and glasses. I needed a frying pan for cooking bacon and eggs, fortunately for only about fourteen passengers. White gloves were part of the service, especially when I served royalty.

Cynthia looked after the Queen, the late King George, the Queen Mother, Princess Margaret, Princess Marina Duchess of Kent, as well as Winston Churchill and the Mountbattens.
   She recalls Sir Anthony Eden saying he was bored and insisting on helping Cynthia to dry the dishes. Initially he had said he would do the washing up, because he had nothing else to do. On another occasion Earl De La Ware, the Post Master General, laid up the tables: 'He put a napkin over his arm and, despite my protestations, insisted on helping. He said, "No, I want to help!" And so he laid up the tables and I served the chicken and he followed with the pommes parisienne.'
   Cynthia remembers many movie-star passengers, like Errol Flynn, who flew with her. 'This was in Nassau when I was starting a catering base there. He insisted on giving me one of his harpoon guns, because I swam on my own a lot. It had a pole with a nail on the end to bonk a shark on its nose if it came too close.' Elizabeth Taylor was on a Stratocruiser to New York. The seats converted to beds so the passengers went to bed 'properly':

→   Elizabeth was young and very beautiful, and every single one of the cabin crew wanted to take her early morning cup of tea, to see those amazing violet blue eyes open!
   I did enjoy the Stratocruisers, which, like the Argonauts, came into service with BOAC in 1949. We converted the seats into beds with curtains, and the passengers changed into pyjamas and nighties. Beds are now in fashion again.

Cynthia also looked after authors such as Agatha Christie and Raymond Chandler.
   Celia Hepworth was now the Head Stargirl, and Cynthia was Deputy Senior Stargirl with BSAA. Later, when BSSA was forced to shut down, she became a Fleet Stewardess on the Argonauts, Britannias and Constellations with BOAC, which had taken over BSAA. Eve Goodliffe spent six years on the Argonauts. She remembers that 'the Yorks were not pressurised and we flew at 10,000ft or 11,000ft. We had cotton wool in our ears because of the noise of the four Merlin engines. By the time we had flown five hours to Lisbon, and eight hours to Dakar we were completely exhausted.'
   Names of the some of the other Stargirls included: Terry Barzilay, Marjorie Tong, Priscilla Vinyalls, Joan Lywood, Eve Branson, Monica 'Twink' Tyndall, Faith Sissman, Judy Bruce-Lockhart, Ann Barker-Mill, Tessa Stevens, Vilma Baron, Margaret Owen, Kay Hutchinson, Naida Smart, Zoe Jenner, Evelyn Goodliffe, Margaret Owen, Kay Bardell, Sylvia Haynes, Jean Fowler, Pat Gummer, June Maddock, Valerie Pennington, Mary Spiers, Maggie Lawrence, Iris Evans to name only a few.
   Those who lost their lives in service were Sheila Nicolls, J. Moxon, Mrs Hetherington, Iris Evans and Lyn Clayton. What tremendous unsung courage and fortitude was displayed

by all the Stargirls. I will take Lyn Clayton as an example. An ex-WRN, she joined in July 1946. A month later a Lancastrian crashed in Gambia, no casualties; the following month the York 'Star Leader' crashed killing Stargirl Mrs Hetherington on her first trip; seven months after that a York 'Star Speed' in which she was flying crashed killing four passengers and injuring other passengers and crew. During 1947 another three Lancastrians crashed. In spite of the obvious risks she continued to fly, as others did. In January 1948, the Tudor 'Star Tiger,' with Lyn and Sheila Nicolls aboard, was lost between the Azores and Bermuda. From a safety perspective, this could not be considered a Golden Age for those spirited stewardesses who flew at that time.

In those early years where there were so many fatal accidents, I quote Harald Penrose who said: 'Perhaps it was the memory of huge war-time losses that made this total seem acceptable in relation to the enormous mileage the three corporations were flying.'

The demise of BSAA occurred in 1949. Two Tudors had disappeared in unexplained circumstances, and as BSAA was unable to establish the cause, the Air Registration Board could not recommend renewing the certificates of airworthiness for the Tudors. Thus with only the Yorks and Lancastrians, which were really not up to the job, Francis Pakenham of the Civil Aviation Ministry recognised that BSAA was no longer a viable company. Under the Airways Corporation Act of July 1949, BSAA was taken over by BOAC. Bennett upset the government by talking to the press about the grounding of the Tudors. He was furious that he was not consulted about this and said so.

This was an awkward time for many of the ex-Stargirls, as they had been used to being the only woman in charge on the aircraft. 'There were many problems with chief stewards when we first moved over. They were not used to working with the girls and didn't like me being in charge of them,' Cynthia recalls. 'This only lasted for six months before I went into recruitment and training. In fact the BSAA crews were sent onto the Eastern routes, known to be the hard routes, with tougher flying and living conditions. But for the BSAA people this was a piece of cake compared to what they had previously experienced.'

Cynthia was later appointed Catering Manager for Iraqi Airways, on a secondment, and later became BOAC's first manager of the new Japanese and Chinese stewardesses based in Hong Kong. BOAC was the first airline to employ national stewardesses, and this was Cynthia's idea. Many other international airlines eventually followed her lead. Cynthia also designed a BOAC uniform, the white cheong sam for the Chinese stewardesses which remained unchanged for more than twenty years.

Cynthia's contribution to women in civil aviation in the late '40s and early '50s, even by today's standards, was quite phenomenal.

## The First Woman to Fly the Atlantic 500 Times

I met Felicity Farquharson when I first began to think about writing this book and was invited to her home, then in Vicarage Gate, London. Although aged eighty-five, she was still as feisty as the young woman who had flown the Atlantic so many times that she made history, having flown 500 times.

After I sat down in her sitting room surrounded by piles of papers and memorabilia, she said to me: 'It's important that someone writes about this early history. We were pioneers in the airline industry and there are so many awful TV programmes that give completely the wrong idea about who we were and what we did!'

Her full name was Felicity Gillian Farquharson Farquharson – 'Intentional,' she said. Had she married she would never have lost the Farquharson. But she never married; many consider she married BOAC instead. During the war she worked with the RAF as a Voluntary Aid Detachment Auxiliary. She was assigned to a hospital in Devon, which specialised in caring for men with disfiguring wounds. They were sent there to be cared for and comforted by the prettiest of nurses, and Felicity was very pretty indeed. Nonetheless, it took courage, optimism, and strength to care for these shattered men and Felicity had vast quantities of all these qualities.

Felicity later became a role model for the airline, where strict grooming standards were demanded. She was renowned for taking great pride in her appearance. In those days an air stewardess had something of the glamour of a Hollywood starlet, and BOAC publicised her achievements with a considerable advertising campaign. Felicity showed me a letter dated November 1944, which sought to discourage her from applying for 'air hostess work' because the competition was so tough. The letter went on to say, 'And the applications are numerous. So numerous in fact that it is possible to secure women for the job with qualifications far exceeding the needs of the job'.

Indeed, that would be the case for many years. The difference between what the profession demanded and the apparent professional and educational levels of these highly skilled women was a cause of endless frustration in the early years. The women struggled to be acknowledged for this and to gain management roles on the aircraft.

In the end, Felicity was accepted. She was one of the very first stewardesses hired, and her first flight was out of New York in December 1946 on a Constellation. Her 100th flight from New York to London took sixteen and a half hours with two stops – fourteen hours in the air. She stopped flying in 1957 and took a ground role. In 1972 she retired after nearly twenty-seven years, the last of the original twelve still working for the airline.


## Lasting Memories and Impressions

Diana Borthwick, who flew in the late '40s on Constellations, said:

> ✈   I thought the aircraft noise was thrilling and the aircraft steps were *very* steep, but we didn't have any comparison. The passengers changed into nightwear [and were] woken with a cup of tea – such leisure. We used silver, crystal, linen napkins and issued scented Elizabeth Arden Blue Grass moistened towels before take off to cool people. No one was hurried. One got to know all the passengers by name and when you were not busy you could sit and talk to them, even play cards. At night stops we would take the passengers on tours.

Diana had been in the WRNS and mentioned in dispatches. She recalls that in her training:

> ✈   We had to go through a pressure chamber to see how we would react in an emergency. We were also tried out on a simulator. There were quite a few air crashes!
>
> So much to do – sailing, riding, shopping, sightseeing, swimming – the greatest challenge was just the fact of flying, although I had done some in the Fleet Air Arm … it was still a thrill as only a minority of people had travelled at that time… The Constellation was a lovely aircraft. I made many friends with the passengers.

In June 2004, I met Olive Marshall who flew on Dakotas, Solent flying-boats, Argonauts, Constellations, Stratocruisers and the Comet 1 between 1947 and 1953. She was an ex-WRAAF radar officer, and resourcefulness had stayed with her. Her first trip was on a Dakota. A return flight between London and Nairobi involved sixty-five hours flying in eight days over twenty-one sectors, rarely above 7,000ft to avoid rough weather. She had never been on one before and was the sole cabin crew. Quite an initiation! The departure lounge was a big tent over on the north side of the old London Airport, which could get very muddy at the entrance.

# THE DAKOTA

### Captain David T. Holloway, Rtd, RAF, BEA, British Caledonia, British Airways

Douglas DC3 G-AGBB

When the Dakota entered service on 26 June 1936 it represented an advance in air travel as significant as the introduction of wide-bodied jets thirty years later. For passengers and crew the Dakota, which was variously known as the DC3 and C47, was a major step forward in design, safety, passenger comfort, amenities, range, speed, and performance. Ask a Dakota pilot about his aeroplane and his eyes are likely to turn misty. He will probably say: 'She is a real lady.' Gentle and reliable, never skittish, she will cope with the worst possible weather conditions. Forgiving by nature, she carried none of the vices shared liberally among contemporary designs. The Pratt & Whitney Twin Wasp engines were not only extremely reliable, but like the robust airframe they coped happily with the extensive misuse and mishandling born of wartime operations.

Perhaps the most significant advance was being able to stand upright and walk through the cabin attending to passengers' needs. Such simple things have long since been taken for granted, but seventy years ago it took visionary thinking, enterprise, and competition to bring them to fruition.

By 1943 BOAC were operating six Dakota flights a week between Cairo and Lagos. By April 1944 there were services between the UK and Lagos, and flights to Algiers had been extended to Cairo. On 1 November 1946, British European Airways (BEA) was formed and many of BOAC's Dakotas and crews were transferred to the new airline. While BEA became the major Dakota operator in Europe, BOAC continued to use the aircraft on Middle East and African routes until 1950.

Although I was privileged to fly 4,680 hours in the Dakota, when the time came to move on I did not miss the freezing flight deck on early morning departures, or the stifling heat in warmer climes. Better equipped, flying at high speed above the most adverse weather, the new passenger jets were a delight to fly, but my first love was undoubtedly the Dakota, 'the First Lady of the Skies'.

Olive was among the first group of stewardesses taken on by BOAC in 1946, one of only twelve recruited by the very first selection board for stewardesses:

➤    I went up before the board along with 300 other hopefuls. The 300 had been whittled down from 3,000 so I was very lucky to be 'one of just twelve chosen'. I was after Felicity Farquharson and Cynthia Arpthorp-White, Viva Barker, Helen Wigmore and Peggy Keyte, who were recruited prior to 1946.

Olive said: 'I was told I was a bit fat. Fortunately the president of the board, Lady Salisbury, was very ample and intervened, and said, "I think she is just right".' This is just one of the many incredibly sexist experiences BOAC was to impose on the women who experienced the interview process over the years.

At the interview Olive was asked how she would cope if they were forced to land on a desert island.

✈      They told me I had to kill a chicken, pluck and prepare it to feed the passengers. I managed to hide my revulsion and said, 'I'm a farmer's daughter', and that seemed to suffice! Later on the training course we learned how if we landed on a desert island, to watch what the monkeys ate and give those to the passengers, and how to collect water by the condensation overnight on the aircraft wings.

But training was not all about food and emergencies. 'I particularly enjoyed the two days we spent at Elizabeth Arden in Mayfair. We were supposed to be able to advise passengers on makeup and even give massages to passengers in flight.'

Olive vividly recalls the antagonism between the stewards and the girls: 'What we should have been told about in the training school was the resentment of the stewards to the invasion by women of their traditional territory.' She continued:

✈      The trainers were inexperienced in training a bunch of lively girls. As these girls were the first in their new training school, my course was called No. 1, and the course lasted for three months.

In our training I remember the acute embarrassment of the elderly instructor trying to remind us to let the roster clerk know what time of the month we expected to be 'unwell' so that we could be rostered accordingly – particularly when the class pretended they didn't know what he was talking about.

**This is a real Dakota stewardess!**

DEAR EDITOR: I refer to your photograph in the April edition purporting to show BOAC stewardesses – and I enclose a photograph of a real Dakota Stewardess in a real BOAC uniform (left). The uniform was very different. Single-breasted, four buttons, brass buckle, stewardess brevet, court shoes and forage cap.

This Stewardess was Olive Marshall. In those days, the girls operated solo, 65 hours flying in eight days, over 21 sectors Nairobi and back, bouncing about in unpressurised cabins and trying to feed passengers and crew out of vacuum flasks. They washed up between meals. – Andy Carlisle, Wokingham.

Our training course also had to do a stint at the Airways Terminal in Buckingham Palace Road, BOAC's London Terminal, as waitresses in the underground dining room, sweltering in uniforms with stiff white collars. We were really used as cheap labour, and on one occasion we had to call on the TGWU, as in an extreme heatwave, this was the summer of 1947, girls were fainting left, right and centre. We had to threaten a strike and the union pledged to call out in sympathy all telephonists, porters etc.

I initially worked on the Dakotas and enjoyed this, although they were pretty rough and noisy. We only flew to 7,000ft as the cabins were unpressurised. Flying at that level often meant you couldn't get above bad weather, so it could be a little scary. And tricky trying to feed and take care of passengers and crew out of vacuum flasks and having to wash up between meals. For passengers flying for the first time this was very frightening. On the Dakotas there were no stewards – just us girls.

Olive was the first stewardess to operate on the BOAC Solent flying-boat G-AHIT to Johannesburg, on 4 May 1948. The Empire flying-boats based at Southampton were employed on the route to Lagos in Nigeria with stops at Foynes, Lisbon on the Tagus River, Bathurst and Freetown. 'Later I flew on the Constellation to Australia, the first stewardess to fly on them. On these trips my greatest challenge was keeping up my stamina!' There were no flight time limitations in those days, and her log book showed sectors of eleven to thirty-six hours, and days of seventeen hours' duration:

✈    I enjoyed the flying-boats. We laid up the tables attractively, using silver service, serving canapés and aperitifs often on the promenade deck. And we were certainly trained in how to serve the passengers. A luncheon began with cream of celery soup, followed by braised ham served with pommes dauphines, creamed spinach and garden peas. The sweet was compote of cherries and cream. Then we served assorted cheeses with biscuits and fresh fruit, coffee and brandy.

I did not do the cooking; this was the task of the steward. We now had the new electrical Crittall ovens, so the courses were served piping hot, freshly cooked. It was a first class restaurant.

The flying-boats were the last word in luxury and sophistication. Comfort was the priority and high standards of passenger care were set and maintained. Passengers could walk up and down the promenade deck, have a cigarette and a cocktail at the bar and more importantly stretch their legs before returning to their seats below in the Solent's interior. As Olive said:

✈    I can only describe it as sumptuous – comparable with the lounge of a luxury hotel.

The ladies room had large mirrors with expensive cosmetics, two dressing tables, flattering lighting, and was off the promenade deck. Further on was a staircase leading to the upstairs seating. On the promenade deck was a library and then the men's cloakroom and beyond this two cabins with six seats which on some flying-boats were beds.

Always on take off and landing the stewards fastened bulkheads to the doors separating the two cabins below so that if water came in it could be contained. All that I have described was below the flight deck. During take off some spray was visible as the aircraft rose on to the forward 'step' before climbing. Touching down, the displaced water completely covered the window and could be a little unnerving, rather more so if the flying-boat did a heavy water landing.

I went on two proving flights and was the stewardess on the first passenger service. It took four and half days to fly from Southampton to Johannesburg. The flying-boat would reach Sicily on the first day, sometimes Marseilles then on to Cairo. We all lunched together, passengers and crew, on a boat on the Nile before flying to Luxor to stay the night. The next stop was the Silver Springs Hotel at Lake Victoria. From here we flew on to the Victoria Falls and then Johannesburg landing at Vaal Dam, south of the city. The final part of the journey for the passengers was a bus to the city.

Our uniform was navy serge with long-sleeved shirts with separate stiff collars, and black ties, navy court shoes and a 'fore' and 'aft' cap. The tropical dresses were dreadful, made of heavy khaki drill, a so-called design by Norman Hartnell. When they were laundered overseas, as they had to be, they were usually starched, and would stand up on their own!

## FLYING-BOATS IN BOAC

### Captain Ken Emmott, Rtd, British Airways

Immediately after the First World War, there was an urgent need to resume and improve communications with what was then the British Empire. Landplanes, landing aids and suitable runways had only been developed for military purposes, so the obvious stopgap aircraft was the flying-boat. An immediate conversion of the wartime Sunderland was readily available, and expensive runways were not required, as there were so many suitable rivers, lakes and harbours eminently usable by flying-boats. Routes were established, or lengthened as appropriate, to Singapore, Hong Kong, Japan, South Africa and Australia using the same BOAC flying-boats which were handed over at Singapore. In those days a flying-boat crew, based at Hythe on Southampton Water, were absent on a protracted trip of up to thirty-eight days away, including 'shuttles' from Hong Kong to Iwakuni, Japan, Okinawa, Singapore and Bangkok. Crews were recompensed for those comparatively long trips by an appropriately long 'stand-off' back home in the UK of some thirty days or more.

The backbone of BOAC's flying-boat fleet was the wartime Sunderland, some of which had been converted to passenger use, and were known as the Hythes. These were four-engined aircraft with a passenger capacity of about thirty people, all of whom were pleasantly accommodated on board at tables, four to a table, making for a sociable day's travelling. So with the newly found glamour of landing and taking off from water; this was always incredibly smooth when compared with landplanes most of the time! Flying on most routes was only carried out in daylight, there being few facilities for night operations at that time. Passengers could therefore look forward to an exciting night-stop after their day in the air, at places such as Luxor on the Nile, Lake Victoria in Uganda, and Victoria Falls on the Zambezi, at all of which BOAC provided some entertainment such as local magicians, conjurers, ghuli-ghuli men, moonlight visits to Victoria Falls etc. Later routes to the Far East and Australia included night operations which were perhaps not quite so romantic as in Africa.

Those fascinating days could not last, of course. Developments in aviation were proceeding apace, unfortunately for flying-boat enthusiasts in the direction of landplanes, with instrument landings, higher speeds, longer range and so on. The flying-boat itself intrinsically had a built-in disadvantage due to the need for a so much stronger, and therefore heavier, construction, with the inevitable poorer commercial efficiency. Improved and larger versions of the Hythe, known as Plymouths and Solents, did not stem the final demise of the flying-boats operated by BOAC, they made their last flights in service in 1950.

Passengers and crews alike regretted the passing of the commercial flying-boat in BOAC. It served during a building-up of air transport in the UK, a glamorous and exciting period for all concerned. For the crews themselves, the special techniques of handling the boats under conditions which never occurred on landplanes, will be fondly remembered.

Olive describes those days vividly:

> ✈ I would go to the Airline Terminal in Victoria London at 6.30 in the morning. By 7 a.m. the passengers arrived and they were bussed to Southampton. It only took two hours, not bad really, and we stopped for breakfast at the Hog's Back on the way. So the passengers really got to know each other before we even were airborne. Once at Berth 50 the passengers went through Emigration and Customs. The flying-boats now were berthed so we didn't need the launches.
>
> We carried thirty-four passengers with about fourteen on the bottom deck and twenty on top. The seats were fully adjustable and the windows were generous in size giving an excellent view. The seats were blue with a darker blue for the carpets. The upper part of the walls and the curtains were in two shades of beige, and concealed lighting gave a feeling of glamour and luxury to the cabin. There were tables between the seats, so four passengers to a table, and then the aisle and then single seats faced each other. There were no call bells as …'there was no need really. I was always in the cabins.
>
> Flying over Africa was always exciting. We cruised at 7,000ft at about 200mph, and the passengers could see the animals below from the promenade deck.
>
> In rough weather this was very different. Hot air rising from the desert had us rocking all over the place and the turbulence made a lot of people very ill indeed. It was the flight engineers who had their work cut out. Repairs down the routes were tricky, standing in a boat which was rocking most of the time as they worked on an engine.
>
> We only flew during the day mainly because at some places like Karachi and Alexandria it was too difficult to land on water at night. The benefit to us as crew was that we stayed in luxury hotels across the world and mostly at the same hotel as the passengers. Needless to say some people got to know each other very well. Later company policy changed … and the crews were put into a different hotel.

When they crossed the International Dateline, the passengers got a certificate. In the late '40s, Olive Marshall remembers that when they crossed the Equator, the captain would often make a quick drop in altitude, as if one was hopping over it so to speak, and an announcement would be made. Many believed that they actually had just 'hopped' over it! Olive recounts:

> ✈ Many passengers, particularly on the South African and Australian routes, were emigrating and not expecting to see England again. They were apprehensive, excited and usually on their first flight, always respectful and so observant of in-flight instructions. And of course after four and a half days and nights with us many passenger never expecting to see England again would weep and hug me on arrival, and then arrive at the lake to wave us goodbye on our return journey to London. Passengers were in awe of us – always so friendly.

Olive married a flight engineer and was allowed to continue flying, which she did for a few years until she decided to start a family. They were never on the same flight and sometimes didn't see each other for often seven weeks at a time. Olive finished by giving me one of her favourite memories: 'I was carrying a tray of food on the top deck of the flying-boat and I tripped over Douglas Bader's legs sticking out in the gangway. Blushing furiously I stammered my apologies. 'Don't worry, love,' he said, 'They're only made of tin!'

Elizabeth Weedon, now eighty-five, was one of ten taken from 2,000 applications in 1946. Her experiences in the Royal Navy and living in China and Malaya were invaluable and she flew in Dakotas, to Lydda, El Adem in the Western Desert where German prisoners-of-war were still clearing the battlefields three years after the war had ended. Her favourite time was spent on the Solent flying-boats. She told me:

✈    We flew off from Southampton, lunched ashore at Marseilles, slept in Augusta and with our thirty-two passengers visited Syracuse, a fascinating biblical city. After lunch in houseboats on the Nile at Cairo, we flew up the river to Luxor and went to the ruined temples in the Valley of the Kings. In withering heat we stayed in the so-called Grand Hotel at Khartoum and in the evening looked at the Omdurman battlefield. We flew up the White Nile to Lake Victoria, landing at Port Bell, and stayed in the Imperial Hotel at Kampala.

Each five-day journey from England to South Africa was an adventure in itself. I enjoyed the remarkable sights of Africa from the air, especially herds of galloping wild beasts disturbed by the aircraft as it flew over Tanganyika Nyasaland, Rhodesia and as we approached the Zambesi, the Victoria Falls could be seen and the roar heard miles away.

She told me that she was the first air hostess ever to arrive in Accra, on a BOAC York with a planeload of English school children who were the first ever to fly to the Gold Coast for their summer holidays. A favourite memory for her was on her return journey when a baby chimpanzee destined for London Zoo was placed in the York. The little creature whimpered and cried until Liz held his tiny hand and stayed with him to the end of the journey.

In November 1946, BOAC was still advertising for stewardesses for its flying-boats. Jean Gordon was one of twelve girls on the first official course to start in 1947. This course of twelve girls (designated as Course No.1) commenced training (along with stewards) on the sixth floor of Stratton House under the redoubtable Joe Lawrence. Unfortunately the Solents were not ready for service and the trainees, like their predecessors, were doomed to working in the passenger restaurant at Airways Terminal, Victoria. In mid-June 1947 two vacancies occurred and Jean Gordon and Marion Burton-Giles at last became airborne.

An interesting comparison with the airlines in America at that time was that whereas the American airlines took every opportunity to promote their girls, BOAC seemed very much opposed to such glorification – until many years later, that is. Such publicity was almost nonexistent, so many names of stewardesses at this time are not recorded.

# THE GODFATHER

Stan Bruce was called many names, some good and some not so good. He was also known as the 'Godfather' in in-flight catering circles. His career had not always been with British Airways and its predecessors. His early days were spent as a waiter in two of the very best hotels, The Dorchester in London and the Hotel Bristol in Vienna. Between these two he could be found at the Adlon Hotel in Berlin. It was there that he was given the name 'Stanislaus aus England' by one of the people he served, a vegetarian called Adolf Hitler.

Stan revealed: 'Getting into the airline industry was not what I intended to do, but giving exemplary service, serving the highest quality cuisine and wine, was what I most liked to do. There was a pride in this and a discipline.' However, when he was an RAF crewman on wartime services on Dakotas, he was spotted by the then Director General of BOAC, Brigadier-General A.C. Critchley, who incidentally was responsible for introducing frozen food to airline catering.

Stan became a chief steward on flying-boats in 1945. Then he was appointed flight steward on the Argonaut fleet, which took over the South American routes from BSAA.

Stan's famous superior silver service was the best in the world, and it provided the other airlines such as KLM, SAS and Lufthansa with some very stiff competition.

However, change was on its way. The then deputy chairman, Whitney Straight, wanted a tray service introduced, the forerunner of our economy tray today. This was when Stan met and worked with Cynthia Arpthorp-White in the many catering trials this innovation demanded.

Stan made his mark thanks to his continuous dedication to improving passenger cabin service and equipment. In 1974 his title was Manager Cabin Service Standards (Overseas Division) and he was awarded the MVO by the Queen in 1976. He was involved in cabin crew selection and one famous anecdote involves his disapproval of 'too many homosexuals joining our airline'. He suggested the question 'Do you like the ballet?' would be an infallible test in recruitment.

When we met up in 2003 and talked over many cups of tea and digestive biscuits, I found out that he was the original designer of the MTB – the mobile tray box, or meal tray trolley, which was to revolutionise the economy meal service, not only for BOAC, but for all the other airlines. Originally these MTBs held a dozen trays for passengers, but by the time they were modified for jumbo use they could carry thirty-six trays or seventy-two afternoon tea trays with tea and coffee on top.

◇◇◇◇◇◇◇◇◇◇◇◇◇◇◇◇◇◇◇◇◇◇◇◇◇◇◇◇◇◇◇◇◇◇◇◇◇◇◇◇◇◇◇◇◇◇◇◇◇◇◇◇◇◇◇◇◇◇◇◇◇◇◇◇◇◇◇◇◇◇◇◇◇◇◇◇◇◇◇◇◇◇◇◇◇◇◇◇

I will remember to my dying day my early days on the Boeing 707 carrying economy meal trays – three at a time – and racing up and down the aisle giving these to passengers. How many miles we all walked doing this, often twice on a sector. Apart from performing a balancing act, the trays were heavy and had hot meals just out of the oven on them. Stan's trolley changed all that. Now we pushed these trolleys up to the front of the cabin and were able to distribute the meals more rapidly and with a lot more dignity and peace of mind.

With the introduction of the Boeing 747, the meal trolleys doubled, then tripled in size and Stan also introduced the gueridon for 747, which was the serving position in the first class where many of the dishes were now microwaved.

In discussions with the author, the girls of the '40s felt that they experienced 'less sexism and harassment' than later became the norm. Many believed that having been in the Armed Forces, both men and women were used to working together, and brought respect on both sides. As Eve Branson said:

> ✈   At the end of the forties, we were a total number of 'Stargirls' in BSAA of around thirty. I never dreamt that forty years later our small band of pioneering women had begun a career that would multiply into several thousands by the end of the golden age and we never imagined at that time where civil aviation would go and I certainly never thought that one day my son would start an airline – Virgin Atlantic. However, the girls in the BSAA were definitely the pioneers in Britain for a fabulous career for women, as we have seen now in the years after us.

So we salute the flying women of the forties who led the way to the Fabulous Fifties.

**CHAPTER 3**

# The Memorable Fifties

*T*he '50s marked the beginning of the glamorous life of flying as a career. Changes were appearing that would culminate in the golden years for BOAC stewardesses. As Brenda Smith told me:

✈    There was such pride in BOAC and excitement. Life after the war was returning to normal. At the time, many regarded flying as the most glamorous career in existence, with the opportunity to travel to exciting places and meet interesting people. Newspaper articles referred to stewardesses as 'the Suntan and Nylon Girls'.

Tourist Class was introduced. In 1952 the seating in an Argonaut increased to accommodate fifty-five passengers. The catering was not too hot, in fact not hot at all. It was a meagre fare of cold open sandwiches, which had to be paid for. Breakfast was a packet of Spangles (a bag of sweets).

The Argonaut.

In the spring of 1952, the de Havilland Comet 1 replaced the Boeing Stratocruiser as the most prestigious aircraft in service. Thus BOAC provided the world's first commercial jet operation. The Comet was fast and quiet. However, three accidents, which happened in quick succession during 1953 and 1954, swiftly obliterated passenger confidence in this aircraft. In two of the Comets, the cabin became suddenly depressurised and the aircraft exploded. These Comet disasters interrupted the jet age. The Stratocruisers reappeared in the North Atlantic run, taking seventeen stately hours to arrive in New York. Lockheed Constellations flew east to Australia and south to South Africa. The noisiest and slowest planes were the Argonauts. They served East and West Africa, India, Hong Kong and Japan. BEA flew the Vickers Viscount, the first turbo-prop airliner in the world. Meanwhile, BOAC had ordered the Bristol Britannia, faster than any other airliner in service. There were great delays in getting these aircraft into service due to early engine flame out problems. They were quickly superseded by the Boeing 707 and the reengineered Comet 4. The Britannia eventually entered service in 1957. Although this aircraft could fly to New York direct in about ten and a half hours, there were two stops – Shannon, where everyone enjoyed the superb duty free shopping, and Gander, a necessary refuelling stop.

De Havilland 106 G-ALYU, Comet 1, at Khartoum Airport.

Camels were not only at Khartoum but also played a part in Kano, Nigeria. Irene Milburn remembers, '… the Shawn of the Emir in flowing robes, on a camel, blew on an enormous horn to keep away the evil spirits brought in by the aircraft. No aircraft could land or take off until this ritual was performed.'

Joan Nourse, who flew on Solent flying-boats and Argonauts, was also one of the first stewardesses to fly on the Comet 1. Publicised as the world's first jetliner stewardess, she was chosen to tour the world to demonstrate the aircraft, including unforgettable flights over the Himalayas. Joan was issued with a navy skirt and tunic, four white shirts and a black tie and two khaki linen dresses with gilt buttons for the tropical zones. She was 'delighted when the collar and tie was replaced by the open-necked white shirt'. Joan was the chief air stewardess on the new Comet route between London and Johannesburg. This was the first jetliner passenger service in the world. She also flew the South American route and her favourite stopover was the BOAC rest house, 'built at the foot of the Andes in an orange and lemon grove'.

For Audrey Cartmell, 25 October 1951 was a very special day. She was posted to No.1 Line, which had been created for the Comet fleet. These were to be in operation about May 1952. Her first Comet flight was a test flight with Paddy Fitzherbert. Audrey says:

> ✈    We were the only two passengers in the cabin. After we took off from London Airport, we climbed very quickly. Then suddenly the aircraft seemed to be hurled across the skies, twisting and turning, then diving steeply before again climbing to greater heights. We didn't understand what on earth was going on, until one of the crew came to see how we had fared. We must have looked like ghosts whilst we tried to rediscover our stomachs. He told us that Captain Linton was testing the handling of the plane under 'unusual circumstances'. We thought the circumstances were more than unusual but after another bout of ducking and weaving, we landed back at London Airport and staggered off the aircraft. It was certainly a flight to remember. I believe the captain was well pleased with the results.

Audrey's first long-distance flight on the Comet was on 14 March 1952, to Johannesburg via Rome, Beirut, Khartoum, Entebbe and Livingstone. The aircraft had flown only nine and half hours with BOAC. She said:

> ✈    This was a development flight so wherever we landed, people would be waiting to see the Comet. Such flights were also publicity flights, with Pathe News filming every aspect of this revolutionary and exciting aircraft. Then in April, we were flown in a Hermes aircraft to Khartoum, to await the arrival of the world's first jet passenger flight – Flight No.113/001. An estimated 20,000 people waited at the airport to welcome in this, the world's inaugural passenger flight.

Audrey and Joan Nourse, who had also been on the first leg of this inaugural flight, were called in to prepare for a very special flight. Joan continues the story:

> ✈    We were not told who the passengers would be, but we both were given a long list of how to address Royalty, Ambassadors, Aristocrats and Archbishops.
>
> We were fitted with brand new uniforms and white gloves to wear and were taken to the de Havilland site at Hatfield. We knew nothing about the flight ahead, as it was all very top secret. As we were doing the finishing touches to preparing the aircraft, a car drew up and out stepped the Queen Mother and Princess Margaret. Among other dignitaries present were Sir Miles Thomas, the BOAC Chairman at the time, Sir Geoffrey and Lady de Havilland, Group Captain Peter Townsend. The reason for the subterfuge was that the Queen Mother was still in mourning for her husband King George VI.

Naturally the Queen Mother didn't want the Press to find out about this special flight which was arranged so that the Queen Mother could experience the Comet. John Cunningham, de Havilland's chief test pilot, was in command. It was a four-hour flight, travelling to the toe of Italy and back, serving a 'picnic' in the air.

Audrey remembers that the Queen Mother was clearly impressed with the Comet's smooth performance. Her Majesty was 'absolutely interested in the whole exercise, including the powder room. The Chief Steward was horrified when The Queen Mother had china tea with milk'!

Horse rider Colonel Llewellyn was also thrilled. He told Audrey that at the Helsinki Olympics, on his famous horse Foxhunter, 'Seeing and hearing the Comet in the distance, before competing, spurred me on to win a gold medal.' The Comet had circled the Olympic Stadium.

Meeting the rich and famous was all in a day's work for stewardesses then, as it is now. David Lean, the Director of *Doctor Zhivago* and *Lawrence of Arabia*, was one of Audrey's favourites. He enjoyed being on the aircraft and was so interested in everything that was going on. One passenger really surprised Audrey. After the passenger briefing she shouted out, 'If it wasn't for the suffragettes, you would not have this job.' It was Lady Astor, who in 1919 had become the first woman to take a seat in the House of Commons, after succeeding her husband as MP for Plymouth. Lady Astor was very much a feminist and had a great interest in women and their professions.

June Blackler remembers: 'the stone jars of Beluga caviar and tins of Dundee cake from the early '50s. On the Comet 1 the passengers were shown how smooth it was by standing a penny on the rim of a Dundee cake tin at take off.' On arrival in New York the aeroplane was sprayed and all food not consumed was put into a large black bag and taken off to be destroyed. Predictably the cabin crew devoured spoonfuls of caviar and finished off the smoked salmon before landing.

Commercial aviation in the early '50s was on the threshold of internationalisation. Many passengers were of different cultures and customs. As Terry Erasmus mentions: 'Once I pushed open the lavatory door to inspect it for cleanliness (another job the stewards let us do) and was amazed to find an Arab with his long brown robe, squatting with both feet on the toilet seat. Not an easy thing to do on a moving aircraft!'

An interesting feature of the early '50s, which was to remain with the airline for many years to come, was the strict discipline and the fear of dismissal for even the slightest misdemeanour. Many of the women I surveyed said that BOAC ruled by fear. This did not bother some of the cabin crew and many got away with more than a misdemeanour (except for the stewards who were caught smuggling gold in the late '50s. They were definitely out). One did wonder if the management really knew what sometimes went on down the routes.

On the aircraft, discipline was strict and adhered to; the captain was 'God'. As Margaret Lloyd puts it, 'In 1952, both the chief steward and the captain wrote reports on us each trip, and you could be "snagged" for anything perceived as less than perfect behaviour, or for incomplete equipment.' The reference to equipment was because the cabin crew had to report three and a half hours before take off.

✈    The chief steward was in charge and the second steward and stewardess counted blankets and linen towels, and checked all the catering equipment for use in flight. I also had to count used linen towels. This was an unpleasant duty, as passengers were often sick, as we did not fly above the weather in those days.

A Royal Flight was the highest ambition a BOAC stewardess had back then, and still is. Usually the flights were awarded to the stewardesses with several years experience. Toni Robinson was sent an urgent message that she had to leave her crew and head to Entebbe. The Queen

Mother had been flying home from Australia with Qantas when their plane encountered engine difficulties.

> ✈   Unfortunately by the time we arrived Qantas had almost rectified the problem. We were devastated. So the crew and I boarded the plane which had been beautifully decorated for the Queen Mother and headed for home. Nearing Rome the flight crew passed us an urgent message that the plane was suffering more problems and we were to pick up the Queen Mother immediately. I was delighted!
>
> The Queen Mother was shown to her seat at the back of the aircraft. I didn't dare look but went on organising breakfast. We took the orders from the staff and word was passed to us in the galley about what the Queen Mother would like. We prepared a tray of fruit and tea. The tea had been put on board in a tin with no name on it, but I could tell it was Earl Grey. A darling little teapot had also been put on board with a sweet crocheted cover. It looked as if a child had made it. I was right, it was the Queen who had made it as a child and given it to her mother. She always took it with her. The tray was passed down the cabin and served by a lady-in-waiting.

The whole flight was very exciting for Toni, especially when per tradition the Queen Mother presented the steward with a watch and the stewardesses with a silver comb and case with her crest. Toni recalls that it was like a dream and 'my head really was in the clouds'.

## On Captains

Hudson and Pettifer in their book about a social history of air travel, say:

> ✈   One interesting thread that runs through the history of passenger flying is the nature of its hero worship at any given time. Throughout the 1920s and '30s, and certainly during the war years, there is no doubt that pilots had almost god-like status, both for what they did and what they were.
>
> An examination of photographs of pilots of the past and of the reality of pilots of the present, as they walk along the airport corridors and to and from their aircraft, certainly suggests that, as a breed, they are good-looking much above the average, although quite why this should be so is difficult to say.
>
> Nowadays – it was not so in the 1920s and 1930s – their appeal may also have something to do with the money they earn. A distinguished income is a great help to a distinguished bearing and manner.

They further this notion by stating: 'Psychologists have gone further and seen the pilot as an essential father-figure. As such, his strengthening, encouraging influence should be all pervasive in the aircraft. If his first task is to fly the plane safely, his second is to reassure passengers that they are in good hands.'

The image of a father figure was fostered and it followed that:

> ✈   The stewardess is mother, waiting on her children hand and foot, listening and watching to see if one is crying or unhappy, always at hand with comforting words and an understanding smile. A steward cannot have this function. He is no more than an airline servant in uniform and his usefulness is limited to efficiency.

This image changed in the late '50s when much of the austerity and aloofness displayed by the captains disappeared, and stewardesses were certainly not regarded as a mother figure anymore – more a sex object.

## ⓞN THE FIFTY-YEAR-OLD TRAIL OF A RED'S RED SHOE

Stewardess Joyce Bull's recollections are told in Jerrard Tickell's book in the chapter, 'My Part in the Petrov Incident'. This was an incredible drama worthy of a John le Carré spy thriller. Joyce was one of the first Australians to be employed by BOAC and was caught up in this dramatic spy drama. I contacted Joyce, in her mid-eighties and living in Melbourne. We discussed the newspaper article 'On the Fifty-Year-Old Trail of a Red's Red Shoe'.

Evdokia Petrov had come with her husband, Vladimir, to Australia in 1951. Vladimir was a KGB agent, but in April 1954 he was granted political asylum by the Australian Government. However, Moscow ordered him to return and consequently he fled. His wife was taken prisoner in the Russian Embassy and was waiting to be flown back to Moscow from Sydney's Mascot Airport on a BOAC Constellation, under the command of Captain Davys.

Joyce recounts the scene of newsreel cameras, jostling crowds and the unprecedented sight of people climbing the fence and rushing towards the aircraft across the tarmac. No one had anticipated the reaction of the Australian people. The Russians' approach to the aircraft was blocked at every point. The two flight engineers stood guard at the aircraft and frustrated an attempt by the people to prevent take off.

The angry crowd was doing all it could to stop Mrs Petrov from boarding. Two stewards who were trying to help her were also being manhandled by the crowd on the steps. Joyce recalls advancing to the platform and suddenly realising that the steps were being pulled away by the crowd. Reinforcements arrived and the steps were pushed back. Mrs Petrov stumbled into the cabin having lost one of her red shoes. Joyce said:

> ✈    During the flight to Darwin, Evdokia Petrov came to the rear of the cabin and I showed her the ladies powder room. She was in her stockinged feet. I told her I was sorry about her shoe and gave her a spare pair I happened to have on board. Meanwhile the angry crowd demonstrations at Sydney had been communicated to Prime Minister Robert Menzies and so began the process of the captain reporting by radio on Mrs Petrov's health, whether she was in fear, and whether she wished to remain in Australia.
>
> On that eight-hour flight to Darwin, I asked her on one visit to the powder room how we could help? I told her that the decision to stay in Australia was hers and that no doubt it could be arranged. She was in utter despair and then we learned that the Russian guards with her were carrying guns. Passengers have to disembark while the aircraft is refuelled, but the Russians were unwilling to do this. Eventually they were persuaded to leave the aircraft. At the bottom of the steps Mrs Petrov was approached by Mr Leydin, Government Secretary and Acting Administrator for the Northern Territory. He offered her political asylum in Australia.

Joyce remembers hearing heavy boots on gravel, shouts and the sound of struggling. One Russian guard had his gun forcibly removed from him and the other handed his over. Meanwhile Mrs Petrov could not be convinced to stay. She believed that her husband had been killed. She was absolutely distraught. Calmly Mr Leydin tried to convince her that this was untrue as a traffic officer unloaded her baggage.

Later Captain Davys, who had been in the office at the time, had witnessed Mrs Petrov take the telephone call that would make her change her mind. Her husband was on the line. She chose freedom and her three Russian escorts left without her. The couple were secretly housed in Melbourne and Vladimir died in 1985 and Evdokia in 2002.

◇◇◇◇◇◇◇◇◇◇◇◇◇◇◇◇◇◇◇◇◇◇◇◇◇◇◇◇◇◇◇◇◇◇◇◇◇◇◇◇◇◇◇◇◇◇◇◇◇◇◇◇◇◇◇◇◇◇◇◇◇◇◇◇◇◇◇◇◇◇◇◇◇◇

## Training in the Fifties

The training school was the 'Convent' at Heston. This four-storey red-brick building became a convent after the Crimean War – and the name stuck. In place of nuns' dormitories were classrooms with aircraft galleys and a mock-up fuselage, in which silver service was practised. It was a draughty place by all accounts. Heather Williams remembers the fingernail inspection every morning and the air/sea rescue training as being all academic, with no practical experience of evacuation down an aircraft chute. She also remembers the experience of getting in and out of a dinghy at Hounslow swimming pool in May 1950. It was twelve weeks of training, and it was only the challenge and excitement of the unusual experience in 1950 of going to work on an aircraft that kept them going, plus the consequent rewards, such as finding a shop next to the hotel in New York that sold nylon stockings! Such a rarity in the UK at that time.

Anne Fullagar recalls that her training in the late '50s was very much on the catering side. She quotes Joe Lawrence, her trainer: '"Girls! Dish and plate appeal. It is of utmost importance. And cleaning toilets. And being aware of the passengers' fear of flying." However, he did not mention that I would be also walking dogs at transit stops on the tarmac'.

Brenda Smith is one of the few stewardesses who actually felt that the training in the early '50s did help with communications with passengers and crew. However, most of the stewardesses I interviewed felt that there were some aspects of flying for which they had not been properly prepared and trained. For example, dealing with drunken passengers and groping male crew members. This was never mentioned during the training and coping with it was not easy at 10,000ft. You had to handle the matter in your own way. It was not an environment where one could simply open the door and walk away!

## And Off They Go!

The real feeling of going away on a flight began in the briefing building. The place was usually swarming with crews, some arriving from flights, others just going out. Friends and wives would be milling about. Those crews in from the Far East were easy to pick out as they would be suntanned and holding baskets filled with tropical fruit. Those from across the Atlantic had that pale and interesting look and were usually clutching the latest American hit record.

Margaret Lloyd recalls how long the days were 'and being reminded that the stewardess was the lowest form of animal life on a crew'. Margaret tells a funny story of an Argonaut stewardess on her first trip being stuck to the loo when an external access panel flew off. The aircraft began to reduce height so she could rise – a nasty experience. Soon after that, a Stratocruiser window blew out over the Atlantic. A quick-thinking steward slapped a tray over the hole, which held the pressurisation until the aircraft descended. After that, crews joked that 'on Strats they use a tray to fix the pressurisation – on Argonauts they use the stewardess's arse'.

Sheila Grant who flew on Argonauts in the mid-'50s remembers the attention to detail concerning the famous Speedbird logo. At that time, the Argonauts were either all economy, or all first class, Monarch with sixty passengers, or Majestic with forty passengers. The Speedbird motif had to be placed at '12 o'clock', facing the passenger on all the plates, cups, glasses. As Sheila recounts:

> ✈  With a five-hour flight say from Rome to Cairo, there was plenty of time for all this. If a first class passenger requested it, the stewardess was allowed to sit and chat to the passenger and have coffee with him or her when she had finished serving. Needless to say, the odd sip of brandy was taken! Fried eggs were served for breakfast. The eggs were broken into paper cups during the night and then at the last minute tipped onto hot round metal dishes and popped in the oven for a few moments by the second steward. Then, reheated bacon was added. The tourist section was introduced in the mid- to late '50s. It was not called economy until years later.

The cosy bar downstairs in the Stratocruiser in 1957, where you could pass a few hours.

Jean McLaren was amused to read the caption for this photograph: 'It is not every girl that gets to make a Prime Minister's Bed!' Jean doing the bed preparation for PM Sir Harold Macmillan and Lady Dorothy on a Britannia for the Commonwealth Tour in 1958.

Kitty Howell flew from 1950 to 1960, and remembers carrying very heavy bags of equipment. She had to report to Aircraft Catering well before departure time to pick up all the crockery and equipment. There were bags of cutlery, a large magazine holdall, heavy tea and coffee pots, plus huge kits of amenities including the Elizabeth Arden toiletries for the powder room. One had to be pretty fit. The meals were seven courses and all the equipment had to be washed up ready for breakfast. Kitty said that on the North Atlantic flights the stewardesses really had to prove their worth. Some of the stewards who had been flying for years did not welcome stewardesses, but as there were now far more female passengers, a girl on board was considered a necessity.

The Stratocruiser had the bar downstairs and Kitty remembers a flight with the beautiful and provocative Ava Gardner. She spent all her time there and every time she saw a crew member she said in her languid sultry voice, 'Come on darling. Join me for a glass of champagne,' which she poured herself, and for the crew member who was passing by.

Diana Furness, who joined in 1950, became a flight stewardess on the Hermes, and sat on numerous selection boards. She felt her experience of the silver service was summed up by the first class bowls which contained three floating rose petals. She said:

> ✈   The trips were long but what a wonderful way to see the world and get to know the passengers. Many of those passengers are still friends today. There was time to converse and genuinely enjoy the passengers. On my training we were asked if we thought that the lifestyle would be similar to the glamorous posters of tropical beaches and palm trees. Well it got pretty close.

As Diana says, 'It was quite fun on the "Strats" with the bunks and finding where the breakfast trays were to be delivered.' Diana Furness' three and half years on the Comet were the highlight of her flying career. 'I loved the Comet. It was a showpiece. The flight crew loved it as it was so easy to fly and the passengers were all so excited to be travelling on it. And a meal service for thirty passengers, no problem.' One of her funniest experiences was a charter from Johannesburg to Livingstone: 'The passengers were all elderly Americans, dressed in transparent plastic macs over their bikinis on their way to visit the Victoria Falls.'

Pam Wolfson flew on many different aircraft but remembers that the Stratocruisers had sixteen bunks that were lowered at the bottom and converted into beds. 'One dear lady drank too much. I looked up to see her walking through the cabin stark naked. I got the chief to sort it out. She then dragged him into the lower bunk with her.'

This was definitely a time when the most challenging task was to keep one's cool and to keep awake. Serving breakfast on the 'Strats' could be a problem. Breakfast in bed on the ground requires a fair amount of dexterity but in the air – well! It took some practice from both passengers and crew.

## Keeping Their Wits

Certainly the stewardesses of the '50s had to keep their wits about them to deal with unusual situations that sometimes occurred. In 1952, a local custom at Istanbul caused Stewardess Chance, of the Argonaut fleet, to make a rare announcement over the PA. The aircraft was bringing the Prime Minister of Turkey and members of his entourage, who had just visited London, home to Istanbul. As he stepped off the Argonaut, a traditional Muslim welcome was extended to him. This consisted of cutting the throat of a large ram at the foot of the aircraft steps. In the passenger cabin, Stewardess Chance announced, 'Ladies and gentlemen. They have just killed a ram at the foot of the aircraft steps. Would those passengers who are not squeamish care to disembark and go to the passenger restaurant? Perhaps those who are would prefer to stay on board, until the tarmac has been cleaned.' No passengers stayed on board the aircraft.

Death on an aircraft can be an unnerving experience. The only way to handle the situation is to do what one can to keep it from the passengers. Pam Wolfson said:

✈   We propped up one passenger who had died with a book and a blanket and nobody knew. On another occasion, a passenger flying alone died. The only solution was to cover him with a blanket and leave a meal tray in front of him. On this occasion rigor mortis set in and the 'passenger' moved, requiring the blanket to be replaced. The crew drew straws as to decide whose turn it was to do this task.

Pam's funniest experience was in Bermuda: 'While leading all the passengers out to the aircraft, I lost my pants. I found them round my ankles, stepped out and put them in my handbag. Great jollity for all.'

Trying to look perfectly groomed for eighteen hours at a time was also a challenge! There were no places designated for crew to rest. The best place to go to sleep was on the mail bag.

The flights were long even by today's standards. Elissa Forbes remembers that the flight from Rome to Nairobi took a good seventeen hours. 'We would take it in turns to sleep amongst the Royal Mail bags, knocking on the sides of the cupboard to be let out. We would have to wait until the coast was clear to creep out. The Stratocruiser had bunks and if there was an empty one and the chief steward was amenable, one was able to grab an hour's rest.'

Another stewardess remembers flying over Hatton Cross on a BEA Viscount when it experienced brake failure before landing: 'We had to pour tonic water, tea and water and anything liquid to hand, then pump and pump very fast in the galley to bring back the brake pressure'.

Flying across the Atlantic on the DC7C at night, to get the aircraft's position the navigator took star sights through a glass bubble at the rear of the cockpit. He stood on steps just inside the cockpit door. Often, a stewardess carrying a tray would collide into his backside. The more adventurous stewardesses were known to put their hands around to the front of his trousers and try to pull the zip down.

'My first trip to Sydney,' Margaret Lloyd recalls, 'I packed my little black dress'. Many of the stewardesses in the '50s always took some formal gear, as they were frequently invited to Embassies for elegant dinners or to various naval functions.

✈   I particularly remember a female passenger, called Mrs Monk, who was returning to Australia with her three small children. Her husband had been killed in a Constellation which had crashed in Singapore a few months previously. The crew had been briefed to take care of her, especially during landings. As we prepared for landing at Karachi in darkness, we suddenly climbed again and proceeded to circle the airport. Apparently, the main wheels had come down, but not the nose-wheel. The Control Tower shone a light on us to make sure that it really had not descended, hoping that it was just a failure of the indicator light. A few sedate dives failed to budge it. After an hour or so using up fuel, we told the passengers to prepare for a belly landing. We removed the exit windows and the door, took all the belongings off the racks and stacked them in the loo. We showed the passengers how to brace for the landing. Not only was it dark, but it was also very noisy without the window exits and door. I was asked by Mrs Monk if I would take one of the children, so that perhaps one would survive. I took the youngest boy – ten-month-old Winston. The captain did a beautiful landing on the grass alongside the runway, guided by car headlights. I handed baby Winston to the ground hostess and Mrs Monk and her two little girls followed. All the passengers clambered out just as if it had been an exercise. (I learned that you do not need a slide for a belly landing – the ground is right there!) We landed about 22.30. At midnight it was my twenty-seventh birthday.

# STRATOCRUISER B–377

### Captain John D'Arcy, Rtd, British Airways

Boeing B.377 Stratocruiser G-BOAC 'Speedbird'.

I started flying Stratocruisers in 1958 with BOAC, having previously been flying Meteor 8 fighters at Biggin Hill with 600 City of London Squadron RAF. This four-engined double-decker aircraft, built by Boeing, was initially used by BOAC mainly on the Atlantic routes to the USA, Canada and Bermuda but was later used on West African routes to Kano, Lagos and Accra, via Barcelona and Rome.

The Stratocruiser was a large aircraft for its time but, as I recall, only had thirty-two passenger seats, all first class, and all with comfortable beds. Downstairs there was a well-stocked bar and cabin crew consisted of three or four stewards and a hostess (not stewardess). Up front on the flight deck we had a captain, a co-pilot, a third pilot/navigator, a radio officer and two flight engineers – quite a crowd!

There were no terminal passenger buildings at Heathrow in 1958 so we used to board the aircraft from tents on the north side of the airfield and then, on most flights across the Atlantic, fly to Shannon in Ireland, where we had dinner on the ground with our passengers before flying to Gander or Goose Bay en route to New York or Bermuda. There were no flight time limitations for aircrew and I remember one flight which took twenty-two hours to get to Bermuda via Shannon Keflavik and Goose Bay. Our destination was New York but bad weather prevented us from landing there so a diversion had to be made.

Many of the captains of the aircraft had been senior RAF pilots during the war or had longer pre-war experience in civil flying. Some were very autocratic in the way they handled their flight crew and seldom allowed their co-pilots to carry out the take offs and landings, so necessary to allow them to build up the necessary handling hours. Hence they became known as the Atlantic Barons.

The Stratocruiser was a fairly slow aircraft and, being propeller driven, could not attain great height. The usual cruising altitude was 12,000 to 18,000ft, which meant that it frequently had to fly in poor weather conditions. The pilot/navigator had to hold a navigator's licence and carry out astro-navigation using a bubble sextant through a hole in the flight deck roof.

I can remember the ground steering was rather inadequate. One had to use considerable rudder in cross-winds and differential braking in cross-winds. But the Strat gave one the feeling that it could stay airborne forever. The Strats always had a very friendly atmosphere between the crew and the passengers. It was de rigeur for as many passengers as possible to visit the flight deck, one or two at a time, and the captain would often dine in the cabin with a passenger on a mutually acceptable invitation. Before taking up flying I had a degree in Law from Cambridge and on leaving was called to the Bar at the Inner Temple and practised as a barrister. I had a rule not to allow very beautiful women onto the flight deck on the basis that if anything went wrong I would be open to the accusation that her presence had distracted me!

Margaret's career in effect was over. She suffered extreme anxiety after this incident and was advised to think about another career, which she did. But as she says, 'I gradually realised that it was not flying that I feared, but having to be 'brave' again.' She proceeded to have a successful career with Lloyd's International Media in New York.

In 1951 Josephine McKay was flying on Hermes aircraft when her most embarrassing experience happened in Tripoli. She went on board to take over and heard a whine from the glory hole near the flight deck area. There was a dog on board, so she asked the cleaners to hand him to her, which they did. She thought a little fresh air was needed and carried him down the steep steps and stood him on the ground. Before she could stroke him he was off into the night. Apparently a lady passenger had said she would only join her husband in Ghana if her dog was there to greet her. Search lights were blazing; people were running around and shouting; the obese airport manager, looking rather tipsy, was trying to join the runners. It was enough to frighten any animal away. She stood around looking and feeling an absolute fool.

✈    The stewards did not help by blaming me for letting the dog out without being asked to. I was really worried. The dog would not have much of a life if picked up by a local. All the dogs I had seen in Tripoli looked starved. The flight left half an hour late – without the dog. I offered to explain to the waiting husband on our arrival, but the captain said that it was his responsibility. I was greatly cheered next morning when I was told that the dog had been caught and would be on the next flight. Apparently, when everything had quietened down, he'd been attracted back by the airport lights. Back in London I was asked to write to Sir Miles Thomas, BOAC Chairman, with an explanation. The husband had been onto him very quickly, in no uncertain terms. I felt that I would like to offer an excuse and told him that the dog had wet on me, as I carried him down the steps, and I hastily put him on the ground. I heard no more. I like to think that Sir Miles had a sense of humour. After all, there was a happy ending!

## The Lifestyle

Bermuda was a favourite place for everyone. In the early '50s, a trip on a Constellation was a three-week service. Crews were based in New York and operated day or night shuttles to Bermuda. As there were no allowances there, it meant that all the crew dined together. Barbara Hume recounts days of beach picnics, riding to and fro on mopeds and lots of tennis. The losers bought the rum for the evening crew party. 'I always played better with that kind of incentive. Rum was only eight shillings and four pence (40p). The mixers were more expensive. However, rum in Trinidad was only three and sixpence a bottle, and so the crew always brought bottles into Bermuda after the shuttle to Trinidad for the long slip before flying back to the UK. Often they overdid the quantity and the Customs Officer on duty would only allow them to bring it in 'if the stewardess went out to dinner with him'.

The hotels were total luxury. Best was The Peninsular in Hong Kong, with Raffles in Singapore a close second. Coming in to land at Kai Tak Airport in Hong Kong, skimming over lines of washing hanging from the buildings, onto a runway jutting out into the sea was quite an experience, especially if you were able to view this landing from the flight deck.

Many people mentioned Beirut as their favourite place. Mary Crosbie says:

✈    Beirut had everything – great hotel (the Bristol), good sporting facilities, fabulous nightlife (the Golden Bar) and superb shopping and mad taxi drivers, especially the ones that took us across the mountains to pick up the service from Damascus in Syria in the late fifties.

In Bermuda we used to stay at the Belmont Manor Golf Club Hotel, where we had no allowances. On one flight a businessman called me over to his seat and asked me where to stay, and my impression of the place. I happened to mention that the lack of allowances inhibited us and confined us to hotel meals. It transpired that I had been chatting to Garfield Weston, the owner of the hotel. The chief steward became very rattled about what I had said as Mr Weston was on the VIP list. Miraculously, within a short time we were granted an eating out allowance, so obviously all had not been in vain.

Many stewardesses fondly remember Dormy House at Sunningdale, where crews did their standby. Sheila Luke reminisces: 'I enjoyed staying at Dormy House, and taking a long walk before dinner. The girls had to walk through a tunnel to an adjoining building and the steward of Dormy House brought tea and biscuits at wakeup time.' At 221, groups would stand around catching up on news of the latest scandal. One could get details of the New York weather or ask how the monsoon was doing in India. I would ask about passenger loads and delays. There was a tremendous liveliness about the place.

June Blackler recalls:

✈    One of my greatest memories was on the evening of the Queen's coronation. I was invited by the Karachi Station Manager, Robbie Trusch Thompson, to be his partner at the British Embassy at Clifton Crossing. It was black tie and cummerbund for the gents and long dresses for the women. The dining tables were set out in the garden, one for at least 200 people. The waiters were lined up on the veranda all in white with scarlet sashes. A gong was struck and they all swooped down the steps to service everyone at the same time. At the end of a glorious day we heard that Edmund Hilary had conquered Everest.

Barbara Hume said:

✈    The ratio of technical crew to cabin crew was quite different on the Stratocruisers. There were seven or eight on the flight deck and only four cabin crew. While the crew had allowances in the major cities, it was often full board in other places, which made for much more interaction with the crews. Of course, we flew on smaller aircraft, had longer sectors, and fewer passengers and much more time to talk to everybody.

In those days, being the only girl on the crew meant that they did lots of 'male' things that they would not normally have had the opportunity to do. Barbara Hume learned to shoot in Montreal and went to wrestling matches and ball games in New York.

In the '50s, stewardesses were called air hostesses and it was the era of the plummy accent. Britain was still suffering from the aftermath of the war. Barbara Hume recalls her first trip, 'feeling so excited in my Hardy Amies-designed uniform', carrying her Globe Trotter suitcase (with no wheels) in her high heels, overnight bag, shoulder bag and being bussed out to the aircraft. Being a disciplined generation, we readily accepted the rulings on skirt length – a carefully measured regulation number of inches from the ground, 'however, some of us were quite capable of putting an extra tuck in the jacket to accentuate the waist. We discovered how to anchor our white blouse with its blue enamelled Speedbird buttons to show the best cleavage.'

✈    I was off to New York. Three thousand miles, fifteen hours and two refuelling stops later I was rewarded with my first view of the Manhattan skyline – a sight that still excites. I love the symmetry, the ordered straightness of the streets and the unique sound of New York. 'The Shelton' on Lexington Avenue became a second home. Soon the Bell Captain was remembering my name. I enjoyed the luxury of my own room, air-conditioned in summer with an en suite bathroom and television. Hotel brochures in England at that time, advertising 'all mod cons' usually translated into 'wash basin in room with hot and cold running water, but bathroom along the corridor'. Most households in the UK did not have a television set.

We were a generation that had been starved of luxuries and deprived of travel by the war. The contrast between England and America was immense. I loved 5th Avenue, Saks, Bloomingdale's, Macy's, the marble hall of Grand Central Station, the drug store soda fountains, and the five and ten cent stores.

There were breakfasts overlooking the sea at the Montego Bay Hotel in Jamaica, dinners in the Cecil Beaton dining room which was landscaped into the cliff with plants, trees and shrubs floodlit, the alfresco Sunday evening buffets at the Royal Victoria Hotel in Nassau, with the tables decorated with trailing exotic flowers, ice sculptures and the 'flamboyant attention-seeking dresses' and hats, of the black choir who came to sing.

'The sightseeing was fantastic,' said Hazel Faulkes. 'The Taj Mahal, The Peak in Hong Kong, sailing in the Jarda Linka in Hong Kong, going up the Bosphoros to the Black Sea, seeing *Aida* in the open air at the Caraculla in Rome. So many memories.' She went on:

> ✈     The Constellation west-bound flights were scheduled with a night stop in Prestwick. This was a gentle start to the trip – a one and a half-hour flight, a crew change and then starting work again the next day. The aircraft arrived early evening and we benefited from a relaxed day (often golfing) and Scottish afternoon tea served in the lounge of the Marine Hotel in Troon. The longest westbound crossing at that time was made by a Constellation, which took off from Prestwick and landed in Shannon, The Azores, Keflavik and Goose Bay where we waited three hours for the weather to clear. The crossing took thirty-two hours and the average was fifteen.

On those long nights crossing the Atlantic, in the breaks away from the passenger cabin, Barbara Hume remembers being persuaded into conversations with the Radio Officer on 'Weathership Charlie' as they flew overhead. He always seemed pleased to hear a female voice, hemmed in as he was by so many oceans and an all-male crew. This customary chat to the weathership went right on into the '60s on the Boeing 707s. However, eventually, sophisticated forecasting with satellites made the old weatherships obsolete.

When crossing the North Atlantic, Toni Robinson recalls that the aircraft's position was determined using weatherships. They gave us their positions and what sort of weather we should expect in their areas. On one flight the captain called me to the flight deck when we were in touch with one of those ships and asked if I would have a few words with the men below us. They had asked to hear a female voice:

> ✈     I put on the headphones and heard a man say brightly, 'Good morning'. I had been up all night and was exhausted. I looked and felt awful but I tried to be bright and amusing. The man wanted to know what I looked like. Not wishing to disappoint him, I made myself out to be like Marilyn Monroe. Maybe it didn't really help since it was some time before he was posted back to terra firma.

Brenda Smith's first encounter with Australia in the '50s was on a trip to Sydney. She went to her room to wait for her suitcase which never came. So she went downstairs to the lobby and the porter was there sitting on her bag. He told her that you always carried your own bag in Australia. His exact words were, 'Got a broken arm or something?' The 1950/51 stopover in Sydney was in a boarding house that overlooked Bondi Beach. Breakfast was two lamb chops, when meat was still rationed in England. Brenda was on the proving flight on the Britannia to Hong Kong and Tokyo. The Britannia was known as 'The Whispering Giant'. She was delayed at nearly every destination. To make up time, they overflew Singapore, causing one local newspaper to head an article, 'NOT A WHISPER FROM THE GIANT'.

# THE BRITANNIA

Peter Riley, Rtd, British Airways

Bristol Britannia 102.

I served seven years in the Royal Air Force before joining BOAC in 1958. I flew single-seat fighters in the RAF so when I went aboard the Britannia at BOAC's training base at Herne Airport near Bournemouth, I thought I'm never going to be able to land this giant!

I did have difficulty landing the Britannia, one of the reasons being that it had a strange control system, on the ground the ailerons and elevators drooped. Many a time at Idlewild Airport, as it was then known, in New York, other pilots called us on the radio to tell us there was something wrong with our controls. When we replied that they were supposed to be that way, some comments were unprintable! When landing the aircraft it was essential to keep power on until it was in the landing altitude. It took me a while to get the hang of this. The aircraft had a very complicated electrical system, referred to in the company as the electrician's nightmare. The early aircraft also had an engine icing problem. In certain conditions of cloud and temperature ice formed in the intakes of the engines. When the aircraft came out of the cloud the ice melted, went into the engine and put the engine out. The modification to overcome this problem took a considerable amount of power from the engine itself, considerably reducing its rate of climb. On an early test flight with executives of a European airline on board the aircraft was forced to make an emergency landing on the mudflats of the Severn Estuary! Needless to say the executives were not impressed!

The Britannia should have been a world beater but a year's delay in delivery due to industrial problems at the manufacturers and numerous delays due to the electrical and engine problems gained the aircraft a very bad reputation. Only one other airline, El Al, bought the aircraft in any significant numbers. El Al operated the Britannia differently to BOAC and regularly made London to New York non-stop. BOAC more often than not had to land at Goose Bay, Labrador or Gander, Newfoundland. However, I mustn't complain as it was on the ground at Gander that I met the stewardess who was later to become my wife.

The Britannia was given the name 'The Whispering Giant' but the comment among flight crews was that it had nothing to shout about!

Brenda also flew on Constellations:

✈ These aircraft had separate lavatories for male and female passengers. The ladies' cloakroom had a settee, a vanity unit and basin and was very luxurious. We had a full load of passengers and were about to serve a meal. I went to the rear of the aircraft and could detect the spicy smell of curry coming from the gents' loo. I told the steward, who went to investigate. There was an

Indian passenger cooking over a primus stove. All the passengers at the rear of the aircraft heard about it, including a schoolboy. Years later, when I was at a function, he recognised me and came over and asked me if I remembered the gentleman cooking on the primus stove.

Rosamund Smith recounts the events of 26 January 1952, when the Egyptian Military took over Cairo. King Farouk and his family left the country for France. Sir Miles Thomas, Chairman of BOAC, got caught up at the airport in transit. Rosamund:

➤　We had been in the Heliopolis Hotel for a slip of a few days. We, as a crew, had no idea of what had taken place. I awoke next morning and looked out the window. It was eerie – not a sound. No cars, buses, trams or people. I went downstairs to learn that the Generals had taken over the country. There was rioting in the city. The famous Shepherds Hotel had been burned down, as well as the BOAC office, and many people were killed. After a couple of days they tried to get us all out. I think there were five crews. It was late evening and we were driven in a blacked-out bus to the airport. No luck. We went back to the hotel. We tried again the next morning, and later managed to board an Eastern Airlines flight, after we had all been personally searched. Part of the crew got off at Athens, and the rest went on to Rome and then by Qantas to Heathrow. It was quite a few months before we returned to Cairo, which became a refuelling stop, and we then slipped in Rome and Entebbe.

Rosamund had other recollections:

➤　In my time, the stewardess always remained with the passengers through delays at all times. After one rather long delay in Iceland, I had been on duty for a very long time. When we took off, the passengers asked the chief steward if I could have a rest. They made up one of the bunks for me and insisted that I got in. After three hours, a passenger wearing my hat woke me up and handed me a cup of tea!

Elizabeth Eker says:

➤　In those days you had to talk to as many passengers as possible and walk around the transit lounges during stopovers and make conversation. This was not such a difficult thing to do as most of the passengers were people going out to work somewhere in the colonies. Some were emigrating, a few going to visit friends and there were also the children going back and forth to school in England. The bucket and spade brigade had not yet arrived.

In the early '50s BOAC passengers had a really decent breakfast including chilled juices, compote of fruit, grilled bacon with tomatoes and freshly scrambled or boiled eggs. There were rolls, croissants, Ryvita, toast, butter, preserves and a tray of fresh fruit. Strong arm muscles were de rigeur as all the service was done with trays. The china and silver cutlery were genuine and so distributing and collecting them was a heavy task, as were the large hot stainless steel coffee and teapots. This was before the days of the elegant trolley service of the '60s. The stewardess's day began by sitting in a wire cage in a prefab near 221 and checking all the equipment that had to go on board, including catering equipment, blankets and towels, before the day's work in the cabin actually began. It was time-consuming and tiring. Headphones used by the flight deck had to be disinfected by the stewardess before departure.

Frozen food was introduced in approximately 1950. In 1952 economy class food was introduced on the 049 Lockheed Constellations. Prior to this, pre-packed sandwiches were defrosted, and served to order. Chocolate bars and cake were also available and monies were collected for this food. One great advantage of the now pressurised cabin, from a catering point of view, was that many restrictions, once considered necessary in planning meals for passengers whose digestion might have been affected by the shortage of oxygen, were lifted.

In the early '50s, the famous Monarch Service was born. Departure was a gracious affair. Madeira and biscuits were served. The passengers were then offered tea and coffee in little individual silver pots. The elaborate seven-course meal service which followed became the pride of the airline. This service was the crème de la crème of airline catering. All the equipment was 'proper' – elegant dining at its best. It remained in first class for many years, improving in presentation, with silver service throughout. The Monarch Service was a benchmark for other airlines throughout the world. Stan Bruce's dream of bringing the style and ambience of the Dorchester to the passengers was a vision that had come true.

## When Fate Played a Hand

Stewardess Monica Osborn wrote about this dramatic desert crash in *Wings on my Suitcase*, introduced and edited by Jerrard Tickell.

In the Sahara desert, on 5 May 1952, BOAC Handley Page Hermes aircraft G-ALDN crash-landed 1,300 miles off course. When I was a training instructor in the late '60s and early '70s, at the airline's Cranebank Training establishment, my boss was Len Smee. Sadly Len Smee passed away in July 2005. He had been one of the stewards on that memorable flight, which carried ten passengers and eight crew. Theirs was an incredible story of survival. The Hermes was on its way to Tripoli in Libya and was completely off track due to gross misreading of the figures needed to set the plane's course accurately at the beginning of the flight. Running out of fuel, attempts to find alternative airfields failed and Captain Robert Langley briefed the cabin crew to prepare the passengers for an emergency landing. On board were a mother and her six-month-old baby, Richard Gurney, now in his fifties. Monica Osborn described that harrowing adventure and the following is a précis of her chapter, 'Ordeal by Sun':

> ✈   We carried out the crash-landing procedures. The desert pack, containing iron rations and tins of water, was put in the rear of the aircraft, near the main door. The escape chute was hooked on to the door and the main exit doors in the cabin were removed after depressurisation. The noise of the engines through these gaping exits was deafening. On impact, there was a bang, a tearing sound, a grinding thump and we came to a complete stop. I had fallen and six-month-old passenger baby Richard was underneath me, unconscious and limp. However, he came round in a minute or two. Everyone scrambled out and the heat outside was like a furnace.
>
> Captain Langley had made a perfect landing, positioning the Hermes between two sand dunes. The aircraft had lost a wing, which lay in bits over an area of about 200 yards, and two engines were lying 20 or 30 yards apart. The propellers were almost bent double, stuck in the churned-up sand. The crew used axes to break into the fuselage and took out luggage to spell out SOS. Meanwhile, the passengers were sheltering from the searing sun under blankets spread over the bushes. Some of the passengers made a fire and an improvised kettle was soon on the boil. The radio officer reassured everyone that the French, whose territory we had landed in, knew we were here.
>
> Later that day I had a moment of panic when half a dozen people came towards us over the dunes. They were Tuaregs dressed in knee-length flowing robes and who strode over the hot sand in bare feet. The captain went out to meet them and an Arabic-speaking passenger communicated our needs. They left and reappeared with a camel carrying a tent, which they erected. Water, which would have to be rationed, was salvaged from a pipe from the galley, everything we could use to hold water was held underneath, including lifejackets. An aircraft was heard. We tore mirrors off the lavatories, the baby's mother and I used handbag mirrors and the radio officer an Aldis lamp, but we weren't spotted. Some of us began to despair as we watched the aircraft disappear into the distance.

Then we heard another plane. This time we set the port engines on fire with the remains of the oil and kept it burning with crates of freight. This time we were seen and the plane swooped over us at 100ft. We nearly went mad with joy.

Then just before sunset we heard the sound of a plane again. This time five people parachuted out, a doctor, two nurses and two wireless operators from the French paratroopers stationed at Dakar. It was a thrilling moment and we shook hands joyfully in the middle of the desert of Mauritania.

Immediately, they attended to the injured. The first officer, who had the most serious injuries, had his wounds cleaned. The engineer officer had his left arm put in a splint, the second steward had the whole length of his right leg in a splint and bandaged. Baby Richard was faring well and his mother was able to mix him some milk. We settled down, but only fitfully, as even at night the heat was overpowering. One of the Tuaregs was outside our tent all night long… He guarded us for two successive nights … but we never knew whether it was to guard us or stop us absconding with the tent.

The following day, a French aircraft dropped water for us. We lost most of the water as it was in petrol cans that burst on impact. There was a desperate craving for water. One of the passengers produced some rhubarb he was taking to Accra. This was cut up into chewable size and was amazingly refreshing. We solemnly chewed and chewed until it reduced to string. Meanwhile, we kept waiting for a French motorised column to reach us.

The third day was hotter and drier than before, and the first officer was getting weaker. The rescue team had come to a standstill fifteen or twenty miles away.

Then, one of the Frenchmen with an African tracker left the oasis where they were camped and found us with the help of flares. Tribesmen arrived with five camels on which we loaded the radio equipment, the desert pack with the tins of water, log books and various other items. Then our journey began. The first officer was getting weaker by the hour.

Two of the tribesmen and a French colonel led us, the crew trudging alongside with the passengers. I rode on one camel, the mother and baby on another and the very ill first officer on the third. When light came there was a fierce sandstorm and we were forced to stop and crouch behind our camels.

We had traversed mile after mile of sand, struggling sometimes almost knee-deep. We skirted around dunes as tall as houses. We stubbed our toes against rocks and jagged outcrops in the dark, scratched our legs on what scant prickly vegetation there was in the yellow wilderness. When the storm passed, we saw a long range of mountains in front of us which meant a detour as the camels could not cross them. We stopped and at last opened our tins of water, the first fresh water for days. Our lips and tongues were swollen. The searing sun had scorched our bodies. The navigator and one of the passengers then set off to try to cross the hills. The rest of us continued the longer way around the hills.

By now the mood had changed. People were walking on badly blistered feet; others were clinging to the ropes dangling from the camels' sides for support, and the flight crew who had injured their backs badly on landing were in extreme agony. After marching for over sixteen hours some had lost heart, or were too weak to go on. All the water was finished. It was their worst moment.

Chief Steward Len Smee and one of the tribesmen decided to continue on. The colonel then took me and Mrs Gurney and her baby by camel towards the oasis where his men were camped. This was a frightening moment for me, leaving and not really sure if I would ever see the others again. Mrs Gurney was extremely concerned about her baby. The sun was making us feel faint and we could hardly speak, our throats were swollen and dry. It all seemed hopeless. I prayed for the safety of us all and especially this six-month-old baby. Then, as if my prayers were immediately being answered, a jeep appeared driven by a Frenchman with Len Smee. An unbelievable moment. Suddenly there was water to drink after five days. Then baby Richard, his mother and I were driven to the oasis of Aoiun Legbar.

When we arrived, the navigator and the passenger were already there, waiting for the rest of our party to arrive. And what a reunion it was.

A strip of desert was marked out, so that a small twin-engined light aircraft could land. Mrs Gurney, her baby and I were the first to be taken out. We arrived at Atar (a French outpost in the desert about 130 miles away) to a huge welcome. Later I was told that the first officer had died in the night at the oasis and had been buried there. It was a terrible blow after he had gone through so much.

## Passenger Amenities and Care

On-board amenities included feather-down pillows, pure wool rugs, fans on certain routes, a variety of reading matter, newspapers, paperback books from the aircraft library, the glossy magazines such as *Tatler*, *Harpers* and *Vogue*, crossword puzzles, playing cards, and bridge scorers. For the children there were books, comics, drawing books and crayons, jigsaw puzzles, games and Junior Jet tuck box kits. Writing material and postcards were carried and correspondence written on BOAC stationery could be handed to the steward and posted 'for you, at our expense'. There were all the famous Elizabeth Arden Blue Grass toiletries of cleanser, toner, moisturiser, hand lotion and hair spray. The male passengers had Yardley preparations, electric razors, safety razors, brushless shaving cream and collar studs. There were also additional items such as eau de cologne, face tissues, toothpaste, toothbrushes, nail and clothes brushes, shoe horns, combs and sewing kits. All this was also available in the economy class.

The Crossing the Line Certificate continued to be popular throughout the '50s.

Helen Gough remembers having to clean the electric razors after use. 'This was really a foul job. On Constellations, we removed the engineer's plug for the sextant in the overhead bulkhead and let the air suck out the previous user's hair.'

In 1957 there was the deluxe sleeper-seat, with leg rests with two positions giving the divan feel.

In BEA, the bar was always the sole responsibility of the stewardess and never the stewards. The task was not finished until the bar paperwork was completed. The money had to tally with the drinks and cigarettes that had been had sold. Being duty free, this was then presented to the bonded warehouse, from where they had been drawn. Margaret Nuttall said, 'I felt this to be rather a strange responsibility for just the stewardesses.'

A day that she will never forget was on a return from a night stop in Oslo in 1952. The doors had been opened and the steps had been wheeled up. She told the ground staff officer, 'I have a King's Messenger on board.' He replied, 'No you haven't.' She retorted indignantly that she had. 'No!' he said. 'You have a Queen's Messenger. The King died in the early hours.' It was quite a shock. King George VI had just passed away.

## The Late '50s

As a sharp contrast to the early '50s, the era of immigration from India, Africa and the West Indies began. Some of the immigrants had never seen a loo. Keeping the loos clean was the stewardess's job and on these flights it was a nightmare.

The 'giveaway' for the first class passengers was a small round, very pretty Wedgwood dish with Elizabeth Shaw mints on them – all so elegant. On the Britannia 312s were pull-down bunks for the first class passengers. The beds were made up by the stewardesses who did a linen check as well. Beds and bunks seem to come and go but are now here to stay.

For passengers in the mid-'50s, flying was a privilege and an excitement. First class passengers consisted mainly of top businessmen, politicians, diplomats, the jet set, company directors, captains of industry, ministers of states, film stars, royalty and government officials. They were mostly travelling on business and were typically British and reserved. There was little, if any, hand baggage, but always a coat and plenty of the sable and mink variety.

Margaret Fairlie, who now lives in South Africa, flew from 1955 to 1965. Margaret says:

> ✈ After eight years you became a Senior Stewardess and had a gold bar on the sleeve of your jacket. This got you no extra pay. In 1965 BOAC were not keen on employing ex-stewardesses in other capacities due to lack of experience. My Flight Capt Captain Alabaster took this up … to no avail. Fortunately this was to change decades later.

Margaret Fairlie proved to be a natural, because she had her first flight after only ten days of training:

> ✈ I was given a day to get my uniform, shoes, gloves. On the Saturday sent by bus to Poole – forty-minute flight (first ever in an air liner) with fifteen engineers under training in Constellations, then on Sunday sent to '221' where I met my crew. The Chief Steward looked shattered when he realised that I had only joined two weeks previously. I was told to use my common sense. Twenty-one days and 100 flying hours later the Chief Steward gave me an excellent report and said that I had proved the training course was a waste of time. I had flown on various aircraft during six years service with the Wrens and of course I was used to working with men.

Margaret remembers Darwin being a slip where:

> ✈ … there was no way they would let you miss breakfast … in those days The Darwin was the only hotel. They'd hammer on the door and shout. So even though you had only got in at 3 a.m. from Singapore, you got up, no excuses accepted, and ate the rancid bacon!

In years past some Aussie hotels had a habit of waking you regardless of your request to 'please be left to sleep'. This was legendary. At the Fanny Bay Hotel in Darwin you got up to answer the door to the tea trolley at 5.30 a.m. whether you wanted a cup of tea or not – no one ever understood this strange Aussie ritual.

Australia was generally thought to have some very strange and antiquated drinking laws in the '50s. Jeannie Lardner recalls arriving in Sydney at 7 a.m. having arranged to meet the boys in the bar about 7.30 p.m. that night:

> ✈ On arrival at the bar, a big bouncer stopped me and said no unaccompanied females were allowed into the bar. I said I was staying at the hotel, but there was no way he was going to let me in. I went back to my room, phoned reception, and asked to speak to one of the boys and said to page him as he might be in the bar. Eventually I made contact and met my escort and went into the bar. The bouncer gave me an odd look but that was nothing to the look on his face when I left with five male escorts.

Shirley Fogg's first memories and impressions of her career begin with the aircraft steps. At the old Champino Airport in Rome she caught her toe on a BEA step and fell from top to bottom, breaking her nose. Negotiating the often rickety steps in the rain and snow in high-heeled shoes was a precarious exercise. For this reason stewardesses were forbidden to carry children or babies down the aircraft steps. To Shirley her job was a crème de la crème occupation. Being the only female among seven men she remembers the crew were always very protective of their 'girl'. The constellation 749 was all first class and BOAC in 1956 introduced the local food of the country to which they were flying: Indian and Malaysian curries, also kebabs and Chinese dishes. The first class meal service always started with canapés and our famous

Lockheed Constellation L049D, G-AHEN 'Baltimore'.

champagne cocktail: 1 Tate and Lyle sugar cube, 1 dessertspoon of Courvoisier brandy and a few drops of Angostura Bitters. Fill the champagne flute with Moët & Chandon champagne and garnish with a maraschino cherry with half a slice of orange threaded on a tooth pick.

The Constellations did the occasional charter and Shirley Fogg once had a party of Chinese Lascars:

> ✈   They did not speak English and were given roast duck for dinner with knives and forks. A disaster! They spat on the floor a lot and this was a culture thing. I had my first party of Arabs who tried to light a fire in the aisle to cook. The use of the old primus stove was a regular happening on the Middle Eastern routes and was one of the many things we were *not* told may happen in the training school.

Barbara Hume remembers:

> ✈   BOAC also operated a charter service taking the colourful party of the Sutherland and Argyll Highlanders on their posting to Georgetown. If I thought I was in a man's world as the only female crew member, I truly believed it on this flight. Even the regimental mascot was a Billy goat. I had access from the flight deck to feed and water him.

One of the questions in the survey was 'what topic should they have told you about and didn't in training school?' This provoked a variety of replies, including mostly about how to deal with certain types of passengers, especially those who imbibed too much liquor before and during the flight. Another was 'how to deal with gay stewards'. This could be tricky! Some of the gay stewards were absolute sweeties, and others downright bitches. Some had either one or two of these reputations, and your only recourse was to get an update down the routes as to how to 'get along' with them.

Working with gay men was a first for many of the stewardesses, who soon learned that their love life was an all-consuming exercise. If two of them managed to fly together it was either going to be a great deal of fun or hell. Gay stewards had a style of speech and demeanour that was quite engaging and before long you almost began to sound like one of them. Some of the stewardesses thought that flying with the gays was rather like having one's sister on board. It was generally acknowledged that a difficulty could be experienced with bisexual stewards, who were usually OK, but woe betide the girl who had fun with one of their partners.

Peggy Thorne joined Barbara Jupp to fly on the first Comet service from New York on 4 October 1958. BOAC had two flights flying simultaneously across the Atlantic and Jeannie Lardner was part of the cabin crew in the Comet 4 from London to New York. This was history in the making. The two aircraft, G-APDB and G-APDC, at 1.36 p.m. crossed the coast off Newfoundland after a flight of six hours and twelve minutes. When it landed at Heathrow, Peggy's aircraft had flown 3,510 miles at 478mph.

On boarding, the passengers were given Madeira and biscuits followed by coffee. It was then cocktails and canapés leading up to lunch. Printed menus offered passengers a choice of food including soup, salmon, Pear Belle Helene followed by cheese, fresh fruit and finally coffee. Once lunch was served it was time for afternoon tea, when assorted mini sandwiches, scones jam and cream, chocolate biscuits, assorted cakes with tea and coffee were served. Passengers were either in first class or deluxe – the expression 'economy class' came later.

Twenty-five years later, British Airways awarded Peggy a surprise Concorde flight to New York and back to help with their publicity for the event.

## One of Our Strict Trainers

Jeannie Lardner joined in 1952 and, whilst having her medical at London Airport, was invited to view the departure of the first Comet commercial flight. 'This was very exciting and the atmosphere was terrific. I thought how wonderful that I am joining this airline.' Six years later in October she had the 'honour of operating on the first ever Transatlantic Jetliner the Comet 4 from London to New York' – a day service to New York. After take off there was a glass of Madeira, lunch then afternoon tea before landing. 'The arrival at New York was something else – people had gathered to watch the historic touchdown and I felt so proud on leaving the aircraft.' BOAC was in front again but not for long.

Many years later Jeannie and her husband did the same sector on Concorde: 'After the long hours on the Strats and the Connies and even the Comet 4, I could not believe it when we landed. I thought what a difference for the crew – no time for crew fatigue,' she said.

Jeannie: 'Many first class passengers were used to having servants and tended to treat the stewardesses similarly, so we learned to give a great deal of help with passengers' children.' Also, in the economy cabin we were experiencing the beginning of the very demanding passenger who expected to be treated like a first class passenger.

Jeannie ascertained that the average working life of a stewardess was about two and a half years and she said, 'Although many join with stars in their eyes, most marry not a crew member, but the boy next door.'

Jeannie Lardner was quite renowned as an instructor and trained close to 1,000 girls for BOAC and many more for other airlines; she seemed to put the fear of God into most of the stewardesses that she trained. Perhaps it was her Scottish brusqueness or maybe she was a strict disciplinarian. Jeannie was my training stewardess, and she certainly had our course on their toes. I like to think I emulated her when I joined the training school later in my career. She had an illustrious career with British Airways from 1952–65, initially as flight stewardess on Constellations 749s. She loved the Connie.

Jeannie Lardner (1952–65) pictured with her crew on her favourite aircraft, the 'Connie'. There were small portable fans on top of the seats – air conditioning in the early days, and hazardous for small passengers!

As she says:

✈ I enjoyed my final years with BOAC as instructress at the Cabin Service Training Unit. Even when we had no classes there was never a dull moment. One day I was called on to appear in a film Max Bygraves was making at the airport. The film was used as an introduction for his new show and I appeared at theatres throughout the UK. Fame at last.

One year I gave several PR talks to groups and thoroughly enjoyed that. To begin with my audience was all females but one day at the Royal Overseas League I found myself facing a mixed audience. I quickly had to change my funny anecdotes.

After she left BOAC she returned to Scotland and became a Training Officer with the Hotel and Catering Industry Training Board in Edinburgh. Her special interest was career talks to young people and they always liked to hear some BOAC tales.

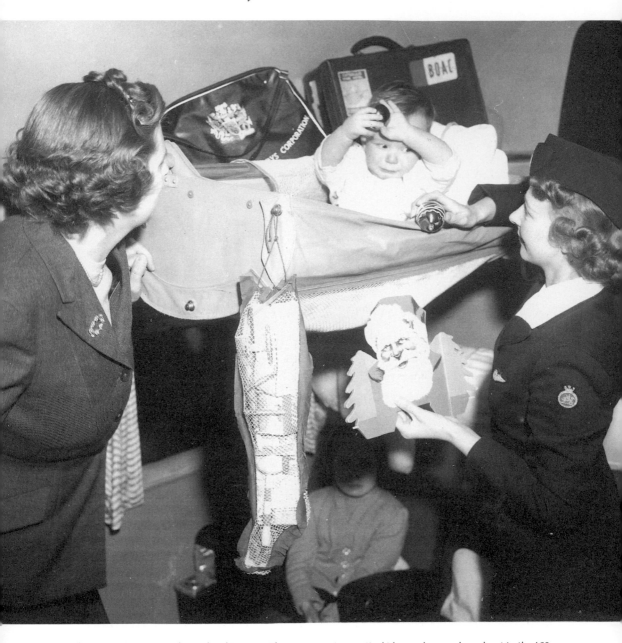

Skycots were not popular with cabin crew. They were an impractical idea and were phased out in the '60s. The Skycot was a total puzzle to erect and many of the stewardesses tried to talk the mothers out of using them. They were small swinging bunks for babies attached to the hat rack and if they were not attached properly, well, you can imagine the consequences! Years later when I had children of my own I realised how potentially dangerous they could be as they were very difficult to assemble and bolt properly to the hat racks. Skycots could only have been invented by a man; totally ridiculous and dangerous contrivances. For nursing mothers BOAC supplied modesty curtains.

Jeannie remembers on Monarch flights, the most luxurious service in airline history at that time, that 'even the flight crew expected silver service for their meals'.

✈    On the Monarch flights the passengers dressed up to fly and for ladies, hats were the order of the day. There was no overhead baggage rack in the forward cabin (berths were in their place) and hats and coats were stowed in the wardrobe stationed at the rear.

On Eastern routes the type of passengers varied according to the time of year. A large percentage was men going out on business and at certain times of year we would have the wives and children. Also a lot of unaccompanied children – they were regular flyers and knew what was what.

Jeannie remembers after a flight with the Emir of Bahrain: 'We were invited to dinner at the Palace. We did not realise it was an Arab dinner, sitting cross-legged on the floor and eating with our hands. A wonderful experience and guess who got the sheep's eye?'
Crew prank:

✈    On a flight from Karachi to Bahrain I was asked to take care of an old woman travelling by herself. She was dressed in voluminous skirts and had a toothless grin and her only hand baggage appeared to be an old shoulder bag. I helped strap her in and held her hand to soothe her agitation. Later I was told by the steward that I had been paying my attention to an amused priest from Pakistan.

Below is a letter Jeannie wrote entitled 'Great Day on Delta Charlie':

✈    Dear Sir: I was one of the stewardesses aboard Delta Charlie on October 4, 1958. It was a very exciting and emotional day for all concerned; when the crew bus arrived at the airport it was surrounded by airline personnel and members of the press, who all wished us every success on our flight.

After a photograph session we boarded the aircraft to prepare for the arrival of the passengers who included the Chairman of BOAC, Sir Gerald d'Erlanger. At 0855 GMT we took off, to great cheers from the passengers. Our flight time to Gander (overhead to overhead) was five hours forty-nine minutes during which time we served refreshments followed by lunch which included Crème de Champignons, Petit Homard en Mayonnaise, Tournedos Saute Rossini, Faisan d'Ecosse Froid Sur Croute, Salad Panachee, Poire Belle Helene, Fromages Assortis and Corbelle de Fruits Frais accompanied by a selection of fine wines and champagnes.

Captain Millichap kept us informed of the flight's progress and there was great jubilation when he announced that we would shortly pass Delta Bravo which was operating the service from New York to London. The Captains exchanged messages and I believe Captain Millichap read 'Jet Speedbird Delta Charlie to Delta Bravo – I have a message from the Chairman of BOAC, Sir Gerald d'Erlanger, which reads "All of us aboard Delta Charlie send our greetings on this great occasion".

Once again there were cheers from the passengers and glasses were charged to toast Delta Bravo, which we passed at 13.36 GMT. Our time on the ground at Gander was one hour twelve minutes and our flight time to New York three hours four minutes. During this sector we served afternoon tea which included Welsh rarebit, hot scones, sandwiches, fruit cake and French pastries. We landed at New York at 1915 GMT and what a reception awaited us there. When we opened the doors we were met with big cheers and clapping by hundreds of people on the observation roof at Idlewild airport.

When I finally left the aircraft I stood at the top of the steps to savour the moment then waved to the crowds. It had been a great day and I was very proud to be a member of BOAC. Stewardess Terri Mullis was on this same flight, and Diana Beresford Davis remembers for the 'first flight of the Comet we lined the runway and saluted as it took off.'

This was a coup for BOAC, as Pan-American, its great rival on the North Atlantic, had plans to be the first airline to operate pure jet transatlantic services.

# COMET IV

### Captain John D'Arcy, Rtd, British Airways

De Havilland Comet 1 G-ALYP.

Between 1962 and 1966 I flew the de Havilland Comet IV with BOAC (British Overseas Airways Corporation). This was the first passenger jet liner to go into operation in very close competition with the Boeing 707 which remained in service for considerably longer than the Comet.

The early days of the aircraft were marred by some very serious accidents including a Comet 1 crash in the sea near Elba and another where a Comet crashed shortly after take off from Calcutta en route to Delhi, both with the loss of all passengers and crew. The cause was eventually traced to metal fatigue and structural weakness of the fuselage which could not sustain the large difference between the cabin pressurisation and the much weaker external atmospheric pressure when flying at normal jet altitudes of up to 40,000ft. When these faults were rectified by design alterations, the aircraft flew safely for a considerable number of years, although the B707 was much more favoured by the world airlines generally.

BOAC operated a large fleet of Comets on all their routes worldwide – North and South America, Australia, New Zealand, Hong Kong, Tokyo and South Africa to name but a few. The aircraft was very popular with both passengers and crew and initially drew a huge amount of publicity and support from the English Press and from the politicians.

The aircraft was powered by four engines incorporated into the wings and typically cruised at .73 Mach. The crew consisted of two pilots, a navigator/pilot and an engineer and cabin crew of two stewards and two stewardesses. This was still before the days of mass travel and cramped seating – the aircraft carried about seventy-two passengers.

I learnt on a very unsophisticated simulator, and initially it didn't even have a visual system. London to Shannon was my very first Comet flight and to be handling the world's first jet after years of propellers was a thrilling experience. It was the Concorde of its time upon introduction and it flew almost at the same speed as the fighters I flew at Biggin Hill. Great fun to fly and so much easier to fly than the Stratocruiser. With the Comet I was flying at the same altitude as the Vampire or the Meteor 8. This was exciting stuff. I can't recall any flying problems with the Comet at all. In fact I never even burst a tyre in my entire career! The actual visibility from the cockpit was considerably more restricted than on previous propeller driven aircraft. This was because the windows were rather small in order to accommodate the additional pressure differentials for jet aircraft. So you wouldn't make a sharp left or right-hand turn being unable to look around the corner.

The variety of routes and the airfields visited were extraordinary. All the fun was going to places like Beirut, Benghazi, Tripoli, Tehran and of course Karachi. This airplane was so easy to fly, these were experimental days and unfortunately the two crashes initially gave a very fine aircraft a bad name.

One of my favourite routes was to Santiago in Chile. The round trip took over two weeks via Madrid, Lisbon, Dakar, Recife, Rio de Janeiro, San Paulo, Montevideo and Buenos Aires. We had stopovers at Dakar, Rio or San Paulo and Santiago and I fell in love with South America. We also carried Chilean stewardesses as part of the crew and without exception they were very beautiful and friendly girls and a delight to have on board!

# The Latter Years

The latter years of the '50s saw the move to Heathrow. The airline offices were marquees, portable sheds and former military mobile vans. Later the mobile vans became prefabricated sheds. The underground to Hounslow West didn't happen until thirty years later.

Smuggling was not really something that the stewardesses did apart from going over the limit with alcohol, cigarettes and jewellery. In 1956, stewards were involved in gold smuggling. Upon arrival in Delhi after one trip, Toni Robinson found that not only did Customs demand the usual declarations from crew but that all crew were to endure a body search. Of course it was BOAC policy at the time that a female had to be present when a stewardess was being searched. When no female BOAC staff member was able to be present in the early hours, the only solution was for the captain to be present. As Toni was stripped of all her clothes, the captain was suitably polite and refrained from watching the process, sparing Toni embarrassment. One of the stewards was actually found to be smuggling gold bars strapped to his body on that flight. Toni recalls noticing him sweating quite profusely during the earlier meal service and figured that it must have been caused by all the excess weight he was lugging up and down the aisle.

Helen Gough flew from 1957–62 and was one of those stewardesses who quickly realised she needed to have a career path:

> ✈    I was offered a golden handshake and this came about if you left between five and ten years and at that time stewardesses were not permitted to stay in after ten years – a disgrace. I used my golden handshake to support myself while I trained as a radiographer. Would I do it all again? Yes, but for two years, not five and a half. It was an amazing experience one gained from this University of Life, no brain work needed. Just what one wants at twenty-plus years!

She also recalls:

> ✈    On my first trip I remember that the second steward (now passed away) was very kind to me. He sat me down after the meal service and served me a meal. I thought this was normal but never experienced it again.
>
> Of all the famous and interesting people that I met, the one I'll always remember is General Montgomery of Alamein. He was in the first class cabin and asked to have me changed as he did not like being served by women. And there was Terry Spinks, a lightweight boxer who had just won a medal. We served the champagne to passengers out of his silver trophy.

Helen Gough went on to become a radiographer, then principal tutor at the School of Radiography at the Westminster Hospital in London. She completed her student bar finals and became a practicing solicitor and was called to the Bar, which firmly dispenses with the notion of the trolley dolly image constantly perpetuated by the media.

Other aircraft in the '50s which must be mentioned were the Vickers Viscount, the Douglas DC-6B and the Boeings 707 and 727. The world's first turboprop aircraft was the Viscount, which entered service in 1953. It had forty-seven seats and was considered a milestone in civil air transport because it was the first British aircraft to be sold to America. It was flown by airlines all over the world.

The pure jet Boeing 707 was in service with most of the world's airlines by the end of the '50s. The propeller-turbine Brittannias brought into BOAC in February 1957 were now being phased out. The airlines were only thinking about jets for long-distance travel. The Boeings superseded the lot. The swinging '60s and the 707s were synonymous.

## Women in Management

Trying to move into management roles at this time was difficult and not encouraged. It was still the macho mindset that the females were only there to provide a pretty smile for a tired businessman.

A cogent remark made by Terry Erasmus was that the only things she had to prepare personally were babies' bottles. 'There was the feeling from the stewards that, "we mustn't give too much responsibility to the girls. They could take away our jobs".'

However, exciting changes were on the horizon. The '60s introduced a burgeoning industry in jet-set travel. The aircraft were bigger, the washing up was less and the glamour of this way of life for all members of the crew reached its zenith.

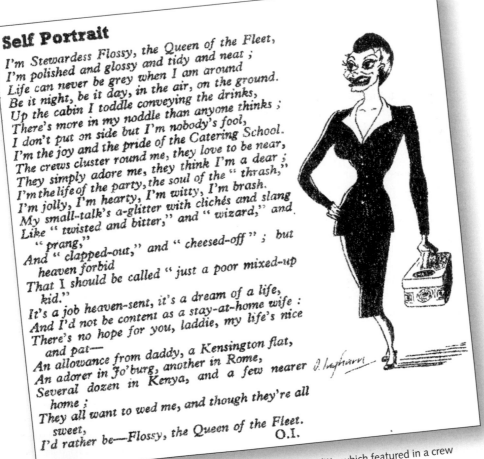

**Self Portrait**

I'm Stewardess Flossy, the Queen of the Fleet,
I'm polished and glossy and tidy and neat ;
Life can never be grey when I am around
Be it night, be it day, in the air, on the ground.
Up the cabin I toddle conveying the drinks,
There's more in my noddle than anyone thinks ;
I don't put on side but I'm nobody's fool,
I'm the joy and the pride of the Catering School.
The crews cluster round me, they love to be near,
They simply adore me, they think I'm a dear ;
I'm the life of the party, the soul of the " thrash,"
I'm jolly, I'm hearty, I'm witty, I'm brash.
My small-talk's a-glitter with clichés and slang
Like " twisted and bitter," and " wizard," and.
 " prang,"
And " clapped-out," and " cheesed-off " ; but
 heaven forbid
That I should be called " just a poor mixed-up
 kid."
It's a job heaven-sent, it's a dream of a life,
And I'd not be content as a stay-at-home wife :
There's no hope for you, laddie, my life's nice
 and pat—
An allowance from daddy, a Kensington flat,
An adorer in Jo'burg, another in Rome,
Several dozen in Kenya, and a few nearer
 home ;
They all want to wed me, and though they're all
 sweet,
I'd rather be—Flossy, the Queen of the Fleet.
 O.I.

Stewardesses always needed a sense of fun, as shown in this ditty which featured in a crew magazine.

# CHAPTER 4

# BEA Memories

ritish European Airways began services in August 1946 with the Douglas DC3 aircraft flying to Paris, Amsterdam, Brussels, Madrid, Lisbon, Stockholm and Helsinki. By 1956 it was the largest airline in Europe. The first post-war stewardess to fly for BEA was the untrained Grace Chester, an ex-WAAF radar operator. During August 1946, she was withdrawn from training to serve aboard a Dakota service from Northolt to Brussels. She remembered that, 'I didn't know what to do or where to put things away. As I recall everything was all piled up around me, large black Thermos flasks of tea and coffee, trays of fancy cakes, cups and saucers and a bar box.' The first to be given publicity was Diana Johnson, who served on the inaugural BEA Viking G-AHOP, a fourteen-seater service to Scandinavia from Northolt on 1 September 1946. Training was carried out at BEA's headquarters at Bourne School, Ruislip, and the passenger buffet in the adjacent Northolt Airport. The first uniforms were second-hand wartime VAD uniforms, which were not too great a fit, and were later replaced by BOAC cast-offs, which fitted a little better.

A number of stewardesses had long careers with BEA and were excellent role models when they moved to training. Among these was Janice Musson, who was Chief Training Stewardess European Division, and who was succeeded by Valerie Leyton Smith. Another eminent stewardess was Pat John, Chief Stewardess Training Regional Division.

In June 1948 the Berlin Airlift began and the Foreign Office asked BEA's charter department to coordinate and supervise the efforts of British civilian airlines. The Russian blockade of all land routes into West Berlin meant that supplies to sustain the West Berliners had to be airlifted over hostile territory. Return flights often carried refugees. Seventeen airlines were involved, including 'Pathfinder' Bennett's BSAA which made 2,562 return flights, flew 6,973 hours and carried 22,125 tons of freight. All in all, civil aircraft flew nearly 500,000 tons of supplies into West Berlin, small by today's standards but a massive effort which contributed to the saving of many lives.

Anne Evans was posted to Berlin for two months during the airlift of refugees. She said:

✈    At the time I joined in 1950 I was the thirty-second stewardess and at twenty-two years of age, the youngest. Most of the other stewardesses had been in the services, spoke another language and were a little older. Towards the mid-'50s physical appearance became more important. Now, at least in BEA, maturity and efficiency seem to be more valued. I remember

# TRIDENT 2

## Captain Harry Hopkins, Rtd, BEA, British Airways

Hawker Siddely HS-121 Trident 2.

Starting 11 March 1964, some seventy Tridents passed through British European Airways, over two decades spanning the 1970s. The Trident wing made it the fastest among airliners. But speed was of little advantage on a short/medium-range aircraft or for economy, so it in fact flew at a high but typical cruising speed. The first model had a meagre take off performance and it was called the 'ground gripper' by crews – hell to get airborne because of the curvature of the earth! Only 117 Trident airliners were sold; the similar Boeing 727 beat it commercially.

The Trident's main asset was its all-weather automatic landing system, in which it was the leader. The first automatic landing with passengers was made in June 1965, in good weather, followed a year later by test landings in real fog. But the final goal was met only at the end of 1971. BEA and Smiths Industries had to work cautiously towards what is now unexceptional – blind landing. For several years the Trident alone could land in dense fog. We, the crew, listened intently to weather forecasts – hoping that visibility wouldn't improve! For then we could land ahead of all the other waiting aircraft.

Pilots sat to watch the throttles eerily closing, and the nose rising in the landing flare, without yet being able to see the runway – only the glow of the approach lights beneath the fog passing below! The pilot did nothing till after touchdown. The care needed in early all-weather flying benefited from a three-pilot crew (two first officers alternated as co-pilot and systems operator). The co-pilot operated the autopilot; the captain would oversee him, and glance up for the runway; the third pilot would keep a watchful eye overall.

In the cockpit a 'ram's horn' control arm replaced a wheel atop the control column – as on Concorde. (You leant over into turns, which gave a 'racy' feel.) The para-visual displays were novel: the rotating stripes of these 'candy-bars' streamed one way or the other in pilots' peripheral vision, to give them a sense of turn – you needed this during fog take offs, to maintain heading without looking at the compass.

The Trident was certainly fast in descending. Engine reverse was usable in the air; with the gear lowered at high speed and airbrakes out. I have seen descents at 12,000ft per minute! Operation of reverse just before touchdown reduced the landing run too. It also cushioned the landing; the line of four wheels each side, on a single strut, always challenged pilots to put a Trident down smoothly.

The Trident family ended with the Trident 3B. This was another odd first: three and a half engines! The small extra engine, above the main tail engine, was named the 'pocket rocket'. It had two settings – idle and take off; it was shut down once the aircraft was settled in the climb.'

The Trident briefly succeeded while it was 'king of the fog'. Its crews will remember it with affection as the all-weather pathfinder.

how formal our training was, still based on a wartime service model. We were expected to stand up when an airline captain entered the room.

Anne remembers only one incident with a chief steward who was an ex-sergeant major and who was typical of that stereotype. 'My only problem with him was that he did not think I called him "Sir" often enough.'

Ingrid Rohr was with International German Services in BEA, based at Berlin's Templehof Airport. IGS flew via the three corridors permitted by Russia to other cities in Germany. 'We were often buzzed by Russian MIGS. Our base was the American and British military clubs, where we were made honorary members.'

On 5 April 1948 a BEA Vickers 610 Viking 1B G-AIVP collided head-on with a Russian Air Force Yakovlev 3 fighter performing aerobatics. The Viking spiralled slowly without control. Four crew and ten passengers died near Berlin-Gatow. The fighter pilot was also killed. The collision was caused by the action of the Yak, which disregarded the accepted rules of flying and, in particular, quadripartite flying rules to which Soviet authorities were parties.

BEA, like BOAC, flew a variety of aircraft in the early years – DC3s, Dakotas, Viscounts, Elizabethans, Comets, the Vanguard and the Trident – with trips lasting anything from three hours to ten days. There was one major difference between the two airlines, a difference that affected stewardesses: their flights were confined to Europe and later the Middle East, North Africa and Moscow. Service was generally more rushed than on longer BOAC flights and there were fewer long glamorous stopovers in exotic places.

A Vickers Viscount G-ARHF, the world's first turboprop aircraft, left Northolt Aerodrome on 29 July 1950 to inaugurate a temporary London-Paris service.

In June 1965 BEA's Trident aircraft made the first automatic landing on a scheduled service, initiating the era of all weather operations. It was the birth of the mass package holiday industry. This became so huge that a separate airline, BEA Airtours, was established in 1970. The responsibilities for this service were carried out for the group by Caledonian Airways for many years.

## A Very Rushed Job

'I joined British European Airways – laughingly known as "Britain's Excuse for an Airline" – in May 1956,' said Pamela Banfill, and she flew with them for the ensuing ten years, four of them when married. Pamela flew on Dakotas, Elizabethans, Viscount 701s and 802s and finally the wonderful Comet 4, and she concludes, 'I have so many wonderful memories of those ten years, and I do feel very privileged to have been part of the truly 'Golden Age of air stewardesses' – all being for me an almost unbelievable fifty years ago.

✈ In BEA we had to fit everything into a comparatively short space of time in order to have all the equipment safely stowed away ready for landing. As we had to start work as soon as possible after take off, walking up the aisle was like going up a mountain while the aircraft climbed to its scheduled altitude, and clearing away during descent resembled walking down a steep slope and required pushing one's body backwards whilst clutching up to six trays between one's arms, so as not to topple over.

We worked six days on, followed by two days off, which meant only one 'full' weekend in seven, and this, combined with working in the evenings and trips away, very much affected our social life.

We would be given our rosters a month in advance, greeted with groans if we had the less interesting routes, or squeals of delight if we had the two weeks taken up with five-six day trips 'down the Med', whether based in Malta and from there going off to North Africa or in Athens and covering the Eastern Mediterranean and Gulf.

The time on the ground at the destination airport was also intended for the crew to take lunch, although often dispensed with and a quick snack taken on the aircraft on the return journey if we had a late arrival to try to make up the time. One captain was known to say to the stewardesses when halfway through her meal and called to the aircraft – 'Don't rush it, dear, just leave it'. There was a huge bonus to missing lunch in Moscow, in that we could exchange our lunch allowance roubles for tins of Beluga caviar.

Patricia Clayton, eighty-six years old, recalls:

✈    In the era of 1946 with Dakotas and Vikings the furthest trip was usually Athens, six hours with a break for refuelling. Food came on in a hamper of individual boxes, and wine was in a steel box. We didn't serve cocktails and, of course, it was all one class. Each passenger was given a cardboard box and tea and coffee were poured into plastic cups from a black thermos. Most of the passengers at that time were business and service people, and, of course, the Queen's Messenger. Although BEA was mainly looking for ex-service people, having been an SRN was the next best thing. In fact in those initial days with BEA some people received no training at all but just went straight onto the aircraft and got on with it. About all we needed to know were currency conversion and a small measure of training with the electrics, for the heating and of course basic first aid.

We had some exciting flights on Dakotas in those early days, particularly when the weather was fog, snow and icy conditions. We would end up at strange wartime aerodromes, many with metal strip runways. The stewardesses would then have to find a canteen somewhere and endeavour to order food and drink for the delayed passengers.

Mary Alexander joined BEA in 1958, and remembers on the Dakota one had to report to the captain and quote: 'Five locks, two locking pins, one pilot head cover, ships papers and thirty-two passengers strapped in, sir.' She went on:

✈    The Dakotas did not fly very high so we flew through some dreadful weather. But this had some compensation, a week spent in Rome or Amsterdam awaiting a new engine, or a week in Vienna delayed due to the weather. All this sounds lovely but the actual working conditions were far from ideal. There was a bar, a large metal box for alcoholic drinks, which were extremely difficult to serve in bad weather. Looking back on those days we all feel as though we were the forerunners of the airlines today. I would not have missed the experience for anything.

On the Dakota there was only one stewardess, Mary recalls:

✈    With the maximum height of 10,000ft flights were frequently bumpy and many passengers were sick – most unpleasant. The captain would offer to 'go around again' if the meal service was not finished. The Viscount flew a little higher; its cruising altitude was between 13,000 and 23,000ft, lovely views on fine days, frightening on stormy nights. The pilots guided the aircraft between huge cumulus clouds whipped up by the storm. Smoking cigarettes was allowed everywhere and there were special ashtrays in the cockpit. I remember a friend telling me he lost all his papers and his silk scarf when yanking open a Dakota window to let out the fog. There was no aircraft heating on the ground and the aircraft in winter would be freezing after standing all night. Progress came when the engineer put a long flexible tube down the aisle that blew out hot air. There was no air-conditioning in airport buildings or on the aircraft until airborne. On the Viscounts it would belt out a loud whistle if turned up too high.

I think my greatest challenges were to give Savoy-like service with inadequate equipment and frequently insufficient time and to keep one step ahead of the 'Rummage squad', Customs & Excise, who occasionally sprang onto the aircraft in search of contraband.

Anne Hartley, a contemporary of Mary Alexander, remembers on a night flight from Heathrow to Copenhagen there was only one passenger, one stewardess and a cargo of animals:

✈    The passenger was taking the animals to Copenhagen Zoo from South Africa. The animals included one rhinoceros locked in a cage and tranquilized, one cheetah, a hyena and several monkeys in separate cages. The man came on board, gave me a loaded gun and told me to shoot the rhinoceros if it moved.

Training for BEA was similar to BOAC training in the early '60s. Mary Gordon said of the RAF film about survival in the Rockies, 'I was definitely going to starve before I skinned a rattlesnake'.

✈    Our evacuation slides in these early days were not inflatable like those in BOAC. Ours were canvas and had to be held taut at the bottom by two strong stewards. For the ditching drill we were supposed to tie our passengers in a circle and sing to them – but not hymns.

Things were fairly ad hoc in the early BEA days. Proper stowage for boxes of ice, coffee pots and teapots didn't exist on some aircraft such as the Vanguard. This was a safety issue which Mary Gordon continually took up with the management. In 1967 the flight time limitations were another issue, particularly with the introduction of cut-price travel. The standard was a twelve-hour duty day and this was not being strictly adhered to. Mary Gordon championed for better flight time conditions, although she felt at the time the only interest in this was in relation to the flight crew. In fact she felt intimidated by the airline's management as crew seen as troublemakers were not welcomed. Your job was on the line if you spoke to the Press about this. Her picture on the front page of the *London Observer* in 1967, even though in the article she was referring to her experience in previous airlines where she had worked non-stop for thirty-nine hours and fifteen minutes, was too close for comfort for BEA and she felt she was being blamed by association.

Mary Hughes recalls that during her training in 1951 all the course had to report to the kitchens at Northolt at 6 a.m. and work two hours in the catering unit before going over to the north side for lectures. When asked what equipment she felt was particularly relevant to her era, but which is no longer so today, she replied:

✈    Cuspidors. Flying so low in unpressurised aircraft was really rough on the passengers. Air sickness today is now a thing of the past. It was dreadful then. Most of the passengers were all one class and there was for a long time only one crew member. We definitely had much more responsibility then.

Two BEA stewardesses who passed away in the late '90s were Katie Gutfreund and Margaret Bellis. Katie was the first stewardess in British aviation to receive the Queen's Commendation for Valuable Services in the Air. A refugee from Czechoslovakia who was determined to fly, she was on the DC3 inaugural to Edinburgh, Aberdeen and the Shetlands, a round trip of about twelve hours. She made history as she was the first stewardess allowed to carry on flying until she was sixty.

Maragaret Bellis inspired her colleagues with her bravery after the 6 February 1958 BEA Ambassador G-ALZU crash near Munich after attempting to take off for the third time on a snow-covered runway and failing to get airborne before the end of the runway. The aircraft was carrying Manchester United's legendary 'Busby Babes', one of the most famous football teams in the world, returning from a match against Red Star Belgrade; eight members of the team died. Of the forty-four on board, twenty-three were killed. After walking away from the wreckage Margaret returned to help others. The aircraft's captain, Jim Thain, wrote to her later: 'Before the Munich tragedy recedes too far into the past, I would like you to know how much I appreciated your magnificent effort during the rescue operations. Your courage was an inspiration to us all. How fortunate I was in having you in the crew.'

## Camaraderie

'Athens was a favourite in those days,' said Pamela Banfill.

✈    Flight crew and cabin crew stayed in the same hotel and there could be as many as five crews staying overnight so there was the inevitable party always in someone's room before going off to the city centre for dinner. We all got to know each other rather well and it used to be said that with so many from different backgrounds and life experiences thrown together, the three topics of conversation common to all were aircraft, cars and sex!

As Mary Gordon says:

✈    Leave a handful of intelligent people together for a few days and they're bound to get up to mischief. I remember for many months the BEA crew hotel in Athens underwent building work. Apart from the constant noise of workmen, there were always piles of bricks and equipment in the corridors. When a crew noticed a stewardess sneaking into their captain's room one night they quietly bricked up the door.

   Athens was really the favoured and much-loved destination, where we would fly out one day, be able to spend most of the next day on the beach, before flying off in the evening to Tel Aviv, Beirut, Istanbul or Cyprus and returning early the next day for more beach and fun at a local taverna in the village.

Helaine Michaels remembers on her training in the early '60s that:

✈    We were a bit amazed that a former BOAC steward was on our course. He had been caught smuggling gold out of India. We had lots of marvellous parties, usually in the captain's or chief steward's rooms. I remember several of us girls being chatted up by the captain in Malta. So while he was chatting up someone else I quickly filled his bed with crisps and nuts. Apple pie beds were also popular.

When Audrey Crome was flying between 1955 and 1958, the captain used to leave the cockpit and go into the cabin to talk to the passengers. Occasionally it would be the first officer. She said:

✈    This was very popular and passengers were pleased to have a chance to meet him and ask questions. They felt privileged to receive this attention. The atmosphere was always very friendly and no doubt we benefited from this pleasant working environment. How different from these days when the crew have to be locked in for safety.

   Our social life was usually an evening meal with the crew once we had arrived at our night stop hotel. The captain usually suggested that we all meet for dinner and as we had to fly off early the next day there was no riotous nightlife, so different to our counterparts in BOAC.

Audrey remembers with great affection the time she spent working as a stewardess for BEA:

✈    The atmosphere among the BEA staff with whom we came into contact in the course of our working day was a very pleasant one, be they cabin staff, traffic staff, air-crew or engineers. We all took great pride in 'our' airline and were proud of belonging to this company. We were, I think, the lucky ones. This was a time when many of our passengers had never flown in an aeroplane and were usually thrilled by the whole new experience and grateful for the care and attention we gave them. It seems to me that passengers in those days were much more pleasant than some of their counterparts today.

# Our Pride in Our Uniforms

All the BEA stewardesses who talked to me referred to their uniforms in some detail. They obviously took pride in their uniforms. *Be Elegant Always* was the title of their grooming booklet.

Audrey Crome recalls:

✈ When I joined in 1955 my uniform was a beige suit. The jacket had three buttons and large patch pockets, worn over a white round-necked blouse. After a few weeks I was issued with a new style beige summer uniform which had a long rolled collar and two buttons on the jacket at the waist, and no large visible pockets, altogether more feminine. The skirt was very slightly flared but fairly straight and mid-calf length, as was the fashion at the time. Our winter uniform was the same style but in a heavier grey material. Summer and winter uniforms were both worn with black gloves and black court shoes. We carried a black handbag. The cap was quite attractive with a cockade and a BEA badge on one side and I found it comfortable and easy to wear. We were also issued with a long grey raincoat for the winter.

Helaine Michaels:

✈ We were the first to wear the box jacket BEA uniform in small checks. I had two winter and two summer uniforms and six blouses and six aprons. You had to provide your own shoes and stockings. But I could claim a laddered stocking on the aircraft and the chit was signed by the captain after a thorough inspection. Of course, in the early '60s and really until January 1971, we didn't have flight time limitations, we just flogged on until the captain made a decision to call a halt.

Judy Farquharson remembers in 1957:

✈ We wore the *best* uniforms ever. A coffee and milk colour in barathea with proper berets with a cockade. The first class was a Silver Wing Service to Paris, fifty-seven minutes to do three courses for fifty people and selling half bottles and cigarettes. On the Dakotas in the late '50s we had to take aileron locking pins and wheel break locks from the ground crew and hand them to the captain and repeat the amount to him.

At BEA Reporting there was a long mirror behind you as you checked in, so the dragons at the counter could see that the seams in your stockings were straight and that your hair did not touch your collar. Your hands were checked for jewellery and nail polish.

BEA stewardesses modelling the early '50s uniform in front of a Douglas DC3 (Dakota).

## A BEA LEGEND

Joan Crane began her flying career in the WAAF as an Air Ambulance Orderly. After training, her duties took her into Europe behind the advancing allies. This was in DC-3s fitted out to carry back British POWs who were too ill to be repatriated any other way. She had logged 320 hours by the end of the war. She joined BEA as an air steward. As she says:

✈  Back in October 1946 we were 'stewards-male' and 'stewards-female'. Training was at Bourne School, Ruislip, admin HQ for the airline. Northolt Airport was within sight of Bourne School. Training was in the passenger buffet and in the manager's dining room. Initially there was no uniform for us, so I dyed my WAAF uniform a dark navy blue. The clothing situation after the war was quite a problem and I also had no clothing coupons left. After a few months BEA issued uniforms and flesh-coloured stockings were permitted. In 1947 a new crewing system meant that we flew with the same crew for six weeks. Weather radar was in its infancy and some of the storms were of such magnitude that it was quite impossible for our tiny aircraft to fly around them. In fact when we took off it was really a question of flying in the general direction, hoping a path could be found between huge cumulonimbus clouds. My log book entry for one flight reads thus:

| | |
|---|---|
| Northolt – Marseilles | 4 hours 13 minutes. |
| Marseilles – Rome | 2 hours 11 minutes. |
| Rome – Rome | 2 hours 40 mins |
| Rome – Athens | 3 hours 42 mins |
| Athens – Athens | 42 minutes |
| Athens – Rome | 4 hours 25 mins |
| Rome – Marseilles | 2 hours 45 mins |
| Marseilles – Marseilles | 1 hour 5 mins |
| Marseilles – Northolt | 3 hours 40 mins |

The DC-3s then took over the English division and the six-week crewing system changed to a different crew every day. Flying in an unpressurised aircraft such as the Dakota could mean that flying above 10,000ft for any length of time could give one a lovely dreamy sensation of floating. This could of course be quite dangerous. At 15,000ft I distinctly recall having great difficulty placing my feet on the aisle carpet, and placing things where I wanted them to be in the galley quite impossible.

By 1948, Joan said:

✈  I was on the Viking. This was a more sophisticated aircraft. The passengers actually got a tray instead of the box, and there was a more effective heating system. There was also the main spar which ran through the cabin, forming a step about eighteen inches or so above the floor. There was a small step fore and aft to facilitate easier passage over it and carrying trays in bad weather courted disaster. One could end up sitting astride it, landing on a passenger's head or face down on the carpet. There was also the added bonus for some male passengers as our skirts were then considerably shorter and panty-hose were not to appear for many years. Some of the fun went out of 'leg-spotting' when our hemlines were lowered.

Flights to Hamburg were always welcome as stockings that were rationed in England were always plentiful there and inexpensive. Joan remembers the Berlin blockade and:

✈  How careful we were to observe the air corridors in fear of provoking any adverse reaction from our recent 'allies'. Gatow was an incredible sight during the airlift. There were so many aircraft

Elegant passengers alighting from a BEA Airspeed Ambassador Elizabethan.

on the ground it was impossible to count them all. It was the most fantastic operation to observe, this entire city's needs being provided by air.

Cabin service instructions are legendary for taking the simplest action and turning it into a thesis. Joan recounts one of these on a Viscount conversion course finishing with '…after which the steward will back the stewardess up in the galley.' One of these instructions was that teaspoons were not to be taken into the cockpit. The stewardess stirred the tea and coffee before taking it in. If not the teaspoons had a habit of falling down between the throttle levers. Joan used to tie her teaspoon to a piece of string for captains who insisted upon a teaspoon for their saccharine.

Then in 1958, like a bolt out of the blue, came the directive that stewardesses would be required to discontinue flying after ten years. Anyone joining after this would have to sign a ten-year contract. Several of Joan's colleagues and Joan had completed twelve years of service. Joan said, 'We were shattered and wondered how it would affect us. Katy Gutfreund and I had no intention of leaving. Most of the others took the money that was offered and left. We were offered jobs on the ground but refused. We refused to go.'

In 1971 Joan Crane received a Queen's award in the New Year's Honours list. So did Katy Gutfreund. However, in January 1976, BEA sent Joan a letter telling her that she would be expected to retire at the end of the month, following her fifty-fifth birthday. Joan said:

✈  I was furious. Katy had received the same letter. The era of Equal Opportunity was here and it was still a battle. The stewards could fly until they were sixty and beyond. There was no equality at this point. We had to take our situation to the Equal Opportunities Committee. I was then advised to take the matter to the Industrial Tribunal. Reprieve was granted when I received a letter dated 25 May 1976, telling me that I could remain a stewardess until aged sixty.

This special concession was for me and Katy alone. Newspapers had a field day and there were cartoons and headlines such as:

'Let's fly the flag…
Fly 'glamour-granny'

The Tristar now appeared, fourteen cabin crew and around 300 passengers. This aircraft had all the niceties I had always dreamed of, eight doors which opened at the press of a button, lovely wide aisles, emergency chutes that did not have to be manhandled but inflated automatically at the touch of a lever. No longer was it necessary for someone to shin down the chute first. And now I felt I could truly call that ballroom at the sharp end the flight deck.

1980 was my last Christmas before retiring. My retirement present, which I requested and was granted, was to fly on the Concorde. Not as a passenger or as crew as I had not done the required emergency procedures, so I was allowed to fly as supernumerary crew.

July 1981 was my last operational flight and I chose Nice for my last flight. I could choose my own crew and it was a Tristar. This meant a large bunch of my special friends. I was made an 'honorary CSO' for the flight. One of the other CSO's told the entire aircraft my life story in a nutshell and on landing there was a great roar in unison from the passengers. Cheering from 300 passengers was a sound I could never have imagined.

◇◇◇◇◇◇◇◇◇◇◇◇◇◇◇◇◇◇◇◇◇◇◇◇◇◇◇◇◇◇◇◇◇◇◇◇◇◇◇◇◇◇◇◇◇◇◇◇◇◇◇◇◇◇◇◇◇◇◇◇◇◇◇◇◇◇

On 13 April 1950, as a BEA Vickers Viking was crossing the French coast bound for Paris, an explosion tore through the rear end of the fuselage. Captain Ian Harvey thought they had been struck by lightning and with extraordinary skill, considering the two enormous holes, turned the aircraft and landed safely at Northolt Airport with no loss of life. Police and aviation experts concluded at the time that a bomb had been planted in the lavatory. It was not until 2005 that archives from Scotland Yard were made public. These show that the Yard ultimately narrowed their investigation to one passenger, Alfred Calmet. He was found to have a record as a conman, and had financial and marital problems. He had told another passenger that he had recently insured his life for F10,000,000. The bomb was a suicide attempt, it was presumed. Fortunately it failed, but a stewardess close to the explosion, Sue Cramsie, was severely injured and spent seven months in hospital. At the time she had noticed an odd smell and was still trying to find the cause when the bomb exploded, tearing the lining out of her handbag and separating the tobacco from her cigarette papers. Sue Cramsie went on to become Chief Air Stewardess for BEA.
(Source: *The Daily Telegraph*, 24 January 2005 – Peter Day & Sally Pook)

Many of the BEA stewardesses, some of whom flew into the '80s after the merger with BA, say that although in many ways their job was made so much easier, they missed the old days for the camaraderie, friendship, and most importantly the very high morale that they enjoyed. It was inevitable that with such small crews everyone helped each other. A general feeling is that today's crews and passengers lack the bonhomie that we all shared so many years ago in that Golden Age.

BA uniform: Angela Threw, Miss BEA 1978. (© Adrian Meredith)

# CHAPTER 5

# The Swinging Sixties

The Swinging Sixties was a wonderfully exciting time to be an air stewardess. As Shirley Swinn says: 'Flower Power had exploded. Mary Quant, miniskirts and boots were all the rage. Chanel suits had arrived. Jackie Kennedy was influential too, as far as fashion was concerned and a new freedom for women began.' It was dancing to the Beatles, and 'Moon River' around the world. The Golden Age was here.

Trips could be as long as twenty-eight days, including lots of time off down the routes. A typical western trip would take one from London to New York, then across to San Francisco or Los Angeles. The next stop would be Honolulu, followed by Fiji, Sydney, then up to Hong Kong. From here, there might be a shuttle to Tokyo. Then it would be home to London, with stops in Delhi and Rome, a total of 23,000 miles, with about forty-nine hours in the air, and with often two to three days in these exciting places.

Exotic eastern trips from London took the crews to Zurich or Rome, then Teheran and on to Karachi or Delhi. Next it would be Sydney via Singapore. Then back the same way. In the Far East, one had between two and ten days in places such as Hong Kong, Tokyo, Rawalpindi and Singapore. The African trips gave you up to five days in the Seychelles, Johannesburg, Nairobi and Dar es Salaam. There were also trips to the Caribbean with (imagine!) six days in St Lucia and the Polar Route via Anchorage to Tokyo.

Crews enjoyed never-ending sojourns by the pool, excursions to places where only the rich and famous had been before, staying in expensive hotels with exotic names such as The Trinidad Hilton, Ocean Park Singapore, the Oberoi Intercontinental in Delhi, the Mocambo in Fiji, the Lexington in New York. There, crews would rest and play. Everyone had unforgettable experiences, such as the huge tropical fruit breakfasts in the Hilton Hawaiian Village right on Waikiki Beach or staying in an authentic Japanese inn in Sengokubara Hakone, or visiting the Taj Mahal, Petra in Jordan, and the famous Treetops in Kenya. Flying gave everyone a chance to see the world.

Other memories are skiing in the Laurentians, when we stayed in Montreal, the opera in Zurich, and the hundreds of churches in Rome.

## Exotic South America

My friend Celia Penny flew in the late '60s and she found it particularly irritating to be asked in the middle of the meal service, 'What are those mountains down there?' The edict was to get the meals out while they were hot. She was embarrassed to confess that once she lost her cool and said to the passengers: 'This is a meal service, not a ruddy geography lesson!'

   The South American route was one long geography lesson. In the early '60s there was a contingent of stewardesses, the fluent Spanish speakers Sheila Donaldson, Mavis Clough, Valerie Birrell, Ann Mottram, Baroness 'Bobby' Von Buseck, Marilyn Tobitt (now Lady Swann), Amalia Ciuvad, Joanne Luchian, Diane Kelly, Lorna Dand, Jill Roberts, Jill Wilson and many others, who flew those routes on the Comet 4. Their flight stewardess in the early '60s was Ann Hughes, based at Santiago. Ann later became a training stewardess in 1964. A typical roster could be London, Madrid, Dakar, Recife, Rio de Janeiro, Sao Paolo, Montevideo, Buenos Aires, Santiago and back again. Mrs 'Ma' Bentham ran the BOAC rest house in Santiago. On arrival the crew were served a large tray of pisco sours in front of a blazing fire. The crew then changed out of uniform and appeared for a sumptuous dinner with wine, most retiring to bed relatively early because of the early morning call. When the crew were called and opened their curtains they were greeted with the wonderful sight of the Andes and the heady scent of orange blossom. The flight crew slipped in Sao Paolo for four days and many of them found it worthwhile to travel over the mountains to Rio. The northbound crew when slipping in Dakar would bring cheap rum from Rio and the southbound crew would provide the 'mixers' for the inevitable party.

## The World was Our Own Shopping Mall

We all had a favourite tailor and jeweller in Hong Kong. You were able to wander into your tailor a few hours after your arrival in Hong Kong and have a fitting. The following day the dresses would be ready for collection and delivered to the hotel. Bombay and Delhi were marvellous places to buy precious stones and a fox fur coat. These items we could get designed to our own specifications in Hong Kong or Singapore. In Karachi there was ivory, onyx tables and crew members who flew into Karachi surely still have tablecloths and napkins from the Cottage Industries Shop. Intricate ivory inlaid pictures and copper from the Middle East, and in Japan, Noritake dinner services accompanied by Japan Sword cutlery and Mikimoto pearls, were all 'must haves' on the shopping agenda. Top of the list was the addiction for French luxury items – Miss Dior, Patou, Lancome, Givenchy and a luxurious silk Hermès scarf.

# BOEING 707

### Peter Royce, retired BOAC captain, remembers the first jetliners

BOAC Rolls-Royce 707 jetliner.

A brown envelope from BOAC was waiting for me when I returned to my flat in Richmond, Surrey, in the autumn of 1966. The letter said that I had been posted from the Comet 1V airliner to the Vickers VC10. This was not good news as I had my heart set on flying the Boeing 707. As luck would have it I found a friend who was desperate to fly the VC 10 so we managed to persuade BOAC to swap our courses. My dream was about to become a reality.

The 707 weighed around 152 tons and could carry 140 passengers at a cruising speed of 540mph for 4,200 miles at a height of 36,000ft.

Before actually flying the aircraft, I had to attend a three-week ground school course to learn about the various systems, such as electrical, hydraulics, engines, avionics, and how they combine to make the plane fly successfully. Exams had to be passed to satisfy the Civil Aviation Authority, before proceeding to the simulator flight deck for another three weeks of intense training.

At last I felt I was getting to grips with all the various nuances of flying this four-engined airliner. A few days after the simulator training finished, I was off to Prestwick in Scotland to finally get to fly the real thing, a really exciting time. The first flight with a senior instructor was unforgettable, and climbing out over the Isle of Mull on a clear day to explore the handling characteristics at several altitudes felt truly magical. It gave one a sense of the power and speed of this beautiful machine.

The first landing on a new aircraft is always a challenge and from the moment I touched down at Prestwick that day, I was smitten. My dream had at last come true.

I was a co-pilot and couldn't wait to gain my command but in those days it was several years before a vacancy one became available. In 1974 my chance finally arrived and it was off to Prestwick again after more hours in the simulator flying the 707 from the left-hand seat. Of course the aircraft had not changed but flying from the captain's seat was different and the added sense of responsibility was very soon apparent. All of us on the course were old friends and we all felt the same way about the 707, a superb machine designed to fly passengers in comfort at speed above the weather.

When I gained my command it was off down the routes to build up my hours as quickly as possible so I could join the training unit and teach others just how fabulous it was to fly this aircraft.

The airline's route structure Airways was worldwide and I was very privileged to cover all of them at one time or another. Compared to today's airliners the B707 was not that sophisticated and flying in poor weather with a low cloud base and restricted visibility was demanding but immensely satisfying. Being 153ft long, the aircraft would wag its tail in turbulent conditions and although there were systems on board to try to minimize this, for the comfort of the passengers the crew would climb or descend into smoother air.

When the Queen flew by 707 to the Pacific in celebration of her Silver Jubilee in 1977, I was in command for the London to Los Angeles sector. What an honour! This aircraft was ideal for this operation and was fitted with a special Royal Flight kit comprising two beds, a dining table and large comfortable chairs. The flight was at night and took eleven hours and thirty minutes and the aircraft performed as predicted without a hitch.

The reliability of the engines was remarkable and in eleven years of flying the 707 I only had to shutdown one engine, which in the '60s and '70s was amazing. It truly was a commercial success and hundreds were built and flown by airlines all over the world, but sadly only a few are still flying as freighters.

Flying the 707 was a joy and a delight, only superseded by the Boeing 747, jumbo jet, but that is another story.

## Living it up on Allowances

Shopping down the routes was a never-ending passion for many. The more adventurous shoppers managed to transport tropical fish from Singapore to Australia. This was before Australian Customs really toughened up. My father had a huge aquarium and spent many happy hours watching his fish. On two occasions, I had a nerve-racking time worrying that my plastic bags of tropical fish were going to burst behind the last row of the first class cabin. By the time the aircraft had reached its flying altitude, the bags were at maximum bursting point, and remained that way until we began to descend. What a relief when we landed. The shark fish survived and lived for twenty-two years.

Allowances in the '60s and '70s were excellent. The general consensus was that you could go away for twenty-eight days and live off your allowances. You could bring lots of goodies home and still not spend a penny over and above your allowance. The extra bonus was that when you got home your salary was in the bank. We had 'never had it so good'. Compared to the salaries of nurses, teachers and secretaries the salary of stewardesses was a fortune.

Andy Bennett remembers her first trip, which was to Washington:

✈ When we arrived at the hotel we were given a crew allowance of $25, a huge amount in those days. I made a list of what I spent including breakfast, taxi to the Capitol and The White House, soft drinks for the crew all round to thank them for taking me out and showing me the sights. At pickup I went up to the Chief and said, 'Here's the money I haven't spent. I've made a list of what I've spent it on.' He just roared, gave me a big kiss and said, 'Put it in your pocket'. Wow, I knew then that I could do the job for a while, as I had thought we only got the basic £9 a week and I had been earning £20 a week in my previous job in a PR company and had saved up knowing that I would have to take a drop in salary.

## *A*N INCIDENT WITH HM CUSTOMS

Philippa Feeney was definitely one of the 'It' girls. She was very tall – in fact over the height limit. Worried about this height restriction, she recalls really working hard at the interview and smiling a lot, which wasn't difficult for her. An independent, fun-loving personality, she had a vivacious, very lively manner and a very striking appearance. Crews loved flying with her, as she threw her heart and soul into the job in the air and on the ground.

Pip Feeney remembers when she purchased a mynah bird:

✈ I bought the bird in Singapore and brought it back to the UK with a stopover in Calcutta. The captain helped get it through Calcutta customs by coughing loudly to cover up the squawk. We put a blanket over it to stop it squawking in the passenger cabin. At Heathrow, I declared the 'bird'

Phillipa Feeney, 1965–68.

alongside other shopping, as a handicraft, as we were allowed to bring these in with no duty. Crews declared their shopping on a green form. The Customs Officer came on board, checked us all off and then we got on the crew transport to go over to the terminal. I was so anxious about my bird that I hadn't noticed that none of the crew had left the aircraft after being checked. They were all waiting to see the bird get off successfully. As luck would have it, we had a fairly new, young and overzealous Customs Officer. He wanted to see the 'bird'. I produced the cage and to my astonishment there was an egg at the bottom of the cage. It had very strange markings on it. It turned out to be a hard-boiled chicken's egg from the first class breakfast menu. The crew had written all over it! The writing consisted of many four-letter words, and 'Get Stuffed!' The Custom's man was so amused in the end that he let me through. I gave the bird to my brother and it lived at Oxford University for the rest of its life, never saying a word.

## More Incidents with Her Majesty's Customs

Sue Thomas recalls the gold smuggling around 1958:

✈   It was when we were on a posting to Beirut. Then we were moved to Karachi where two stewards were caught. I had a police escort and they were convinced that since I was the only female on the crew I would reveal all. The stewards were imprisoned out in the desert. We took a BOAC bus and lots of goodies and went to visit them. Not a good idea as we nearly got the sack. I seem to remember they were pardoned when the Queen did a trip out that way.

They were luckier than Sally Wigram. Sally was the epitome of the disciplined stewardess, beautifully spoken, very pretty with dark curly hair and had served in the Royal Navy as a Wren. So she certainly knew about obeying rules and doing the right thing. She was in fact a model stewardess until a devastating incident that cost her her job. She explains:

✈   Having been laid sick for a week in Singapore, I was feeling pretty weak but decided I was well enough to work my way home. On leaving Bahrain for Heathrow, the first class had been taken over by one of the Sheik's sons who was on honeymoon and taking his new bride to see London, Paris and Rome. It was a special occasion and we made an extra effort to ensure they had superb service.

On approaching Heathrow, the young Sheik insisted he give me a gold necklace. On seeing his reaction when I said, 'Oh but I couldn't accept,' I realised it would be an insult to decline his gift and thanked him. After landing, they had so much hand luggage and no one to help them so I made many trips up and down the gangway with their luggage and then wished them a wonderful holiday. At this point I was told we were to go to the Sheds. This is where the crew is carted off to Customs, where officials will look through everything in our luggage to make sure we are not smuggling items. I showed the gold necklace to the young Customs official and said it had been given to me on landing and therefore I had no time to fill in the declaration form. He got very excited and rushed off to get a more senior official. Meanwhile my captain and the rest of the crew had gone home. I was left all alone and feeling very sick and weary. The next thing I knew, I was off to the police station, where finger-prints were taken and I was released on bail until the case came up in court a few months later. Even an expensive lawyer could not get me off as I did not fill in the Custom Declaration form and I was charged with smuggling. So I was left with a criminal record and no job. This was a harsh and devastating ending to a new career.

However, I feel that BOAC was still reeling from the gold smuggling stewards and determined to make Sally a scapegoat.

Cartoon by Oni Wyatt.

Generally smuggling was not really something that the stewardesses got into apart from going over the limit with alcohol, perfume, cigarettes and jewellery. The gold was left to the few stewards who were prepared to take the risks.

## HAVE YOU GOT YOUR 'LITTLE BROWN ENVELOPE'?

There was a custom that many brown envelopes containing a monetary gift of 100 dinars was passed to stewardesses for merely attending a party. This practice was stopped in the early '70s, when the British newspapers got hold of stories about these beach parties.

Oil was first found in Bahrain in 1932, before many of the other Gulf States, so Bahrain was moving forward into a faster and more sophisticated pace of life.

Celia Penney recalls:

✈    I was one of the many stewardesses in the sixties who enjoyed the generous hospitality provided by the Ruler of Bahrain. As usual, we had been invited to his 'beach house' (with solid gold taps in the bathroom) during the day. Two of us had then been invited to a party at one of his other palaces in the evening. The chauffeur turned up for us and we had a very pleasant evening with His Highness and other members of the Royal family. The rest of the crew knew we were going and we had been subjected to the usual banter about concubines, harems and sheep's eyes, but we knew we were safe.

During the evening, the Ruler invited me into another room and presented me with a very delicate pearl necklace. He explained that before Bahrain had become an oil state, one of its main sources of revenue had been from pearl fishing. Now that the revenue was no longer needed, all the pearls that were fished belonged to him. These 'trinkets' were then given as gifts to some of his favoured guests. I was thrilled to accept such a beautiful present.

At the end of a very pleasant evening (where no sheep's eyes or concubines had been in evidence) we were driven home. We were both given a large sum of money, as apparently His Royal Highness had enjoyed our presence. We had done nothing to 'earn' this money apart from being present and dancing with our hosts. Honestly!

We knew these gifts were quite common but were still rather embarrassed about it all and consequently did not tell the rest of the crew. We also thought they might have been just a teeny bit jealous.

For the same reasons, we decided not to declare the money and gifts when we arrived at Heathrow – perhaps wondering if Customs would think we were on the game. I hid the pearls in the lining of my skirt waist band and sewed the cash (about £500 – a lot of money in those days) into the lining of my hat. I can't remember what the other stewardess did with her gifts – something similar I presume.

We had not been out of the country for long and were only allowed two tots of alcohol each. It was the custom for the stewardess often to give her allowance to a member of the flight deck (or a steward) if she was not taking any alcohol in. He then could have four tots, although officially two were hers. On the Customs form I declared my usual two tots and the first officer carried in four. If anybody asked, which they never did, he would say that two were mine. I confess that I did not declare the pearls on the Customs form.

We landed at Heathrow and unusually were suddenly called over to the Sheds by Customs for a surprise search. I was shocked. This had never happened to me before and I was petrified they would discover my pearls, but knew they never did a strip search unless they were really suspicious. What did they know? Were there secret X-ray machines around? It got worse. I was singled out for a full interrogation and taken to the Interrogation Room. Room 101 in *Nineteen Eighty-Four* had nothing on this. It was like something out of the KGB. A female Customs Officer stood at the door (presumably to stop me from escaping) and there were three others surrounding me. I could feel the pearls boring into my waist and the £500 scorching my head. I felt like confessing all – even before they started the interrogation. I remembered *Nineteen Eighty-Four*: 'Anything but the rats!' I thought. But I kept my cool. How could they know? They started asking me about my alcohol declaration and where were my two tots. I said that the first officer had them (which was true) and wondered why they were making such a fuss about two tots. This was before the days when Customs had other things to worry about, such as heroin, cannabis, guns, terrorists, chemical weapons and dodgy meat from Africa. Then they informed me that the first officer, although only declaring two tots on the form, had been found to have in his possession nearly a full bottle. Sin of all sins! 'Naughty man,' I thought, 'but what has all this to do with me?' I soon found out. Trying to avoid getting into trouble, he had told Customs that it was mine and he was carrying it for me. What a dirty trick, I thought. I had no hesitation in telling them the truth and that he had coerced me into declaring two tots for him. They believed me and let me go, complete with pearls and money. It was bizarre but very, very scary. My days of smuggling ceased from that day. Don't know what happened to the first officer. I hope they sacked him. I still have the pearls.

Cartoon by Oni Wyatt: 'the fruit and veg challenge'.

Australia has to be the toughest country apropos quarantine in the world. First-time passengers landing at Darwin watch with amazement as two Darwin ground staff, usually 'bronzed Aussies' in white shirts and shorts, stride through the aircraft cabin each with a spray killing any bugs that may have unwittingly been carried from the previous port of call. Fruit is an absolute no-no; it cannot be imported and penalties are severe. One fairly new first officer was given an exceedingly hard time by the senior captain. Thoroughly fed up, he sought revenge by putting a first class orange in the captain's briefcase. This particular captain was one of the few whom everybody dreaded to fly with. Fortunately the captain's bag was not inspected; he was very lucky! This notorious captain, nicknamed Captain Blade, imposed all sorts of restrictions on his crew, always wanting to know what his crew brought on board with them. It was invariably shopping of some kind, but woe betide you if you had not asked his permission. Oni Wyatt recalls bringing a sheepskin jacket onto the aircraft at Sydney. Captain Blade spotted this. She hadn't sought permission to bring this coat on board and he insisted that she offload it. Oni simply gave it to a ground staff member and that was it.

This obsession with crew shopping extended to Nairobi where shopping in the market for fresh exotic fruit and veg was always a big perk. Each cabin crew and technical crew invariably took back to England a basketful of avocados, pineapples, mangoes, guavas, coconuts, paw-paws and so forth. On one particular trip the cabin crew neglected to ask Captain Blade for permission. To the crew's amazement the captain, who also had a huge basket of fruit, insisted that all *their* baskets of fruit go into the hold. The crew always put their baskets behind the last row of passenger seats as they knew that fruit in the hold would not survive the trip from Nairobi to London – and they did not. At London, the crew baggage was unloaded onto the crew transport and with a nod and wink from a member of the cabin crew the captain's fruit basket came to an untimely end, as the crew transport 'accidentally' reversed over it.

Dealing with Her Majesty's Customs in the Golden Age developed in many the art of obfuscation.

## The Glamorous Erratic Lifestyle

Before the jumbos, crew social life could be very lively and much looked forward to. There was this strange yet successful social phenomenon that the job carried, which meant that a group of ten to twelve total strangers would meet and almost immediately become a team for the length of the trip. They could become very close, work together, eat together, go on excursions together, shop and swim together, work on the aircraft and do a whole lot of other stuff together, if the spirit and the body were willing.

The catch cry once everyone had registered at the hotel was 'Whose room?' followed by the famous phrase, 'Bring your own glass!' The room parties were legendary. This not to say that everyone drank like a fish but there were quite a few cabin crew and chaps at the sharp end who did enjoy more than the odd drink! The aircraft oxygen came in useful for many cabin crew who needed to buck themselves up the next day in preparation for a long flight!

All the alcohol for crew parties down the routes was supplied courtesy of BOAC. Many a cabin crew dinner party in the UK would offer fine wines and champagne courtesy of BOAC. Christenings and weddings were the grateful recipients of studied plans of attack to dispose of surplus vintage aircraft stock. The dilemma that could occur in flight was if there were only one or two first class passengers. The auditors must have been very shocked at the amount of alcohol one or two passengers could consume. New cabin crew were told that by their second trip, 'You will be bringing a bottle for the room party. If you do not drink yourself bring it in for the rest of the crew.' In fact, if you did not turn up with a part bottle from the aircraft at a room party you were considered a social pariah.

Knocking off aircraft supplies meant that even the odd gold three-tiered trolley could disappear from the aircraft along with Dundee cake, Beluga caviar, smoked salmon, Elizabeth Arden and Yardley toiletries, hot house grapes and other fruit and cheese (including the stilton jars). All found their way into many homes. Alcohol, cigarettes, coffee, tea and Kleenex also disappeared. The desperate ones also helped themselves to all the dry stores, Heinz baby food, toilet rolls, Holbrookes sauce and Colmans mustard. I hasten to add that not all cabin crew regarded pilfering as a perk. However, it was de rigeur to strip the aircraft when arriving into Calcutta. Biscuits, Bovril, biros, cereal, Cow & Gate powdered milk, Farex and Heinz baby food all found their way to Mother Teresa's orphanage.

America is strict about foodstuffs coming in. On the Monarch flights in the '50s and '60s the first class meal was a lengthy and elaborate affair. Cabin crew coming into New York had to dump all the leftover food – including Beluga caviar, hot house peaches and Belgian grapes. This regulation also included flowers and at that time a red rose was placed on the passenger's table along with the silver and glassware.

I had a very charming and inebriated Trevor Howard on board. He thoroughly enjoyed every morsel of his food and the Chateauneuf du Pape. As I went to clear away he took my hand and said he wanted to give me a little gift. He then graciously presented me with the red rose from his table, the same rose I had initially placed there, and kissed my hand. I couldn't keep the kiss but I still have the rose, crushed and dried, as I was determined to smuggle it into New York and keep it forever. A true brief encounter!

Sitting in the right-hand seat of a 707 as a stewardess was the second greatest thrill for me. I was training for my pilot's licence at White Waltham, in an old Auster. My instructor was an ex-Spitfire fighter pilot and his black Labrador was always on the back seat, often licking my neck as I was doing my circuits and bumps. Fortunately the passengers on the 707 were not aware that I was piloting their aircraft and the cockpit door was shut. Although the automatic pilot was engaged in manual mode, the captain in the left-hand seat almost convinced me that I was in charge of this powerful machine. There was a slight bump as I took over his 707 and he said: 'You are now in charge.' Tremendous. I loved it. What a buzz!

Glamorous as all this was, there was a downside to this erratic lifestyle. It made the forward planning of important social engagements almost impossible. Standby was compulsory for all the crew. The worst part was when you had to be at the airport within one and a half hours of the call, packed and ready to go. You could suddenly be sent anywhere. For many this became such an inconvenience that they left. This lifestyle also was not conducive to relationships at

Cartoon by Oni Wyatt: 'the perils of standby'.

home, as they were difficult to maintain. Stewardesses were always seen as unreliable and 'always rushing off somewhere exotic'. Marilyn Cox:

✈    Being owned by BOAC rather than working for them finally drove me out. Cabin crew then had no idea what they would be doing after their current trip until they got back home and found their next roster on the door mat.

I left without giving notice and was told by the airline not to darken its doors again, but I was back six months later. Ironically, I was back soon working for my old BOAC boss in reservations, and twenty years later finally left the airline, having achieved a senior position in marketing in a very different British Airways.

A contrary opinion, and I might say quite an outburst, came from Cynthia Langstaff:

✈    If there was a 'Golden Age' of airline stewardesses I believe that would have been well before my time. Ours was never a profession since qualifications were not uniform and the selection process was very ad hoc and depended on the staffing needs of the airline at the time; nor could it be classed as a career as when I joined in 1962, I was told that my employment would only last for ten years, when I would be given 'the golden handshake'. This was sexual discrimination at its very worst. Another example of this was that in seven years of flying I never came across a woman in charge of an aircraft cabin, other than a visiting cabin service officer. We always had to defer to the male of the species, many of whom were semi-illiterate or prancing queens.

Another aspect of life as a stewardess was the blatant sexual harassment from flight deck, stewards, bosses and passengers, which in the '60s was not only rife but considered normal. The girls put up with this, including being overworked and underpaid, in order to 'see the world' and in the '60s there was still a little residual glamour – probably inspired by the uniform – to make it seem as if it was all worthwhile. A Golden Age it was not.

The universal perk for us all was the 10 per cent fares we were allowed as staff, which also meant our parents and brothers and sisters could use them too. I remember using this ten percent when I left London on a Friday night, flew to Singapore arriving Saturday morning and that night went to a ball on the HMS *Terror*, a grand Royal Naval ball, hopped on the plane on Sunday and was back in front of class of trainee stewardesses on Monday morning. That is the longest distance I ever travelled to a ball.

Passenger service in the '60s was indicative of a bygone age. Passengers who boarded in the economy cabin were shown to their seats. Stewardesses used the words 'Sir' or 'Madam' while doing so, thus setting the tone. White gloves were worn and cabin crew, in those days, helped passengers stow their hand baggage and their coats (neatly folded) in the open hat racks. The slogan was 'BOAC Takes Good Care of You' and we did. Jeannie Lardner, the instructor, had drummed into us all that if you saw a sleeping passenger, to cover them up with a blanket. It is said that a stewardess in the economy cabin walks eight miles between London and New York.

## New Stewardesses

After 1964, there was a huge intake of cabin crew, mainly stewardesses. The 707s were going around the world and the wonderful new VC10s were doing Africa, the Middle East and the North Atlantic. The stewardesses were getting younger. Many were only nineteen, twenty and twenty-one. Looking back, many realise now how very inexperienced and unprepared they were for such a sophisticated and worldly career.

Being street (or air) wise was not something that could be taught in the training school. This was the era where the women employed at nineteen and twenty years of age would not have had the same experience of working with men as the stewardesses of the '40s and '50s, who had had wartime experience.

Virginia Sheehy had many flying highlights in her ten-year career including several Royal Flights. She was there for the tape-cutting ceremony for the first Concorde prototype at Toulouse, one of the many public relations projects in which she played her part representing the airline.

She was, she admits, a 'very by the book' stewardess and certainly a role model for the many new recruits that had joined in the mid-'60s. Certainly the innocence of the early '60s showed in their faces. It was a quick learning curve for these naïve young women who had led a reasonably sheltered life with little preparation for the job socially, emotionally and psychologically. To convent girls, like Virginia Sheehy, the world of BOAC was an eye-opener. Despite stories of many of these young, inexperienced stewardesses being taken advantage of, there were, as Ginny recalls, many generous, kind and respectful passengers. 'Every time one man came to London he gave me a Chanel handbag and wined and dined me in the best of places. There was no ulterior motive, simply a wonderful platonic relationship.'

Australians were so proud to be BOAC stewardesses. Gay Halliday was one of eight originally employed to crew the Australian end of the London to Sydney flights. Based in Sydney they flew the Sydney–Singapore/Sydney–Auckland/Sydney–Hong Kong sectors.

When BOAC advertised in Sydney for Australian-based stewardesses over 2,000 girls applied. They were sent to London for training. Gay remembers Jeannie Lardner being very dismissive of the Aussie girls: 'You colonial girls …' Gay objected to being called a colonial.

The other Aussies with Gay were Joy Fawcett, Terry O'Conner, Jean Scott, Wendy Hart, Ann McNicoll, Shan Clarke and Meg Hulbert. UK stewardesses were then sent to Sydney on three-month postings. Later came the option to be London based and this was the cherry on the grapefruit for several of these Aussies.

Virginia Sheehy recalls her trainer saying: '"We don't want any of those Hunting Clan tricks. Hands off the back of the seat please." She was in the mock-up and had her hand resting on the headrest.' Hunting Clan Air TSP (a charter airline) became British United Airlines and there was the feeling that stewardesses from other airlines were not really welcomed in BOAC.

## The Early '60s Uniform

Ninety per cent of the survey recipients said how proud they felt to wear the BOAC uniform and to be part of BOAC. It was the image.

The forage cap style was smart but difficult to wear for some. If you had the regulation off the shoulder bob bouffant hairstyle of those '60s days, sprayed to withstand walking to your aircraft in a blizzard, invariably when you took it off there was hat indentation in your hair.

I redesigned mine soon after I got my Wings by unstitching the side flap just a little to give it a jaunty look. Tess Curtin, a flight stewardess, stopped me and asked me what had happened to my hat. I pretended that the stitching had come undone. I don't think I fooled her one bit and every time I went on service I would be ducking and weaving so that she didn't spot me. I thought the BEA hat was much smarter.

The hats and gloves, which were always to be worn, worried the stewardesses as the loss of either or both was a disaster.

Anne Rossi told me:

✈ Before a twenty-three-hour flight to Sydney the cleaners didn't return my hat. I went on the trip without it. Nobody said anything but I nearly had a heart attack when I saw Mr Lawrence, Head of the Training School, standing at the top of the steps in Singapore. I passed him and he didn't notice or say anything. I was very relieved.

Annetta Markman: 'My greatest worry was getting to 221 and not having my hat with me. I used to have nightmares about it for years after.' Many of the girls mention a recurring dream while they were flying. It was either getting to the airport and having left their hat behind or being in a plane about to land on a busy street and they are 50ft or so off the ground when the wings fall off. It is amazing how many of the ex-stewardesses managed to keep their hats when they left the airline.

In the late '60s, we were given a new uniform designed by Clive. It was a navy short dress with a detachable white Peter Pan collar and a neat box-style jacket, with a lovely wool coat and boots for winter. For summer there was a pink and turquoise dress with a mandarin collar and a zip in the front, four inches above our knees. This was a huge contrast to the previous military-style uniform.

Once the '60s were in full swing, we were all taking up our dresses so as to not look so out of fashion. We wore them with navy tights (Wolfords) as we all know dark stockings are very flattering to the legs. The summer dresses were so short that when you lifted the passengers' hand luggage into the overhead lockers (which we used to do in the Golden Age) you almost showed your knickers. There was a craze at one time to flaunt knickers that said 'Fly Pan Am'!

Angela Froude said:

✈ In Blantyre, Malawi, we had to cover up our short dresses in a long full-length wraparound skirt just to go ashore and sit in a crew room for a four-hour turn round. However, in those days there was no such modesty in Jeddah or any other Saudi city and we happily walked around in skirts barely covering our backsides at times.

Many stewardesses wrote about the paper dresses. Oni Wyatt:

✈ This was the time of the insane paper dresses, which you cut to the right length (subject to your interpretation) and then wore under your winter coat out of a freezing New York, doing the Caribbean and Bermuda shuttles. They were thin paper shifts with palm trees on them and a huge sun right over the left breast! We had a fresh orchid to wear as a corsage. The trouble was that one drop of water on the dress would be soaked up like blotting paper. It would then rapidly disintegrate!

Celia Penney says:

✈ It was a silly publicity stunt. They wanted us to look like the exotic Jamaican stewardesses – as if we ever could! We were constantly trying to dodge drunken male passengers trying to set the dresses alight. We never quite got the length right when cutting them and the American men would try to shorten them with their own scissors. They also kept asking for things from the hat rack. I suppose it would be called sexual harassment today but that condition did not exist then. We mostly were good humoured about it. Girls would sue today and need counselling.

Katie Smith remembers:

✈   We wore them with lime green pumps and had a large flower in our hair. I really regret never having a photo taken in one of them. They did not last long and were an absolute disaster. Whoever thought them up I wonder? It can't have been a woman. They had to be cut to a length just above the knee. Someone else always had to do this while you stood there still and straight. The loaders at New York became very adept at this!

Another stewardess commented:

✈   We wore these dresses with care. They tore easily and spilt vinaigrette dressing made them transparent. There was also a huge sun or flower over the left boob. Lifting your arms up to help a passenger reach the hat rack was asking for trouble – this was the time when one wore the frilliest of underwear. I didn't mind any of this but I lived in fear of the cigarette lighter. The paper dresses were allegedly fireproof. However, the general consensus was 'what a daft idea'.

Paper dresses in flight were also used in TWA. These were much more extreme than BOAC's These paper outfits reflected the destination: a French gold lamé cocktail dress, lounge pyjamas for New York, a Roman toga and the 'serving wench'.

## Hair & Hat Dramas

Grooming standards caused consternation for many of the stewardesses. Each time a stewardess went on service, she was supposed to see her check stewardess and this is when the hair and hat dramas could begin. Management decreed that hair had to be off the collar and 'when the hat is worn, hair must not be visible below the peak'. It was to be worn 'in an upswept style, must be swept back from the face to the crown of the head, thus ensuring that the hat is worn at the recognised position i.e. forward in direct contact with the forehead.' All rather pedantic. Exaggerated bouffant, curls or chignon on top of the head and loose pony tails were not allowed. Considering that the '60s was the time of the 'exaggerated bouffant' there were some battles over these constrictions. Sarah Forsyth, who had the quintessential *Tatler* look, remembers being most upset at having to get her long and immaculate hair cut on the training course.

The biggest changes in the '60s were how we wore our hair. A young Vidal Sassoon was a household name. His angular, carved, sleek haircut was the height of fashion and for those whom it suited, looked stunning. BOAC turned a blind eye to this radical new cut and the stereotypical hair off the collar look had had its day. The '60s also saw the birth of backcombing. This frazzled haystack, with a little thatch combed over until your hair billowed around your face, came into fashion. As if this was not enough, the hair piece became mandatory, carted around in a little box in one's cabin bag. What were we thinking? By 1963, sexy was the whole point. We were kittens with false eyelashes and great sweeps of black eyeliner.

Hong Kong produced magnificent human hair wigs and we all bought pieces and swathes and half wigs and full wigs to cover our hair. A boon particularly for those with long hair with the task of putting it up at 1.30 a.m. The perils of wig wearing in the late '60s and early '70s were numerous as the wigs could let you down – particularly if doing a lifejacket demonstration when you pulled the lifejacket back over your hair or bending quickly into the ice bucket. Or scrabbling around a passenger's feet helping them to find something. Needless to say securing the wig was always an engineering feat.

# *L*ONG HAIR SUFFERED THE WORST

Carol White on her training course was reprimanded for coming in one morning with her hair down, as she was going out in the evening. She was then shown photos of short hair but refused to even contemplate cutting it. She said:

✈   When I finished training, I was punished by being put on Argonauts. I worked out of Beirut. Argonauts, the only two left in service as the runway at that time was not long enough for the Comets. There was only one service a week, which flew to Abadan and Kuwait. We then had a week slipping in Beirut. There were wonderful nightclubs and the casino. We stayed in the Bristol Hotel and enjoyed fine dining and dancing every night. We did twenty-two hours on duty from Beirut-Abadan-Kuwait-Abadan-Rome. This was thousands of miles away from London and hair inspections – it was great. What a punishment! (See p8 in the colour section)

IF YOU WANT TO GET AHEAD, GET A HAT: Headgear through the ages from the rakish tilt of the 1940s Stargirls of British South American Airways...

...to the stylish forage cap with its jaunty cockade worn from 1954 at BEA...

ON PARADE: The smart Wren-style uniform which took the BOAC name around the world in the 1940s — and is that a Dakota we spy behind them?

NIPPED AND TUCKED: Post-war austerity, with a hint of the New Look, influenced the 50s style.

ELEGANCE ABROAD: The BEA look introduced in 1960 was to last for seven years.

...By 1967 the women were in "a small oval-shaped hat" by Hardy Amies...

...who also designed the Tutankhamen style which took over in 1972...

...In 1978 came the Baccarat Weatherall bowler...

...followed in 1985 by Klein's structured beret.

# Uniform trends

KITTING out 20,000 staff in a new uniform was never going to be anything but a challenge. You can, as they say, please some of the people some of the time, but you'll never please all of the people all of the time.

However British Airways, never one to shirk a challenge, has tackled it head-on by giving every one of its customer contact staff the chance to have their say in the new look that will be unveiled next week.

If the uniforms on this page are anything to go by, it will be a uniform of its time, reflecting some of the current fashion statements. It will also have been designed with the views of the wearers in mind—suitable for different shapes and sizes, versatile for different climates, comfortable, practical and stylish. And, of course, embodying the quality and excellence for which British Airways stands all over the world.

It all takes time. It was more than a year ago that a survey of passengers and staff revealed that it was time for a change in the airline's front-line image. The current uniform, designed by Roland Klein, has been in use for eight years, as long as any of the uniforms pictured here from previous decades.

Initial discussions with Purchasing led to a small project team of managers representing all frontline areas, being set up in March.

Co-ordinated by a pilot, Captain Michael Palmer, it included Margaret Brandon and Belinda Macdonell from Cabin Crew, Doug Atkerden from Ground Ops London and Lynne Pon-

THIS time next week 20,000 frontline staff across the airline and across the world, will have seen the uniform designed to take them into the next century.

We look back at how uniforms have changed through the years, how they reflected the fashions of their time and the image of the airline, and to whet your appetite for the launch by Lord King, the Chairman, of the new uniform next Thursday.

tet from Gatwick, Margaret Stitt and Rosemary Gibbs from Uniforms, Lindsay Todd and Mark Russell from British Airways Regional, Gerrie Smith from Design and Eric Burdon from the Americas' marketing team.

Around 27 designers were considered at the outset, but with some concerned about the constraints of corporate wear, others worried about timescales or mass manufacture, and others simply reluctant to compete for the appointment, it was July before nine, covering the spectrum of corporate and couturier design, were ready to present their outline designs.

At the same time a questionnaire went out to all 20,000 cus-

tomer contact staff, seeking their views and preferences for a new uniform. More than half responded, providing invaluable feedback which was made available to the three designers shortlisted on the basis of their enthusiasm, design ability and understanding of both staff needs and the company's need for quality and controlled cost.

The three designers spent September and October meeting, listening to and talking to a cross section of some 600 ground staff and cabin crew at work in London, Belfast, Manchester and overseas in Paris, New York, Hong Kong and Dubai.

By November they were finalis-

MILITARY LOOK: Right, the BOAC look for the 1950s lasted into the '60s with slight modifications.

ing their designs, taking into account the views they had gathered, and two weeks ago were ready to present a catwalk show to an invited audience of around 100 uniformed employees of all grades, who filled in another questionnaire on their particular likes and dislikes about each one.

"The vital element in the whole process was for the designers to meet the staff, and to talk to them to develop their understanding of what was needed," said Michael. "Ours is a very difficult set of shoulders to mantle as the uniform is being worn by so many people, and it was essential for the designers to find out first hand what staff feel has been missing and what considerations should be taken into account."

You can see the results for yourself in next week's *British Airways News*.

KLEIN DESIGN: The current uniform was designed by Roland Klein and launched in May 1985, reflecting the more informal, fluid influences of the decade.

FLYING HIGH: Hardy Amies' uniform, introduced in 1972 for BEA, lasted through the merger with BOAC and into the first few years of British Airways.

SEVENTIES STYLE: Summer shift dresses in coral and turquoise, knee boots. A-lines and zip jackets set the style of the '70s for BOAC staff with the uniform launched in the autumn of 1969.

CITY SLICK: The pinstriped suit by Baccarat Weatherall was the first uniform designed for British Airways, and introduced in May 1977.

THE WAY THEY WERE: How the men's uniforms progressed from the '30s and the 40s to (we think) the '70s.

TEA TIME: The in-flight look for stewards working on BOAC's Constellations in the 1950s.

*British Airways News,* January 1993.

Oni says:

> ✈    Another aspect that makes me smile is that in the '60s and 70s, we often wore wigs. To
> pull on a wig was so much easier when you were arising at two in the morning in Karachi,
> once again suffering a powercut. Hong Kong did a great line in nylon and real hair wigs, plaits
> and tizzy bits. But they were so hot.

The grooming and glamour overhaul was a standard procedure which all stewardesses knew to expect,
and some with apprehension. This visual component was intrinsic to the perfect stewardess.

## The Supernumerary Flight

Your supernumerary flight was such an exciting experience. Your first flight after all that training.
Suddenly you were actually going to be on a real aircraft doing all the stuff that had been theory
for six weeks. My first trip was to Washington DC. Walking up the aircraft steps my heart was
thumping with anticipation. I wanted to be the best stewardess in the world. Imagine my feelings
when the senior steward came up to me after a few minutes on the aircraft, as I was preparing
the 707, and said: 'So you're Australian?' I had already introduced myself but not mentioned that
bit so I said, 'Yes I am'. He replied: 'Well, I'd like to tell you that there are only three types of
stewardesses – the Good, the Bad and the Ugly,' and then he walked off. I never forgot that.

The crews delighted in breaking-in new girls by playing tricks. Maths was never my strong
point so the first time I had to deal with several different currencies at once (in those days
passengers paid for their drinks) I was dreading it and mentioned it to the steward down the
back. I had worked out quite a few conversions in my head but was nevertheless very nervous
and apprehensive about making a total fool of myself. As it happened, the whole exercise
couldn't have been simpler. Before I even attempted to tot up drink order totals the passenger
had added it up and whipped out on almost every occasion the exact money. I was so relieved
and said to the steward how wonderful all the passengers were and so helpful. He just smiled
and said: 'Is that so?' Coming into Idlewild one of the passengers in the very back row rang
the call bell and I bent down to hear him whisper to me, 'I think you can take that notice off
your back now.' I raced to the loo and reached around and found a piece of paper which in big
letters read: THIS IS HER FIRST TRIP – BE KIND.

On another occasion Jean Heath said that the chief steward told her:

> ✈    It's your job to feed the dog in Lower 41, which was a small hold underneath the 707s
> flight deck that was accessed by moving the navigator's seat. I was given a bowl of food and a
> torch and shown the way. Of course the navigator followed me. Another ploy was to be given
> a 'dipstick' and told to check the level of the toilets during flight. Naturally I fell for it.

Oni Wyatt recalls:

> ✈    The lavatory of the VC10 had a cigarette disposal ashtray, covered with a flap. Unknown
> to the passengers, and carefully kept from us new recruits, was the fact that you could lift
> another flap at the front, outside of the door. If you timed it right when the female occupant
> was seated comfortably, and you had a practised aim, you could angle a soda siphon to give a
> good squirt right up the unmentionable. So, yes, I got caught! It was absolutely shocking! But
> you had to laugh! The rats!

Lorna Dand's first flight was to New York. After a diversion and delay at Shannon the aircraft
flew into a long bout of turbulence. As she felt exceedingly unwell, the crew suggested that she

lie down on a spare first class bunk. When she recovered, she found that the crew had stolen her skirt. As she had to make the PA announcement for the landing in New York, she did it with a blanket wrapped around her: 'Eventually I had my skirt returned. It made me less naïve in the future. We had a wonderful *esprit de corps* and we were all careful not to talk to non-flying people in too glowing terms about our wonderful lifestyle for fear of appearing boastful or blasé.'

One stewardess, Shirley Dakin, remembers that her supernumerary flight was to Accra in Ghana:

✈   Chubby Checker was on board; he took a shine to me and wanted to take me out in Accra. I remember the chief steward was very protective of me and told Chubby that he certainly could not take me out as I was on my first trip and the crew were all going to look after me. It was a lovely introduction to flying and being with the crews.

## 𝒜 TRICK PLAYED ON STEWARDESSES

After taking off from Tokyo, I spent the whole sector back and forth through the cabin unaware that a notice from the bathroom of our hotel, the Tokyo Prince, had been pinned to the back of my skirt, which read: 'This seat has been sterilised for your protection.'

I was on my first trip back to Australia and hadn't seen my family since I had left a few years earlier. So coming into Darwin I was starting to get very excited. The next stop would be Sydney and then up to Brisbane – and home. Coming into Darwin the first officer asked me if I would like to see the Southern Cross. I jumped at the chance and pressed my eye to the eyepiece of the periscopic sextant. I couldn't see a thing and felt rather a fool. He suggested I use my other eye, which I did and there it was, the fantastic Southern Cross. I was thrilled and went back to the first class cabin to find that both the senior steward and the galley steward seemed to have difficulty looking me in the face and there was a lot of turning away and smiling. I wandered out into the first class cabin to see if anyone wanted anything prior to landing. All the first class passengers were also suppressing smiles and looking away. With everything in order for landing I did my briefing and, prior to taking my crew seat for landing, popped into the loo. Imagine my horror and embarrassment when I looked in the mirror to see two black circles around my eyes. The first class passengers had been tipped off. Everyone was in on the joke.

'XVC10 Jen'... cartoon by Oni Wyatt

Shirley Fogg: 'I was offered a carton of orange juice by the senior steward. I downed it in a flash and saw the steward raise his eyebrows. It was half full of gin.'

One of the popular tricks played on new girls in Darwin in the early '60s was being told she had to press the crew's trousers when they arrived at the hotel. The stewardess acquired an iron and ironing board from housekeeping, and set about her task. Fortunately for one girl, an experienced stewardess called in on her and expressed astonishment at what she was doing. The trousers got pressed but with creases down the sides instead of front and back, and with the bottoms of the legs sewn up!

Helaine Michaels:

✈     I frequently had a soda syphon squirted up my dress, hence I always flew with a spare pair of knickers in my bag. Our standbys were done in the old Queen's building at Heathrow and were often hilarious as they involved captains as well. The goings-on between two settees pushed together were interesting to say the least but it was all innocent in the early '60s.

I remember a trick that was played on me. All my normal uniforms were pinched in a Moscow turn round and I had to operate the flight in boots and leggings which was the Moscow uniform at the time. The crew had my uniforms and gave them back a few days later.

---

## A BRIDGE BETWEEN OLD AND NEW
# THE VC10

### The late Captain Roger Gorton, BOAC VC10 pilot

Vickers VC10.

I joined BOAC in 1966 and was chosen for the VC10 on the basis that I was more likely to succeed than if I went on the B707. The course was made up of two captains from the DC-7C, senior co-pilots from the Comet and Viscount (the latter having been on loan to BWIA in the Caribbean), new pilots from Hamble and myself from an Independent Airline flying Avro 748s.

The hours of simulator training were not to my taste as it never seemed like an aircraft and was spoilt by instructors introducing problems for you to solve! At first sight it seemed very big, and for me, lacking propellers. I duly finished the flying training and was launched on the third world, new co-pilots being sent east from London.

At that time the Standard VC10 flew east and the larger Super VC10 mainly across the Atlantic, the latter version of the aircraft still being delivered. Both aircraft were operated by a captain, often ex-wartime, two co-pilots, one at least holding a navigation licence, and a flight engineer, usually the crew negotiator and fount of all useful knowledge on and off the aircraft. In the cabin there was a purser plus two stewards and three stewardesses, one of whom was often a 'national', for example an Indian or Pakistani girl if those countries were en route. Passengers enthused over the aircraft as it was more comfortable and gave a smoother ride in all weathers compared with other contemporary four-engine jets. Indeed some pilots reckoned the aircraft could land itself, though I found the aircraft and myself always needed help from each other.

In those years 'going east' included Africa, the Middle East, Iran, the Indian sub-continent and Singapore. Captains had more authority than now to decide the best course of action since communication with London was often non-existent as indeed it could be with the destination until almost overhead. In addition, especially in Africa, many airfields were severely lacking in landing aids for four-engine jets. In Accra the only runway lights might be paraffin goosenecks, at Khartoum it helped to know in a sandstorm that the bridge over the Nile was just about in line with the runway and at Blantyre awkward winds and a narrow runway could make for interesting approaches and take offs.

Sometimes Colombo would have a local difficulty. The copper wire for the lights and landing aids would 'disappear' to a local market, making it helpful to be able to use the aircraft weather radar to map the coastline and find the lagoon beside the airfield. And a mention for Rangoon, which was the last place I knew that kept an old BOAC custom. While the aircraft was being refuelled, tea and cake was provided in the terminal 'on the house' for the pilots (and the flight engineer if he had time). Unfortunately Rangoon fell out of the network when a management captain not used to its features had a problem landing and the airfield was declared not suitable for operations. This in spite of the fact that ordinary line pilots had been coping with it for years.

Compared with modern standards many hotel and city facilities on the eastern routes were very primitive. This resulted in crews being more sociable than in later years, whether it was visits to the Pyramids, the Taj Mahal, horse riding in the hills north of Tehran or just meeting up in the bar – or a room if the country had decided to be 'dry' because it was having an international conference that week or there was a sandstorm raging outside.

As time went by and more VC10s were delivered there was a consequent expansion of the fleet route network – eastwards to Hong Kong, Tokyo and Australia, westwards to the Caribbean and South America and farther west to Australia across the Pacific via Los Angeles, Honolulu and Fiji. I used to carry an old school atlas and it seemed the VC10 was reclaiming the red of the old Empire!

The best about the VC10? The crews and the destinations.

## The Graceful Swan, the VC10

Said Angela Froude:

✈   Taking a flight was a special occasion and the passengers dressed up and looked smart and not casual. Ladies sometimes wore hats and gloves. We did too. We were very proud to be British and flying with BOAC, the best airline in the world. There was a great sense of excitement before, during and after every flight. It was all a great adventure.

The VC10 and the Super VC10 arrived and those who flew on the VC10s aircraft still regard them with great affection. The VC10's inaugural flight was in April 1964 to Lagos. On board were Stewardess Josephine Dixon, Senior Stewardess Tess Curtin and Stewardess Sue Graham. The Super VC10 made its inaugural flight across the Atlantic a year later with Senior Stewardesses Tess Curtin, Susan Graham and Madge Nixon.

But the aircraft did have some idiosyncrasies. Judy Black says: 'I always had to remember to shove a fork in the handle of the fridge door on VC10s, otherwise the entire contents could fly out on take off. It happened on one occasion with a Crew Flight Inspector sitting in the front row. We scraped caviar off the floor and served it without him seeing! Thank heavens for that dividing curtain!'

Judy had a spirited and lively career in BOAC from 1964 to 1969. She encapsulates her memories:

> ✈ Flamingos on Lake Naivasha, dancing to the tune of *I left my Heart in San Francisco* while actually there, receiving a proposal of marriage at the top of the Ngong Hills in Nairobi, falling in love with a helicopter pilot in Lagos, driving the Ruler of Bahrain's Stingray (before I had passed my test), shopping in Hong Kong, falling in love with the handsomest hotel waiter in Rome, falling in love with the handsomest MEA man in Beirut Airport, getting engaged to a lawyer in Pretoria, riding a stallion across the desert by the Pyramids to an oasis for dinner, being chased by Africans in a remote village with machetes for taking photographs of them, being in a taxi which accidentally ran over a little boy on the way to the Taj Mahal and subsequently being imprisoned by the locals and not knowing our fate.
>
> I am horrified now to think how easily we cabin crew drank during a flight. For example, we had a pre-flight bottle of champagne before take off. We were mostly more interested in enjoying ourselves than looking after passengers.

This comment arose a lot, but it certainly contributed to the party atmosphere. And many passengers wanted this. Katie Smith: 'I was on VC10s mostly and we absolutely loved the aircraft. They were very beautiful; rather like a sports car – pretty but uneconomical! We always had such a good relationship with our passengers as there was no in-flight entertainment. We *were* the in-flight entertainment.'

## Our National Stewardesses

The introduction of National Stewardesses had begun in the mid-1950s with the employment of Japanese girls based in Tokyo and then Chinese girls based in Hong Kong. At first they were supernumerary cabin crew but later they were designated 'Stewardesses B' and replaced British stewardesses along the Far Eastern routes. They wore national dress and had the languages necessary for the growing number of regional passengers. The Indian and Pakistani stewardesses wore the traditional sari.

By the late '50s Chinese national recruiting and training was well established. Patricia Jones said that Mi Ling, with BOAC for many years, was the chaperone and supervisor. Mi thought the airline did not appreciate that no respectable Chinese family at the time would have dreamed of allowing a girl to become a stewardess. The result – one jumped ship and another was hiked out of the bed of a Qantas skipper. It was bitterly cold and these little Chinese girls used to arrive for training clutching hot water bottles and moaning.

The '60s saw a major expansion of BOAC cabin crew. The stewardess was now no longer the sole female. There were usually three and the third stewardess was sometimes a national stewardess – Chinese, Japanese, Indian, Pakistani, South American, Jamaican or South American. For the European girls it was a marvellous opportunity to get to know these women, their families, culture and customs.

The Japanese stewardesses, which BOAC introduced in the mid-'50s, were renowned for their demure demeanour, gentleness and perfect femininity, always evoking a peaceful aura. The first BOAC Japanese stewardesses were recruited by Cynthia Arpthorp in Japan and sent to London for their training. In 1954 they stayed at Dormy House where they 'tried to get used to the English food'.

Michiko Masuda was 'very proud to be a BOAC stewardess and flew the Tokyo–Hong Kong and Tokyo–Honolulu-San Francisco-New York routes. Meals were served from a trolley and drinks included sake for the passengers, who were mainly Japanese businessmen. In 1968, many

For passengers travelling eastwards there were a variety of uniforms. The national stewardesses added an exotic quality. (© Adrian Meredith)

Japanese started travelling in tour groups to London and Europe, favourite destinations for honeymooners.

One had to be a university graduate at that time to become a stewardess and Michiko recalls: 'In Japan, to be the air stewardess is still the dream of most girls.' She considered herself unsuitably trained when one American passenger asked her to name a suitable doctor in Tokyo for an abortion. 'Once when I was driving the car in BOAC uniform to Haneda Airport a policeman saluted me. This was the funniest experience in my life! My best experience was doing PR at Heathrow Airport with the famous British film star, Dianna Rigg.'

Yoshi Ishikawa enjoyed the fun she had doing public relations work for BOAC in the US to promote the new Pacific routes. Her position was mainly in the first class ('and in my time

The first Japanese stewardesses, Nachiko Sagawa, Kazue Tokoroda, Takako Shiozawa, Mineko Nakayasu, and Fusako Ogisu, in a publicity photograph taken in 1955 at Haneda Airport on arrival back in Tokyo with an Argonaut in the background.

women passengers in the first class did not wear trousers') serving sake and Japanese tea. The main task of the Japanese stewardesses was to look after the non-English-speaking Japanese passengers. Yoshi, as did all the other Japanese stewardesses, wore the traditional kimono on board. The consensus by these stewardesses was that it was totally impractical to work in and changing into it was done on board in a cramped lavatory. All her colleagues like herself were a novelty on board the aircraft and the subject of countless photos taken with passengers.

✈   I remember when BOAC was to start the Pacific route. I was sent to Honolulu on Pan Am, to take the BOAC flight out of San Francisco. However the permit for BOAC's Pacific route was delayed week after week. Two of us stayed in Honolulu for three months. Eventually we both went back to Tokyo on Pan Am again. It was the best paid holiday I have ever had!

BOAC in 1958 was the first international airline to introduce Indian stewardesses on its flights, even before Air India, and initially the traditional sari was the official uniform in the air. The sari was pure silk marina green with gold borders and these stewardesses gracefully rustled and glided up and down the cabin.

Hijacking of aircraft was a new terror weapon and Indian stewardesses acquitted themselves notably on our VC10s at Dawson's Field in the Middle East. Another Indian stewardess, Jennifer Suares, was awarded the Chairman's Commendation for her part in the evacuation of the 707 aircraft at Heathrow in 1968.

✈   Stewardesses came from all over the vast territory of India and Pakistan from a variety of backgrounds and religions. One of the most enjoyable aspects was the recruitment and selection. Basic training was done in London. All other aspects of their day-to-day admin from four different bases involved a great deal of travelling to keep in touch. Another interesting facet was the research and assistance in the design of their uniforms, especially the colourful sarees.

So said Peggy Thorne, who completed her career as a cabin crew recruitment officer in London. Tall, elegant, with a laconic sense of humour, she was known as the 'Duchess' and reminded me of the headmistress of my old school, Glennie, in Toowoomba. A little imperious, the gentlest soul beneath this exterior and definitely a role model for the women, Peggy Thorne became another prominent woman who made inroads into the management section of BOAC well before the Equal Opportunity Act when there were very few chances of promotion within Management Cabin Services. She had a thirty-one-year career with British Airways: thirteen years as a stewardess and ten years in charge of Indian and Pakistani stewardesses.

Despite the tag of Golden Age there were also tragedies: crew and passengers losing their lives in incidents, disasters and tragic circumstances. Inevitably, over the years accidents have occurred and flights came to grief. From every accident a lesson was learned. This is the price of progress.

## A Woman of Courage

In Squadron Leader Beryl E. Escott's book, *Twentieth Century Women of Courage*, 600 heroines from many walks of life are documented: Amy Johnson, Odette Sansom, Jean Batten, British astronaut Helen Sharman and Barbara Jane Harrison, GC (posthumously), known to her family as Jane. Jane was the youngest female recipient of the George Cross. The George Cross, the highest civilian award for gallantry, ranks alongside the Victoria Cross, which is only awarded for gallantry in battle.

Jane Harrison was twenty-two when the BOAC Boeing 707, G-ARWE, caught fire soon after take off from London Heathrow on 8 April 1968. The blazing No.2

The Whiskey Echo crash.

engine fell from the aircraft leaving a fierce fire burning on the port wing. Two and a half minutes later Whiskey Echo made an emergency landing at the airport and the fire intensified.

Jane was working with Ros Unwin and Jennifer Suares, the Indian stewardess. Jane's duties in an emergency were to help the steward at the aft station to open the rear door and inflate the escape chute and to help the passengers at the rear of the aircraft to get out. When the aircraft landed Jane Harrison and the steward opened the rear galley door and inflated the chute, which became twisted so that the steward had to climb down it to straighten it before it could be used.

Once out of the aircraft he was unable to return. Jane on her own manned the exit and organised the passengers to get out of the aircraft. One can only imagine her feelings of intense fear, sublimated by the discipline of the ingrained knowledge of what to do in these situations. She encouraged some passengers to jump from the aircraft and others she pushed. With flames and explosions all around her, escape from the rear of the aircraft became impossible and she directed her passengers to another exit while remaining at her post. Jane was finally overcome by smoke trying to save an elderly disabled passenger, seated in one of the last rows, and whose body was found close to that of the stewardess. Jane will always be remembered for her heroism and bravery. She performed her duties exactly by the book and saved many passengers' lives and is an example of selfless devotion to duty and courage, as are all the other members of the crew. Passengers praised her calmness and courage. Although she could have saved herself, she gave her life attempting to help the disabled passenger. For her gallantry, Jane was awarded the George Cross posthumously – the fourth woman to be so honoured.

Before 1940 there was the Empire Gallantry Medal and four women had won this before its name was changed. Three were awarded the George Cross for service in enemy-occupied territory during the Second World War. Thus Jane was the eighth woman to receive this medal.

# 8 April 1968 – Flight 712

Boeing 707 G-ARWE taking off for a flight to Zurich made a forced landing at London Airport. Sue Smith says:

✈    When I left flying I joined the BOAC purchasing department at Hatton Cross. On April 8, I watched with horror as the 707 Whiskey Echo landed and stopped within sight of my office window. The No.2 Rolls-Royce Conway engine had suffered a compressor disc failure during take off, causing a major in-flight fire. During the brief period in which the aircraft was airborne, the engine actually fell off into one of the reservoirs in Staines. After landing, the fire intensified and from my viewpoint, as the whole aircraft became engulfed in black smoke with little fuselage visible, I feared a tremendous loss of life and remember a feeling of terrible impotency in not being able to assist the crew.

The 121 passengers escaped in 90 seconds from this blazing crash at Heathrow. Five passengers were lost and the skilled airmanship, strict adherence to well-learned safety procedures and the fact that the first leg of the flight to Australia was only to be as far as Zurich, were the major factors in saving so many lives in this incident. It was at 1,000ft when there was an explosion. The inner port engine burst into flames and fell off with part of the wing. This plummeted into a water-filled gravel pit at Thorpe, Surrey. Crews flying to Europe usually have only about 22 tons of fuel at London Airport. However, it can carry 72 tons of fuel. Therefore had the Boeing had a full fuel load the fire after it had landed would have been far more severe and, of course, the aircraft would have been far heavier to handle. The pilot, Captain Charles 'Cliff' Taylor, had only four minutes to bring this blazing Boeing down and because of his presence of mind only five of the 126 people on board died. Captain Taylor did this in 3 minutes and 32 seconds. Sir Miles Thomas, Chairman of BOAC, said: 'By immediately doing what must have been a very difficult tight circuit a complete holocaust was averted. It was a brilliant example of British airmanship at its best, sad though its necessity may have been.'
One of the survivors among the crew of eleven, Stewardess Rosalind Unwin, twenty-four, nursed a scorched face and forearm as she told how she walked through choking smoke to soothe frightened children. The former children's nurse, said:

✈    I just did what we are trained to do. The smoke was choking, thick and black, and the heat was absolutely awful. Captain Taylor did a marvellous job of getting the aircraft in as he did. It all happened very suddenly. There were lots of children aboard the plane, flying to Australia with emigrant families. Naturally they were pretty scared. But we had been trained to act as I did, so it seemed sensible to stick to the routine and try to keep calm. The intense heat scorched my face and my right forearm. I did not notice it at the time. It was just the terrible smoke that choked me and everyone else. I kept thinking of the children. I was pretty scared myself.

## 𝒜 LEGEND IN THE SIXTIES

There are not many industries today where the people who work for them also become legends far beyond the confines of the industry itself.
Even in the early '70s, passengers would ask me if I knew so and so. They would immediately go into raptures about what a fabulous stewardess she was, her repartee, her gracious service, her knowledge of fine wines, her wit, her beauty, her great legs. And would I pass 'my best wishes on to her'.
Asked if she has any regrets in life, Rowena, aka 'Bunty' Harker, responds with a rapid, 'Yes, of course'. It's hard to imagine that a person who has led such an extraordinary and intriguing life could possibly harbour any regret. Rowena's life story seems fit for the silver screen, with over ten years of travel as a

BOAC stewardess, a master of three languages, time spent as a Bluebell Girl, a French au pair, a Dorris Girl in Beirut, a wife and mother, public speaker, Festival Artistic Director and a renowned beauty.

The name Bunty Harker was given to Rowena at a young age, as she proceeded to dazzle baby contest judges with her baby bunting beauty. Pictures of Rowena in her twenties and upwards still reflect this classic beauty, and no doubt assisted Rowena in her bid to become a Bluebell Girl in Las Vegas. In those days, Bluebell Girls were usually English beauties, whose bodies were believed to be more balanced than those of young women in other European countries. Rowena, and twenty-seven other young Bluebells, travelled to Las Vegas to entertain. After a year in America, Rowena returned to England before being tempted by the idea of joining the Doriss Girls and headed to Beirut. Rowena loved Beirut, and it loved her in return. The food, nightlife, people and opportunity afforded to women in the '60s led to Rowena and her fellow Doriss Girls remaining there for ten months.

Rowena on a day off in New York.

It was upon returning to England after Beirut that the idea of constant travel, a steady income and a new experience drew Rowena to flying. Rejected by Pan Am due to her 5ft 10in height, Rowena headed to BOAC, who accepted ladies of taller stature. It was aboard BOAC Britannia 312s, and later the more modern VC10s, that Rowena travelled to most parts of the world. Not only did Rowena's travel afford her a bevy of experiences but it also left her with many friends. Rowena continues to travel to maintain these lifelong friendships.

Rowena preceded the feminist bra burning by several years on a VC10 test flight. The flight had been diverted via Cairo to Lagos and was running around three days over the estimated flight time. In order to stay 'stewardess-fresh', Rowena did her own laundry in Lagos. Due to the 95 degrees humidity, Rowena's laundry failed to dry completely and while her stockings and uniform were bearable, her bra remained saturated and unwearable. On board the VC10 return flight, Rowena decided to put the bra in the plane oven for four minutes to dry out. After just over a minute, smoke began to billow from the galley. This sent the captain and engineer running in with fire extinguishers, before Rowena had the chance to solve the situation herself. The captain soon emerged with the charred bra covered in white foam, much to Rowena's embarrassment!

Rowena's reminiscences include refusing to date Cary Grant, who had the bravado to ask the BOAC beauty out. Cary Grant was the sole passenger on a flight from London to New York in the early '70s. One of the young stewardesses approached Rowena and asked if she could possibly be introduced to Mr Grant. When Rowena asked why, she said that he had dated her gran many years before. Whilst Cary Grant was not brave enough to admit this dalliance with the stewardess's grandma, he certainly had the courage to constantly request that Rowena join him for dinner in New York. Rather than damage his ego, Rowena invented a boyfriend that she pretended she was going to meet in New York. Mr Grant became so persistent that Rowena then announced she was marrying her boyfriend and her web of lies grew from there!

Like all other BOAC stewardesses at that time, Rowena's time in the sky ended abruptly on her thirty-sixth birthday, after ten and a half years. Unfortunately, Rowena's birthday came just three months before the Equal Opportunity Laws abolished this regulation. Rowena recalls foreseeing the regulation change and mentioning it to the BOAC personnel officer, who commented, 'Oh, but the law won't apply to BOAC'.

---

I will always remember another personality whom I shall call Karen Laver. She was tall, flamboyant and imperious. Her makeup reminded one of a kabuki dancer, very white. She had a certain disregard for the uniform regulation. Karen was never keen to wear her hat as it spoiled her exaggerated high bouffant hairstyle. She would often wear black stockings, not the uniform regulation colour, if she felt like it. Every time I flew with her she was an A stewardess in the first class. One of my boyfriends at the time was a passenger on one of her flights. In those days after take off the A stewardess drew the curtains separating the first class passengers from the economy class. My friend in the economy class said to me: 'When she drew the curtain across she had a look on her face which said "when you have earned enough money you can be up here too".' This notorious stewardess and I did several New York trips together and I was fascinated by her supreme self-confidence and the way she managed to get her passengers to behave impeccably. There was absolutely no nonsense when she was in the cabin.

Many were quite in awe of her and God help you if you got in the way of her acerbic tongue, which was also witty, when the situation was called for. Two stories attributed to her circulated around the routes. The first one deals with a first class passenger from New York to London who was demanding all sorts of attention. After a few hours of this attention seeking, this lady asked Karen: 'Do you know what the servant situation is like these days, dear?' She replied with great dignity: 'I'm sure Madam will have no difficulty whatever in finding a situation.'

Charlie Drake, as many people would remember, was a man of small stature and a comedian. However, his humour didn't always go down very well, particularly with this stewardess, who was at least 2ft taller than he was. He asked her what she would say to a little f***? She replied: 'Hello little f★★★'. Even the flight deck did not escape her eye. A captain said to her: 'Stewardess, I do not like your perfume,' she replied: 'Captain, I don't like the dirt under your nails but I won't say a word.'

But I will remember her for her very pale complexion, because she *never* allowed an ounce of flesh to be touched by the sun. She would walk to the aircraft in the hot Caribbean with an umbrella and always wore her white gloves.

In fact history recalls that American passengers used to ask if she was on board when they checked in: 'Is Karen Laver going to be on this flight?' Her eccentricity was adored by the American passengers! In fact she was almost a celebrity in terms of how passengers remembered her and asked you if you knew her, although many passengers had only met her once.

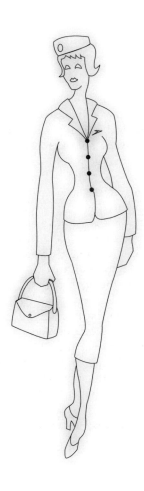

## CHAPTER 6

# The Golden Age Continued...

## Entebbe Experiences

As I recall, BOAC, and any airline that flew into Uganda, never felt entirely safe. The country was ruled by a lunatic who reputedly had several heads of his wives in the fridge and none of us wanted to end up the same way. At the time I flew into Entebbe, I was sent on a ridiculous mission. The ruler, Idi Amin, had just issued a statement that our stewardesses were not to be seen in mini skirts. This posed quite a dilemma for BOAC as all our summer uniforms were pink and turquoise mini dresses. They were short as was the fashion in the '60s, and with navy blue tights looked most effective. I was to report on this current phobia of Idi Amin and come up with a solution. The stewardesses were unwittingly putting politics in jeopardy if we continued to wear our minis. The captain was well aware of this problem and basically it amounted to the fact that the girls would have to remain on the aircraft. This was an impossible situation and a solution that would never be allowed. Meanwhile all the passengers had disembarked and the crew were left wondering: how do we sort this one out?

I stood near the captain, who had taken his jacket off, which meant that all the crew could take off their jackets, which we did. I made the suggestion that we all tie a male crew member's jacket around our waists. The skipper went along with this. So three stewardesses walked, heads held high, feeling utter fools, determined not to trip or let the jacket fall until we had checked into our rooms in the hotel. There was not a murmur from operations. What this did mean was there was a solution and we were always going to be able to cover our legs. This is what the dictator had decreed and oddly enough, that seemed to be the end of the matter. BOAC never received another signal about our 'inappropriate uniform'.

## Trade Unions

The formation of the unions for cabin crew in the early '60s caused much dissension. The majority of the stewardesses did not come from trade union backgrounds. As one of the stewardesses, who flew in the mid-'50s, said: 'I wouldn't join anyway. It was not an acceptable idea for a young lady with the concept of duty.' Furthermore the typical stewardess at this time came from a middle-class upbringing which did not encourage pro-union ideas.

Audrey Cartmell: 'I was lumbered as representative to the Transport and General Workers Union – attended one meeting in London speaking truthfully – and was asked to leave by the TGWU.'

The TGWU wanted all cabin crew to join the union automatically. Many found this idea dictatorial and undemocratic. There was also the counter argument that if you did not join you would receive the 'benefits' anyway. The majority of the stewardesses found the whole union movement not really their cup of tea.

In the early days there were no flight time limitations or provision for 'rest' as only basic take off and landing seats were available. As Peggy Thorne says: 'An uphill struggle with management to improve this resulted in a few of us forming The Air Hostesses Association, which eventually affiliated to a trade union for representation. So our voices would be recognised.'

This issue began to be addressed in the '60s. Up until the mid-'60s, joining the TGWU was voluntary. Many did not do so, echoing the words of Delia Green: 'the Transport and General Workers Union I did not join as I had accepted the conditions when I joined. For a while my name was on a list of non-union members on a notice board in 221, as an intimidation tactic I imagine.'

In fact there was a great deal of intimidation to join the union and most of the female cabin crew found that they had to reluctantly join, whether they wanted to or not. Those who refused were told that other cabin crew would be forbidden to fly with them. The union wanted all cabin crew to join the union automatically when they were in the training school. Three people abstained from joining the union for their entire time in British Airways. These were Mike Heath and Phyllis Hall and myself. Several years ago, I recounted to them the occasion when we three were called in by the TGWU to be finally persuaded. Each of us was put in a separate room and told that the other two had changed their mind. I didn't relent, despite this betrayal by my two colleagues. When this ordeal was over, we said to each other 'Why did you change your mind?' As it turned out, none of us had fallen for this ploy. The result meant we were exempt from the union. However, from then on every cabin crew member automatically had to join the union. For us to be exempt, a deal had been struck with the management.

It was certainly upsetting for many stewardesses, who were told that no one would fly with them unless they were members. British Airways made it very clear that they wouldn't accept any resolution that required them to 'suspend from duty or dismiss from employment those air cabin crew who are not members of a Trade Union.' This was a conundrum for stewardesses, who were receiving in January 1969 correspondence from the Transport and General Workers Union saying that they must be a fully paid up member of a bona-fide Trade Union or Association by 1 March 1969. 'If not, then those who are members will refuse to operate with non-members from this date.' Initially only stewards belonged to the TGWU and very few stewardesses.

By late 1969, the London Air Hostesses Branch was formed by stewardesses, run by stewardesses, with the aim to get the stewardesses' terms of service improved by the Corporation. It was then part of the General and Municipal Workers Union.

Life was unbearable on board if you were flying with a union steward and were not a member. Many stewardesses found it easier to join the union and there were some like Sheila Luke who was quite adamant: 'No, I did not join a union because I did not believe in striking.' Eventually the cabin crew branch of the TGWU was named the British Airlines Stewards and Stewardesses Association.

Vicky Radcliffe: 'We were advised during training to join – which I did, but I never attended any meetings as I was not interested in union activity. The stewards were usually more active than the stewardesses and some were quite intimidating with their ideas about the "rights" of the cabin crew'.

BASSA was an old-style union and not very pleasant, according to Andy Bennett. By the time Stephanie Moore finished flying, 'It was 100 per cent obligatory membership. I recall several awful strikes where certain stewards didn't help the cause by arriving in a Rolls-Royce.'

Susan Thrush featured on the cover of the *BOAC
Cabin Crew Bulletin*, summer 1972, the same year that she won
the Miss Speedbird competition.
The very existence of the competition
for stewardesses reflects the airline's emphasis on beauty
and glamour.

Sylvia Ladley and Jean Haines in the Hounslow swimming pool for rescue training.

Aircraft evacuation training in the '60s, a part of the extensive air-sea rescue training.

'Getting our Wings'.
The brevets which in past times were proudly attached to uniforms by newly graduated stewardesses. They are certainly redolent of another era.

Be it known to All Men
that I
**Phoebus Apollo**
being Monarch of the Sky even as my Uncle
Neptune is Monarch of the Sea,
am
*Lord of All things that Fly*

be they insect, bird or man himself - from the smallest solo gnat to the largest Trans-continental Air Liner; from the prehistoric pterodactyl to the post-atomic rocket; from the first swallow stooping round for a companion to make up a summer to the maximum effort swarm of bees formating on the queen; from the rarely grounded swift to the temporarily airborne hen; from Flying Officers to Red Admirals; from box kites to balloons; from night fighter bats to dive-bombing seagulls; from flying fish to flying buttresses;

Be it further known that I, Phoebus Apollo, being the Sun God, am Master also of the Equator on which the sun never sets; and that as the Equator is the Biggest Line in the world, so am I Lord of All Lines.

Be it yet further known that those who shoot about the sky in aircraft may in so doing Cross the Equator, and thus be held to have

*Shot the Biggest Line in the World*

and should henceforth be set apart from all those who have not.

...this document testify

LONDON-RHODESIA AIR MAIL
SERVICE 1932-1962

ZAMBEZI RIVER

**RHODESIA & NYASALAND**

1/3
POSTAGE

EMPIRE C CLASS
FLYING BOAT 1937

Printed in Gt. Britain.

'Crossing the Line' certificate given to passengers in the early '50s.

The Short Empire flying-boats
were used to carry mail to Britain and
the British Colonies
in the 1930s and the 1940s.

3

The Solent 2, Short S.26.

Janice Musson,
BEA Chief Training
Stewardess. (© Adrian Meredith)

Collectors' items now, the BOAC fan, part of the passenger amenities for tropical climates.

Virginia Sheehy on the cover of the flight information booklet behind every seat.

Before the moving map of today, passengers had this bulletin which they passed to each other by hand!

WELCOME ABOARD

Bienvenue à Bord
Willkommen an Bord
Benvenuti a Bordo
Bienvenido a Bordo
مرحبا بكم
歡迎各位乘客
ご搭乗ありがとうございます

FLY TO AUSTRALIA BY

B·O·A·C & QANTAS

| TOTAL TIME (OVERHEAD TO OVERHEAD) | LONDON TO GANDER 5 hrs. 49 mins. | GANDER TO NEW YORK 3 hrs. 04 mins. |
| TOTAL DISTANCE FLOWN | 2450 mls. | 1142 mls. |
| AVERAGE AIRSPEED | 472 m.p.h. | 450 m.p.h. |
| AVERAGE GROUNDSPEED | 420 m.p.h. | 370 m.p.h. |
| AVERAGE HEADWIND | 52 m.p.h. | 80 m.p.h. |

Time on ground at GANDER 1 hr. 12 mins.
Thus total time airborne LONDON to NEW YORK 10 hrs. 13 mins.

Millie Fisher, Martin King and Don Foster in a publicity shot for the first class service in the cabin crew mock-up at Cranbank.

The winter swinging sixties uniform. Lydia Lawrence and Veronica Collen-Smith. Designer Clive.

Carole Hardy and Geraldine Fuller in the swinging sixties. In came mini-skirts, boots and trousers. Carole in the summer uniform.

The paper dresses in 1967.... Flower Power in the Carribbean on the steps of a 707.

No. 19    MARCH 1969

cabin crew bulletin

In the hippy '60s, passengers on Carribbean flights were served rum swizzles in 'trendy' beakers with umbrellas, fruit and flowers and, for the Polar Route, these pretty slippers and drinks coaster.

The three-dimensional Glenys Lister is modelling the re-vamped 'paper dress' made up in a lightweight woven fabric – much more practical than paper!

'RUM Swizzle'

1 measure Rum
½ measure Lime Juice
½ measure Sugar Syrup
1 Dash Angostura Bitters
Crushed Ice

Garnish with
Orange Slice
Cherry
Swizzle Stick

Serve with a straw

BOAC

Carol White (1959–1960) doing her punishment in Beirut, still with her luxuriant long locks.

In the early '70s, the Sari the Indian stewardesses had worn for many years was replaced and Eileen Carson is modelling the uniform, to conform with a modified type of national dress. Designer Clive.

Japanese stewardesses wore kimono in flight. (© Adrian Meredith)

From the BOAC booklet about the new training school at Cranebank and the new uniform of the late '60s. Wigs (and they worked) were handy for hiding the banned long hair!

# Boeing 707 Whiskey Echo
## 8 April 1968

Capt John Hutchinson's log book.

Photo courtesy of Capt John Hutchinson.

Children (called Junior Jets) adored their log books signed by the Captain of their flight every time they flew.

Carol Hardy and colleagues from El Al and Air Lingus pose in the 9ft intake of the massive Pratt and Whitney engine.

Katie Smith's shocking pink Jaguar! The only other pink customised E-type Jaguar in the world was ordered by Hollywood film star Tony Curtis after having seen Katie's!

Carol Hardy, pictured at the launching ceremony, was the ambassadress for the airline.

Boeing 747-100 at its
role out in Everett in
Washington State in 1968.

Andrea Bennett and those
long legs!

Julia van den Bosch
was the longest-serving BA Concorde stewardess
from 1976–2003.

She flew more hours than any other Concorde stewardess
either on British Airways or Air France.

Concorde: the small interior of the cabin. Nick Brett, Auli Wroe, Jeff Anderson, Lesley Runnalls, Stuart Davie, Glenys Gilliott.

Concorde Wingwalkers:
JFK Airport, New York,
USA. First Officer:
Tim Orchard.
Cabin Crew: Ruth Tait,
Glenys Gilliott,
Cyn Hopkins,
Sharron McVeigh,
Lesley Runnalls,
Nieves Gutierez.

Concorde at the North Pole: Rovaniemi Lapland. The Arctic Circle runs straight through the airport. Peter Skidmore, Glen Palmer, Joanne Lee, Lesley Runnalls, Ellie Carson.

Veronica Collen-Smith, who was part of the crew for HM the Queen's trip to Riyadh.

The start of the Royal Tour, 12 February 1979 and finished 2 March 1979. HM the Queen arriving in Riyadh.

The Queen Mother with Lord King, Viscount Linley and Lady Sarah on board Concorde for her eighty-fifth birthday. (© Adrian Meredith)

The Concorde twins: Estelle and Elaine Moffatt. (© Adrian Meredith)

Concorde: Adrian Meredith's favourite photograph...
curvature of the earth.  (© Adrian Meredith)

## Flight Time Limitations

For many years cabin crew did not have flight time limitations, unlike today where there are rest rooms or 'Wendy Houses' (small cabins for crew for sleeping) and private areas to have a quick nap. Particularly in the '40s, '50s and early '60s, people were often on duty for twenty-four hours at a time, sometimes longer. The only recourse was to find a spare seat and be given permission to have a little rest. On the 'Strats' there was a bunk, but many people said that the 707 was the best for a quick nap. 'Boeings always wagged their tails to rock you to sleep,' said Wyn Behenna.

## Working with Stewards

One topic stewardesses should have been told about in the training school was how, as the only female member of the crew, we were supposed to please both cabin crew and flight deck. Or how to choose between them when it came to socialising. We were prepared for most things in training but not this.

Vicky Radcliffe says:

> ✈ Some of the older chief stewards had been on flying-boats, or in the Merchant Navy. And many of the BOAC cabin service stewards had come from the pre-war Cunard liners – 'from off the boats'. They could be sarcastic and unkind to young crew members. Some of them were alcoholics and drank on duty. There was no procedure for reporting them or making a complaint. We were basically too scared of the situation. I knew of one instance where a fairly new stewardess did make a report. The poor girl was hounded out of the airline within three weeks.
>
> It was only my sense of humour that got me through some situations. For example, one of the stewards started calling me Miss Roedean and although it could be slightly hurtful, I think that it went with the territory. I refrained from calling him 'Mr Hackney' or even 'Hackneyed'.

On the other hand Shirley Dakin maintains:

> ✈ The stewards were usually great fun. I always remember leaving the galley to go through the curtains to serve the passengers with tea and coffee and the steward sweeping back the curtains would say, 'OK darling, you're on,' as if in a theatre production. You then went into the cabin with a smile on your face. At other times the steward would put the wine basket over his arm, sweep out into the first class cabin saying, 'I'm going to the shops darling. Do you want anything?' As one gay steward said to me: 'This is not a job, darling. It's a performance.' With him it was.

'There were naturally clashes with all the different personalities involved. Some chief stewards were very scathing about the girls not taking the job seriously enough and some of the gays disliked girls on principle,' says Sue Brown. This was a frequent comment. To many of the stewardesses it was a career, and one they took great pride in. Stewardesses became adept at adapting and ingratiating themselves if necessary, to some most unpleasant personalities.

There was a very famous chief steward, recalls Andy Bennett:

> ✈ He was acid and hated women… A real wasp, venomous … and for obvious reasons I will have to call him Derek. It would have been handy to know about him … he was a real bitch. Stewardesses would call in 'sick' to avoid flying with him. But most of the gays were wonderful and great company.

However, tolerating the odd obloquy from the stewards, we soon learned, was part of the job.

Some stewards were downright lazy and would love to just sit and watch you rush about. The usual thinking was you were fair game. And there were chief stewards who were condescending and mean, described as 'little Hitlers', and it seemed to give them a great deal of pleasure if they made you cry. There were the complete alcoholics, who sat down with a drink in one hand and a cigarette in the other for the whole sector and said, 'Get on out there and get them trays out as fast as you can, doll.' These stewards were about as useful as an ashtray on a motor bike.

In my surveys there were frequent comments about the chief stewards being lazy or old queens who wanted to be alone with their new young stewards, who begged us not to leave them. The girls did their best to protect the young lads.

Yet in the late '40s and '50s, it was accepted that the captain and the chief steward both did reports on their crews In the late '50s and into the '60s, when there were more cabin crew, it was not uncommon for the stewardess to hear these words from the chief steward, 'You be nice to me and I will give you a good report.'

Celia Penney recalls:

> ✈    Many of the chief stewards were lovely. Some were really funny and some were kind but some had a reputation for being rather spiteful. Down the routes, the flight deck often desired the company of the stewardesses. It could get very awkward. If the chief steward did not have a chip on his shoulder about the flight deck and the captain was without delusions of grandeur, then the camaraderie was excellent. They would set the tone. If the chief steward disliked the flight deck, he could make life very difficult for the cabin crew if they fraternised with them. The best trips were when the stewards and the flight deck got on and we all went out together.

These clashes were inevitable, as there was in the majority of cases a huge disparity between male and female cabin crew in relation to education and background. There were many mentions of this 'shock to the system' by the stewardesses, who had been theatre nurses, ward sisters, teachers, managers and used to responsibility and running their own show. Now suddenly they were being treated like idiots by chief stewards, who hovered around telling them how and watching them perform the most mundane of tasks on board the aircraft. Often taking 'orders' from these people was both galling and irritating with every take off and landing a drama.

There were many marriages between cabin crew, as many of these men cut a dashing figure. Not all stewards were pogglethorpes. In fact some senior stewards were absolute gentlemen. If you saw their name on your roster you knew that the trip was going to be total fun from beginning to end. Also these senior stewards or pursers saw the entire crew as a team and social separation was not on their agenda. This made every trip a holiday, full of fun and laughter and happy passengers joining in. Wondering how you could take the money was a comment made by many. Unfortunately there were not a lot of them.

Two senior stewards who were a total pleasure to fly with come to mind instantly and one would have easily thought they were first class passengers had they not been in uniform. Jack Bury was one such gentleman, considerate, great sense of humour and caring. I remember once in the Lexington in New York all the crew, except two, were in the crew transport. Jack went off to find them and eventually two very sorrowful cabin crew members staggered to the transport. Jack was between them holding an elbow. There was a tearful stewardess and a guilty and sad galley steward. It transpired this was their last trip together. He finally had to accept the inevitability that his first child was almost due to arrive and she, the utter hopelessness of the whole affair. They had sought solace in many G&Ts.

As we all know, the eight-hour rule of no grog before a flight is sacrosanct. Here was a dilemma. Already late, we decided as a team to 'carry' these two back to London. Legally we were two cabin crew short. If the skipper knew, he didn't let on. Skippers were not in the habit of snooping around before a flight. We bundled our colleagues into two back seats and there they stayed. The steward had passed out, the stewardess intermittently having a quiet sob. And the wonderful Jack suddenly became a galley steward, something he had not done for years, and he threw out those trays with the speed of a one-armed paperhanger. I took the B stewardess's place and was racing to keep up with him. The steward in first class quietly did the whole service on his own. Later Jack and I tucked into some leftover smoked salmon and an orange blossom and he said, 'It's good to keep your hand in Libbie. I hear you are going into the Training School. Well, half those people in there couldn't even hold a tray. So keep your hand in.' I never forgot those words and when I had the opportunity to go down the routes when the training season was over, I always made sure I worked on the aircraft – if only to prove it to myself that I hadn't forgotten what to do.

The other memorable gentleman was Don Foster. He was the suavest steward to grace the skies. He also became a great success in another airline, Emirates, and enjoyed a stellar career transferring the best of BOAC to their training school. With many of the stewards it was de rigeur for us to have a champagne cocktail before the passengers boarded, setting a party mood. These same stewards would often make sure the flight deck had one on arrival. We can see from the differing opinions above that experiences with stewards amounted to a two-way bet.

## SOME OF THE GREATEST CHALLENGES

On a return trip from Nairobi, one of the duties of the first class stewardess was to undo the cellophane wrap off the large fruit basket. Some of the senior stewards liked you to spray it with soda water to give it that fresh appeal. I did this and frightened a 7in lizard out of its life. It quickly ran up the cabin interior to the first class hat rack. I mentioned it to the captain as he saw me clutching my heart in shock. 'You're sure it wasn't a snake?' he asked. 'Definitely not,' I retorted. 'I know a snake from a lizard!' 'Well,' he said, 'in that case we are not delaying the aircraft to hunt for a harmless lizard.'

However, this lizard had the annoying habit of popping its head over the edge of the hat rack. Two of the first class passengers, who were a little worse for wear when they boarded, found this most disconcerting. Every time they tried to tell the steward or me that there was a lizard in the hat rack and we looked up, it had disappeared. This led them to believe they were hallucinating, as none of the other passengers appeared to have seen it. This was not entirely true, as passengers from East Africa were used to reptiles of all varieties and simply took no notice.

A far more alarming incident happened on the London to Nairobi flight. The meal service was finished and we were bedding down the passengers. There was no in-flight entertainment in the early '60s, and so with the blinds down and the lights out, we were hoping that everyone would go to sleep. It was a VC10, such a wonderfully smooth and quiet aircraft. I was sitting on the crew seat at the rear having a cigarette. Out of the dim light, an attractive woman in her late twenties appeared and said she had a problem. She was holding a round basket and said: 'I don't want to alarm you but my snake has escaped.' I could feel my heart thumping as I repeated: 'Your snake?' 'Yes, I'm a snake dancer and flying to Nairobi to work at the hotel.' It dawned on me that the snake could be slithering down the aisle in the darkness. I had a cabin bag a crane could barely lift, as I took all sorts of items for my own personal survival. Fortunately, one of the items was a torch, so I gave this to her and said: 'You start searching at the front of the cabin. Try to act normally and don't disturb the passengers! I will start from the rear.'

I really had no intention of searching for that snake. She now had the torch. I positioned myself up on the back galley bench with feet off the floor. However, the shock was too much for my bladder and I had to scoot to the loo. As I opened the door, there it was quietly curled around the base – 'trying to get cool', the dancer explained to me. I watched in amazement as she gently picked him up and replaced him in the basket. At first, all of the crew thought I was having a joke, but I was as white as a sheet, so eventually they believed me. Luckily the engineer officer had a piece of rope in his bag so we got the woman to tie so many knots around her basket that Houdini himself would have had a problem.

The list of challenges that faced the stewardesses of the '60s is long. Here are a few:

✈  'Trying to look glamorous after an eleven-hour crossing and having to serve breakfast.'

✈  'Stewardesses were not allowed to be married, so a few got stuck down the routes on their wedding day.'

✈  'We lived in sheer luxury on the ground when on service, but the bad side of flying was perching on an air larder at 3 a.m. trying to stay awake and then having to smile at breakfast. Now that was a challenge.'

✈  'How to cope with jet lag without taking sleeping tablets?'

Trying to keep healthy and avoiding 'gippy tummy', particularly in places like Teheran and Bombay. Staying polite and staying sober were mentioned often and finally, Shirley Swinn said her greatest challenge was 'to have the courage to leave a life and world that I loved – but you could not fly and be married in those days.'

The reality for stewardesses to keep their jobs meant they had to exude allure, maintain the perfect body, convey passenger care, be friendly but not too familiar, competent but not intimidating, all this performed so that the job looked effortless.

## The Flight Deck

The flight deck were a great bunch, the majority very young and the older ones ex-RAF and wartime pilots. Then there were the ex-Fleet Air Arm pilots. These fellows had a special charisma all of their own. We were flying with a mixture of men who were debonair, quite odd, cocky, egotistical, aloof, absolutely lovable, eccentric and overgrown schoolboys.

Marilyn Cox recalls a problem with the flight deck that Carol Dakin also experienced. On a flight from London to Nairobi she had had to put up with a lot of grief from the flight engineer all the way. He was constantly pawing at her and requesting to know what colour her knickers were. She had taken it all in her stride and was now standing at the hotel bar having a drink. Farther along the bar was the engineer, who had made the trip over from the Norfolk Hotel deliberately to continue his campaign. This particularly unprepossessing character with red hair, red beard and pink skin lurched over to her with a pint in one hand and reopened the banter. Without hesitation, she grabbed a pint off one of the other guys, stuck it in his other hand and before he could gather his wits, undid his flies, ripped down his trousers, pulled out the elastic of his boxers and tipped first one of the pints he was holding down into the void, and then the other. He stood there with soaking trousers around his ankles, while the whole bar erupted in hysterics. Needless to say she had no more trouble on that trip.

Joyce Hogge wrote about problems with the flight deck, 'that were occasionally caused by over-inflated egos. I was once reported to the Queen Bee for telling the First Officer that I was put on the aircraft to serve passengers and not to pander to his wants.'

Many considered the pilots could be quite aloof and demanding. The RAF types with handlebar moustaches, hail fellow well met attitude who strutted. In the latter years pilots were sleeping in separate hotels and having separate transport.

We had to look after all the flight deck's needs and there was a tradition that on landing we took champagne and orange juice to the flight deck – in a paper cup.

The call sign for all BOAC aircraft was 'Speedbird', followed by the flight number. I was on board a flight into Kingston, Jamaica (the paper dress days) when a young first officer had a momentary lapse of memory. When calling the Control Tower, he inadvertently used the call sign 'Blackbird'. He assured the captain that it was an innocent mistake but the cabin crew knew that it was a bet. The Control Tower at Kingston didn't seem to pick up on it – thank goodness.

Andy Bennett recalls an incident going into Rawalpindi: 'We got struck by lightning and it balled through the fuselage. The flight deck had white knuckles on landing and in those days, the early '70s, we all had drinks on landing. Large brandies all round.' Another incident occurred at Heathrow on take off when the aircraft flew into a flock of ducks which set fire to one of the engines. On asking the captain later how he felt he said he was fine as he went through it every six months in the simulator and this was better because he didn't have a training captain breathing down his neck.

## Junior Jet Club and Children

Stewardesses became very involved with unaccompanied children, either returning to boarding school or going home for holidays. The captains were a significant part of this marketing operation, and many took it very seriously. They would come into the passenger cabin and always meet and talk with the children – the Junior Jets. Of course, the biggest of thrill was being invited on to the flight deck, which was also very popular with the parents.

The children's Junior Jet log books had to be filled in and the captain signed them all, quite a task in the school holidays.

Kay Bailey operated the 'Lollipop Special' from Heathrow at the start of the Christmas holidays, where she:

✈ … would organise several of the 'would-be-stewardesses' to serve the barley sugars and go round with the Junior Jet Club info. We once had an enforced stop in Jakarta with sixty unaccompanied children. We were put into private houses scattered all over Jakarta. To crown it all, it was the monsoon season and when we turned on the taps, green slime came out. We eventually managed to round up all the children and continued our journey to Australia.

These large batches of children either caused mayhem or were enormous fun. Bearing in mind that there were no video games or movies, the stewardesses were on the go keeping everyone from strangling each other or dying of boredom. The 'would-be stewardesses' among the children, of which there were always many, were quite a bonus. They would serve orange drinks, water, Coke and skilfully use the silver trays. They really concentrated on getting the seat numbers correct for this task. I used to give them the order pads and off they went. I would have at least half a dozen on the go serving only a few rows at a time – their own rows. I am loathe to admit it, but they also had great fun wiping down the loo hand basin, replacing loo rolls and giving out blankets. The whole task often meant that they wore my hat. I used to give my 'would-be-stewardesses' a squirt of my Miss Dior perfume as well.

José Langrick says her worst experience was when acting as an escort to thirty unaccompanied children (including one little girl with special needs) travelling from Heathrow to Hong Kong for the Christmas holidays. Due to bad weather they diverted to Formosa (now Taiwan):

✈ We arrived in a tremendous downpour and were taken to a hotel for the night. Of course, we were not the only aircraft being diverted and the hotel was heaving with guests. When we were at last allocated rooms, many of them didn't have any beds. The staff did their best – 'We bring beds'. They did – from a storeroom covered in dust. I was extremely relieved next morning to find that all thirty-two children were back on the aircraft to Hong Kong.

'...*Abroad, Hongkong, Cedric Clifitta-Jones (7yrs) above 2 EF*.'

Cartoon by Oni Wyatt: stewardesses dreamed of stowing
naughty children in the overhead lockers!

Clare Weston remembers immigrant charters to Australia when children were airsick:
'We'd even rinse the clothes out and wrap the kids in blankets. The aircraft atmosphere
was dry enough for the clothes to be ready for them to wear on disembarking. The ladies
powder rooms on the 'Brits' were known as Ching's Chinese Laundry on those flights'.

The children's pets were also frequent flyers. The pet hamster, mouse and occasional frog flew
with their young passengers – usually on them, or around their necks. If one escaped, there
were always plenty of catchers, as all the unaccompanied children were always seated together.

Oni Wyatt recalls one particular incident:

✈   The Mai Tai cocktails were decorated with orchids (often garnished with infernal ants!)
and straws – a rum-based drink served in a 'bamboo' beaker. We took round these drinks on
trays to the economy passengers to set a holiday atmosphere as we flew down to the islands.
The worst day was when we'd set all the trays out in the back galley with one tray with drinks
minus the rum, since we had lots of children on board. I had thought it would be nice if the
kids had a similar decorated drink to their parents. Plus a few people didn't want an alcoholic
drink anyway. Guess what? Off went my friend with the wrong tray. Too late the other lot

had gone to the kids. There were some decidedly jolly infants rocking around that fortunately short flight, in holiday mood indeed.

### The Mai Tai cocktail
*2oz white rum*
*1oz lime juice*
*½ teaspoon of orange Curaçao*
*Add crushed ice and garnish with a spear of pineapple, mint and orchid*
*Serve with a straw and swizzle stick.*

## '60S MYTHS

Airline folklore always improved with the retelling and crew parties down the routes were a great source of rumour and exaggeration. Here is one apocryphal example. When BOAC began the Moscow services in the late '60s, 'Reds under the beds' was a constant theme for the crews on those flights. A crew in Moscow suspected that their room was bugged, so a search began to find it. Under the carpet in the centre of the floor a metal plate was found. The flight engineer then carefully removed the plate and exposed the wires. He disconnected these and in the room below, the dining room, the chandelier fell to the floor.

The '60s was the culmination of the Golden Age. Glamorous BOAC girls were competing well in the beauty stakes against their American counterparts, such as Mandy, Candy and Randy, who were the 'Fly Me' girls for United Airlines.

Myth and folklore accompanied many of these very sophisticated girls. One such beauty was Gillian Ritchie, an ex-model and a former BEA stewardess. Gillian attracted men wherever she went. She was in the movie *The Games* directed by Michael Winner. 'My boyfriend at the time picked me up in a Ferrari on the tarmac and Winner was outraged. Perhaps it was because he didn't have one and I only had a minute role, if you could call it that.' Gillian also served Ursula Andress in the movie *Perfect Friday*: 'BOAC allowed us to be used in movies – presumably this was good advertising.'

There is always associated with the truly glamorous girls an aura of myth and folklore about their lives. Gillian Ritchie recalls walking into a crew party straight from a flight where several crews were sipping their G&Ts and gossiping. The topic in progress was a wild stewardess everyone had flown with. This girl never stopped: she was collected by a Ferrari in Rome, whisked away on horseback in Lagos and stalked by a mercenary from the Belgian Congo, who asked her to marry him and presented her with a machine-gun belt of live bullets on the aeroplane as a love token. All of this on one trip. Gillian exclaimed: 'Who is this woman?' They all cried: 'Gillian Ritchie.' 'But I am Gillian Ritchie and it's not true,' she protested. 'Well not exactly – they didn't all happen on one trip anyway.'

She said: 'Having flown for six years one naturally had adventures like everyone else. I presume condensing these down to one trip made it a good story for everyone. My poor reputation!'

Gillian did a three-week standby at the Lexington hotel in New York City with her London flatmate, Willa Grainger. She explained:

✈    This was a big mistake. Having done the Met, the Modern Art, the Guggenheim etc. we would sit out the afternoon standby with a bottle of port and lemon squash and play backgammon. Two weeks on and getting twitchy, we took to afternoon activities. Took a helicopter ride around Manhattan, rowed a boat in Central Park, skated at the Rockefeller Centre and then we discovered the racetrack at the Aqueduct. When it became apparent that neither of us was available when the call finally came, we were packed off to the UK never to fly together again, but it was a great holiday.

When I was flying in the '60s I kept hearing stories about the stewardess who had been given a pink Jaguar as a gift by a passenger – and at that time a racehorse was also added to the list. It was a Corporation rule that we were not allowed to accept gratuities and for most part we did not do so. However, every so often it was almost insulting to the passenger not to accept. On the Middle East flights all the crew received very generous gifts from the various Rulers and these were allowed. We carried a first class passenger from New York and on all occasions he would always have a bottle of perfume for the stewardess. I can remember I was introduced to my first bottle of Nina Ricci L'Air du Temps and every so often I buy myself a bottle in memory of those many kindnesses I received. But back to the Jag. And here is the story as told to me by Katie Smith:

✈     I went out with an Arab Sheikh for three years during which time he asked me what my dream car was and I said a shocking pink E-type Jaguar. When I got back from a night flight from New York, he asked me if I would go with him to the Jaguar showroom in Park Lane before I had my much-needed sleep. The salesman wanted to know what I meant by 'shocking pink'. I finally found a ball of knitting wool in just the pink I had in mind and when I took it into the showroom the salesman asked if I wanted to knit the car a jumper. I said no but I would like a car that colour; he turned white at the thought of it. It was the joy of my life (as was my flying) and for my fiftieth birthday Khalid bought me a model of an E-type (but not in shocking pink!). We are still in touch after all these years.

Many rumours abounded about what happened to the pink Jag. According to the *News of the World* the Sheik, in a fit of jealousy, had it sunk in the Thames; others claimed that Katie had wrapped it around a tree. All were quite untrue. The reality was a bit more boring, according to Katie:

✈     I left BOAC to get married (I was one of the first stewardesses to be asked to stay on after marriage but it was not considered the done thing then!). My husband was rather jealous of the E-type and its associations and as he already had a new large Rover, and it would be our second car, it was just too expensive to run and with great sadness I sold it. It's funny but in retrospect I wish I had kept the car and never got married, but hindsight is hardly a science.

## Buy Me a Beer in Karachi

One of the most popular stopovers (slips) was in Karachi, Pakistan. Many crews, if asked where they would like to be for Christmas if they were on duty, would say Karachi. Accommodation was the rambling Speedbird House quite near the airport. In fact, it was the shortest ride anywhere at that time from airport to resting place, perhaps two minutes. This was a hotel specifically for airline crews and named after the BOAC emblem. It was not particularly glamorous, rather like an old Australian outback motel. In fact the Qantas crews renamed it 'Birdseed House', doing the anagram bit on the sign in front, and it would stay like that for days.

The stewardesses' rooms were known as Virgin's Alley. The rooms were quite simple, just a wardrobe bed, and a table lamp. The showers were located between the rooms, so you had to remember to lock the other side when you entered. In some of the rooms were suspiciously drilled holes, so one got very adept at taking a shower in the dark. The temperature was sometimes 110 degrees Fahrenheit, so the overhead fans were always on. When the air-conditioning units were installed it was like going to bed with an engine running.

When I talked to Peggy Thorne about humorous occasions she remembered the time she was in Karachi and had been chatted up by an attractive Australian, who was a BOAC captain. They had been out to dinner, which was in the rest house, so not exactly out to dinner. After Peggy had gone up to bed, to her embarrassment he banged on her door and said, 'Open up Peg'. She ignored it. More knocking and the shout, 'Open up, Peg'. She pulled the cover over her head and wished him gone but still he persisted. 'Come on, Peg, open up,' until finally another Qantas stewardess got out of bed, opened her door and yelled: 'For Christ's sake open up and let him in so we can all go back to sleep'.

Only Qantas and BOAC crews stayed there and on occasions the odd (unlucky and surprised) passenger needing to be close to the airport.

It was the scene of much rivalry between the two airlines, epitomised by a lot of very long and loud parties, ribald jokes against the other airline, and inventive schemes to keep just about everyone from having a good night's sleep. However, everyone remembers it fondly as a haven where there was the best breakfast at any time of the day or night after the long flights from Singapore or Rome.

You were also allowed to take a few beers into this Muslim country then. So the crew always took in their full quota as the rest house did not serve alcohol. As many of the slips in Karachi were up to three or four days, the few beers we had brought in didn't last long. However, crews were never ones to be daunted by this. Somehow endless amounts of grog seemed to appear like magic and the parties continued. For some crew members, three or four days without a gin and tonic was sheer torture, so various systems were in place to alleviate this. One of the most common was to transport your gin in Elizabeth Arden skin tonic bottles, and a few Schweppes tonic bottles and simply hope for the best at Karachi Customs.

The one thing all the stewardesses knew about Customs in these parts of the world was that that their attention could be taken off the job at hand by putting your most sexy lingerie at the top of your case. It meant that many bottles of 'skin tonic' slid by their expert eye. All in the cause of duty.

On one flight into Karachi the task of bringing in extra Gordon's gin was mine. The names of all the crew were thrown into the captain's hat and I got it. It actually meant if I messed up (and got caught) I would lose my job. I put my permitted number of beers in a cuspidor (sick bag) plus several bottles of Schweppes 'tonic' in my bag. Now there was the small problem of getting it through Customs.

Every member of the crew had a part to play if it looked as if I was going under. Contingency plans ranged from fainting, bribing Customs with BOAC pens, a very bad coughing fit, to a fall. However, the underwear usually did the trick, so all attention was focused on my M&S lingerie. We were the masters of diversionary tactics when it came to getting the extra booze into Karachi.

Credit must go to Qantas for initiative in keeping up the gin supply in Speedbird House. These stewards never seemed to run out of booze! On one BOAC flight, I actually saw their plan in action via a charming Aussie steward, who, fortunately for us, worked for BOAC. He had the whole operation in hand. His story to Karachi Customs was that he had been instructed to take a particularly excellent brand of British hosepipe into Australia from the UK for his old dad, who was an avid market gardener. He brought this hosepipe into Karachi in reasonably sized pieces. As we knew of the plan, it was de rigeur for the other stewardesses and I to just get on with the job and leave 'our man' to do his gin thing. He came prepared with two sound corks, and the aircraft supplied the Gilbey gin. So while he contentedly filled his piece of hosepipe with gin on the plane, we looked after the economy cabin – minus one steward.

The next hurdle was Customs at Karachi, where we were only allowed a few beers each. The gin-laden hosepipe went into the steward's white coat bag, which he casually flung over his shoulder. The best diversionary tactics were from the stewardesses. Again the odd seductive item of lingerie on top kept all attention away from the steward with the hosepipe. It never failed. This particular steward told me that initially he had two bits of hosepipe and the empty piece was the one that was scrutinised. After that the dad/market gardener story was accepted without question.

The snooker room and party room vibrated with activity. Did we ever sleep? Probably. Certainly it was a place for hangovers and midnight feasts and pranks. One captain woke with a start to find himself sharing his room with the dhobi wallah's donkey, which had been tied to the hand basin, complete with its cart. Someone had got the cart through the door by removing the wheels.

I will always remember the bearers, more British than the British. Always so smart and proud in their white uniforms with polished buttons and wearing white gloves. I used to walk in feeling utterly scruffy, while they were always so spic and span. My white uniform blouses were always whiter when I left and my shoes polished.

One of the most popular and more rotund bearers had the name of 'Humpty Doo'. Karachi was such a touch of the 'Raj' – like living in another era. Hazel Faulkes also has the fondest memories of the bearer's curry and the Head Bearer, The Major: 'He had been in the Gordon Highlanders in the war. Such a lovely man.'

We were pampered and so well fed. The bearer's curry arrived ready right on seven. How we all loved it – well, most did. There was afternoon tea by the pool with many bearers carrying trays of teacups and yellow cake. It had an old-fashioned atmosphere, redolent of Graham Greene and Rudyard Kipling. A passing of a time when flying was embarked upon with some sense of adventure, with a pioneering spirit that dwelt in those modest establishments.

I always felt I rejoined my flight a lot heavier than when I had alighted a few days previously. Kathleen Fuller says: 'The bearers were also so welcoming and one could have bacon and eggs at any time of the day and curry, of course.' Enid Hewitt recalled: 'We had to share an internal communal bathroom, sometimes with a Qantas steward. Needless to say, our connecting door was always firmly locked.' And Celia Penney adds: 'Massages, pedicures and eggs and bacon at three a.m. Basic accommodation, separate sleeping quarters, a limited menu and set meal times and totally looked after by a caring paternalistic staff – it was rather like a co-ed boarding school, but with no rules, teachers or lessons! Amazing!' Jane Briggs: 'Christmas in Karachi was great! We used to fill a garden hosepipe bought in Hong Kong with gin. So – great parties!'

Memories of playing tennis and snooker by floodlight at midnight, Bunda boating and fishing, riding camels on the beach, picnics on the sandpit, catching and cooking crabs. Diane Johnston experienced the bunda boat sinking when all the cockroaches from the bowels of the boat rushed up – into her hair.

Oni Wyatt:

✈ I remember it always seemed to be 'Meatless Day' when I arrived, dying for a good bit of chicken curry at the Karachi Guest House. The elegant turbaned bearer would gravely bring us dahl and rice. Then I would go to a ground-floor room and try to sleep, while the ancient air-conditioning system would clunk through the night and I would probably find the usual streams of ants using my cabin bag as a reconnaissance stop off for edible goodies. And who could forget the 'The Corn Man' and his magical corn cures? He smothered your feet in red dye and then sucked through a straw and produced the corn. It was a grain of rice.

Judy Black used to gather up all the flight deck's meals that they had not eaten at two in the morning, such as lamb chops, plus the leftover cream, and take them off in Karachi to feed the dozens of cats hiding under the bushes in the middle of the night, going around quietly calling them, otherwise the ants would storm her room if she kept the food until daylight.

Susan Bannerman:

✈ I was in Speedbird House in Karachi for the 'strike' in the early '60s. This lasted nine days and our captain organised a tennis match between Qantas and BOAC. Of course after nine days 'the bar' ran dry but to our amazement the first officer found a crate of Pernod. I was also in Speedbird House when the Duke of Edinburgh stayed there while on a visit to Pakistan. He came into the bar before dinner, where there were about eight BOAC crew standing and drinking and about ten Qantas crew sitting at nearby tables. The Duke managed to have a quick polite word with every individual before leaving for a dinner engagement.

Cartoon by Oni Wyatt: 'Battles with Insects'.

Feeding the pye dogs in India and Pakistan was frowned upon. Immediately when the doors opened, these forlorn animals were waiting for you to throw out the galley door leftover lamb chops and bread. It seemed all the dogs in India and Pakistan were fed by incoming aircraft.

Pam Wolfson (1953) recounts:

➤ In the early days of Speedbird House, the rooms did not have their own lavatory, so one had to walk in the stifling heat down the outside passage to a long row of 'thunderboxes'. Here you sat with a fan overhead and hoped that your bottom wouldn't get tickled by the 'bog wallah'. He came along to empty the bins and if you had the bad luck and the unfortunate timing to be there at that time, you got your bottom tickled with a feather broom. It was a most constipating experience.

On the same theme here, a Comet in the mid-'50s landed at Karachi in a most robust way and a Pakistani ground staff waiting on the fuel truck was heard to utter this apocryphal statement: 'Oh my goodness, aircraft shitting all down runway' as the washroom waste valve loosened on landing.

Speedbird House became a much quieter place when the Qantas crews pulled out. They were missed by the bearers, who found them all utterly quixotic with their pranks.

In the early '70s, the rest house was closed down. It marked the end of another epoch. As the *BOAC Cabin Crew Bulletin* said:

✈　　Remember the warm moist smell of yellow cake at teatime, your own personal insect spray, the tinkling of tea cups by the pool as the sand clouds gather beyond the rose bushes, midnight feasts of eggs and chips, never to be forgotten commune-sized parties – and king-sized hangovers! Just a two-minute 'bus bounce' from the airport. The bearers more British that the British and smarter than any of us, uniform types, their moustaches waxed, buttons shining, brandishing white gloves, attending to our every whim. They whisked away our dirty laundry and dusty shoes, and patiently answered the plaintive cries of 'Bearer' along Virgin's Alley. No longer will we hear across the tarmac 'Buy me a beer in Karachi'.

## Memorable Impressions

Lorna Dand: 'The contrast of arriving at Hut 221, a prefab, and then giving Monarch Class Service on board. In earlier days we could slip through a gap in the perimeter fence to get to 221. In 1963, they gave us a new reporting building, but we still called it "221".'

Standby was usually for a whole week and you had to be at the airport within an hour and a half of being contacted. 221 was a great place to bump into friends and swap news. Everyone met and laughed and reminisced before and after their flights. On a return flight, you could look up the roster for your next flight.

On Britannia 102s, we had Jamaican and Indian stewardesses to cover local routes. It was common knowledge that some did not have the same hard work ethic as the British cabin crew. The Jamaicans especially were known to say immediately they boarded the aircraft: 'I'se Victoria – I'se tired.' This was the all-time joke. They quickly found a spare seat at the back of the cabin, covered themselves with a blanket and went to sleep.

'Friendships were made in an instant at 221 and a crew either gelled or didn't. Friendships were also severed at 221 on return very quickly! –"known as the 221 divorce",' remembers Irene Tait.

Linda Cowe recollects: 'The nice thing about coming down those steep aircraft steps, particularly in a warm climate, was that every airport was different and different countries had different smells. Now you get off the airplane, and walk along a corridor – you could be anywhere.' She continued: 'Rome – driving along the Tiber early in the morning before the rush hour started was never to be forgotten.'

Vicky Radcliffe:

✈　　Lovely memories of the helpfulness and kindness of hotel staff in India and Sri Lanka. The Fijians were 'Gentle Giants', bargaining with the Chinese in Hong Kong and the Arabs in the souk. Horror at the poverty in India, South America and Africa. On my first trip to Calcutta, I asked the Indian stewardess about the hordes of people sleeping on the streets and she said that it was 'the Indian way of life'. A great culture shock to a Westerner, but also a great learning curve and hopefully a lesson which encourages more tolerance.

Mary Patterson:

✈　　As an A stewardess, I had to give a briefing over the PA. Instead of saying, 'There is a call bell above your seat,' I said, 'there is a Call Girl above your seat.' I can still hear the great eruption of cheering. On a later trip I was demonstrating the life jacket and the whistle had been removed and had been replaced with a tampax.

Such opportunities. I didn't really appreciate them at the time but certainly do now. Visiting the Taj Mahal, rafting down the Rio Grande from Port Antonio to Rafters Rest in

Crew reporting at 221 for passenger and technical briefings. Incentive BOAC booklet of April 1968, a publication for airline staff.

Jamaica, driving through the Blue Mountains near Sydney, travelling for several hours on a bus from Teheran to Isfahan and being taken to a waiter's home to see the carpet weaving, a chief steward and I being the guests of the Maharajah of Baroda – wonderful, wonderful memories. The terrific camaraderie. I learned so much from my flying days, including how to handle people from all walks of life. This stood me in good stead in my 'life after flying'.

For many of the girls the exotic places like India, Africa, the Seychelles, Australia, the Caribbean often had the downside of a plethora of wildlife, mainly flying insects and, of course, the ground variety of spiders, lizards, snakes, moths and geckos. In fact, getting used to bugs of all kinds was quite a challenge. Darwin was famous for the Fanny Bay Hotel (where you would be woken up by the staff with a cup of tea whether you wanted one or not at 5 a.m.) and its cockroaches. These flew in the window and as one captain said: 'They are so large they could land at the airport.' The trouble was that these cockroaches got into your sponge bag, for example, and at the next slip, Sydney, you got one hell of a fright as they flew out.

Jill Edmonds commented:

✈    The distinctive aircraft smells and Elizabeth Arden hand lotion. The noise of the engines starting up. The noise in the rear galley of the Comet was deafening (that's probably why we had to have our ears checked each year). Hats and gloves (white for summer and navy for winter) were a must and after more than thirty years, I still have recurring dreams about arriving on the aircraft without my hat. We wore our uniform with pride.

Helen Beresford Smith:

✈    The exciting experience of being escorted into Amman by two fighter planes on each wing. They had been sent by King Hussein of Jordan, when we had his brother on board.

I received a gold Omega watch from the Sheikh of Bahrain, just for carrying a relative of his. The generosity of the Sheikh of Bahrain was legendary. In his time he must have given away millions of gold watches to all members of the crew. Many of them had several!

On the eastern routes, we were fortunate enough to be made honorary members of private country clubs such as The Saturday Club in Calcutta.

In Bahrain: 'In the Middle East having all the lecherous Sheiks waiting for us to arrive at the guest house,' says Shirley Swinn, 'and the crew parties at the Sheikh's beach palace. My experience of the generosity of the Sheiks was being collected in a yellow Rolls and driven through the desert to his beach house where there were buckets of French champagne, a table groaning with food, the latest disco music, plush red seats … everything you could possibly want. The captain suggested I dance with him and I can remember he was so small and with me in dancing heels, meant his head was buried between my breasts. Their generosity was overwhelming and our hosts didn't drink!'

Heather Bradley a tall, very attractive Irish blonde, remembers:

✈    We were housed in the '60s in the Gulf Aviation rest house. On my first trip in 1968, I went to the bar for a heart sharpener with the rest of the crew and was almost immediately approached by a very friendly Baharni, who was hoping that I would 'join somebody very important for half an hour in a darkened room'. This description was given to me after I questioned him as to who I would meet. I then went off to my room, after refusing this invitation. There was soon a knock on my door and a man was standing there with tray of rings glistening at me and again he suggested that I should spend time with the same very important man. I said no thank you and again there was another knock and this time a note pushed underneath. It was the manager of the rest house saying if I wasn't going to spend time 'with the important one' then how about dinner with him and a nice present. I said no to it all ... but there were amazing parties at the palaces in those days.

Angela Froude had a rear evacuation slide implode on a very rough take off from Bermuda on a 707:

✈   It filled the entire galley area with a great roar, trapping the crew. I ran and got the first class carving knife and rushed back down the aisle, being thrown all over the place. I then stabbed the slide to deflate it. The passengers thought it was all most amusing.

Jenny Maxwell remembers that her best experience was:

✈ ... when I looked after Merle Oberon, the star of *Wuthering Heights*. I spent a long time with her. She was enchanting and I helped her prepare her hair for the reporters. As a gift she gave me her sunglasses, which I still treasure. I then received an invitation to visit her and her husband in Mexico, which sadly I never accepted.

Caroline Chambers says: 'I left the airline to settle down. I would only have left this fantastic life to settle down and marry, certainly not for any other job.'

Nothing quite compared with the attraction of working in the air, flying aboard a modern aircraft with the responsibility for service and safety in your hands – and being paid to do it. There are, of course, the many other benefits such as free travel, free stopovers abroad, the chance to work as part of a happy, friendly team, a chance to meet different people every day. Nothing could equal it.

By the end of the '60s there was the continual buzz about big jumbos joining the fleet. Many of us could not imagine how this was going to work – over 300 passengers at once! The concept seemed almost impossible. The surging '70s arrived and once more a vast leap in civil aviation was beginning.

# CHAPTER 7

# Liaisons – Dangerous or Otherwise

*A* strange and perhaps unique feature of aircrew life is the depth of involvement that forms when people are working together, flying around the world for several days at a time, only to return home and literally never bother to telephone or make contact again. Days and nights of spoken intimacies and confidences, as well as sexual liaisons, are mostly discarded without so much as a wave at the end of a trip at 221. The nature of the job makes this almost inevitable. Each new flight brought with it an ingredient of sexual tension which either fizzed up or faded away. Suffice to say there was a lot of harmless frisson and flirting. Working together in the close proximity of an enclosed community thousands of feet up in the air inevitably produced various levels of intimacy, sexual liaisons and shared thoughts and opinions, with the end result that your fellow crew members often knew more about you than those you left at home. Many of the crew parties were held in hotel bedrooms which provided the setting for many shared intimacies, fuelled by copious gin and tonics that somehow appeared out of crew bags.

Conversely, arriving back at London Airport these relationships were for the most part discarded in what was known as the 221 divorce. 221 was the name given to the building (originally an old Nissen hut in the early days on the north side of Heathrow Airport) in which one signed off, collected your mail, perhaps the next roster, and bade farewell. There was little time for standing around as suddenly the reality of home, wives, children made this part of the trip a quick exit and a vague wave.

'The way in which the crew became an entity once Heathrow was left behind, became a nucleus of its own until the return, when abruptly we resumed our home lives', put so aptly by Shirley Fogg, is one of the fondest memories expressed and experienced by stewardesses.

Then, of course, there was nothing nicer than finding you were flying again with one of these people at another time and you took up almost where you left off. There were several downsides to these airline liaisons. There existed an unspoken, for the most part, rivalry for the favours of the female. Many of the stewardesses objected to the fact that it was assumed that they were obliged to socialise only with the cabin crew. This didn't go down very well with a lot of the stewardesses who then found themselves having to cope with 'petty jealousies, particularly from cabin crew with regard to flight crew' and many commented that this was something they wished that they had been more prepared for when they began flying.

Colgate toothpaste even got into the act.

Backbiting and intrigues on a long trip could turn a twenty-one-day flight around the world into a nightmare. For many this was their greatest challenge, 'being consistently friendly and nice to passengers and both crews, cabin and flight.' It certainly added another dimension to the word 'teamwork' if you were considered a 'flight deck' girl and had to work harmoniously with stewards who regarded the stewardesses as part of their package.

Many of these trips resulted in either marriage or long and often heartbreaking affairs (and in retrospect, this was a waste of time and life). For young, innocent twenty year olds the sight of a handsome man with lots of gold braid on his arm could knock any bird off her perch, and these experienced flying Lotharios knew their stuff. There was a great deal of truth in the statement 'I'm a single man once the wheels are up!' and opportunities to be the consummate philanderer abounded.

Some of the male crew, whether it was flight deck or cabin crew, seemed to board the aircraft in a state of perpetual heightened passion, which found a natural environment in an aircraft fuelled by champagne, caviar, beautiful girls and glamorous passengers. They also had the added advantage of what is called the 'miracle of male compartmentalisation' and were able to have several affairs running simultaneously. When this was discovered, revenge produced some phenomenal results. One such discovery led a stewardess to ring her pilot, who was thousands of miles away, using the telephone at his home, where she often resided, and leaving the call connected for three weeks.

The most glamorous of the lot were the ex-Fleet Air Arm pilots; bags of charisma, every one of them undeniably handsome, with a kind of panache that guaranteed them lots of attention. The person allocated to do that on board was the A Stewardess, otherwise known as the 'bird in first class'. It was mostly her duty to look after the flying crew, usually after the first class passengers had had their meal. On the odd occasion there were captains who insisted that they were attended to only by the senior steward, but these were very few, usually the oddball skippers it was best to keep away from. Despite popular mythology the stewardesses did not do this job simply 'to get a captain'.

The captains were always conscious of the necessity to have their crews getting along harmoniously and many of them were renowned for being great party givers and social organisers, in places like San Francisco, Honolulu or Beirut where there were slips of several days at a time.

There was usually a great feeling of camaraderie between pilots and stewardesses. We certainly depended on them to get us there in one piece and they looked to us to take care of everything that went on 'down the back' with the help of the stewards and to advise them of any incidents pertaining to the aircraft and passenger safety. There were endless cups of tea, meals

.. Make sure Tech always get something to drink ..

watch it –!
one of those
nursing types again.

Cartoon by Oni Wyatt.

garnished with tasty extras, Nescafe whipped up to frothy concoctions as they sat in the cockpit for endlessly long hours. The most exercise the flight crew did was when they pandiculated at various intervals. As many of the girls said: 'They deserved spoiling.'

In November 1946, when the first stewardesses were posted to the North Atlantic run, BOAC issued press statements that they were stewardesses *not* air hostesses, wanting to avoid the 'glamour and frivolity' tag. There were restrictions as to where they could sit, work and move on the aircraft. Whether she could be allowed in the galley or heaven forbid the flight crew compartment. David Beaty writes in *The Water Jump* that a legacy from most of the American airlines stated that for the stewardesses '*entry into the cockpit is very emphatically laid down not to exceed 30 seconds*'. The result was that the British order said they were to stay in the passenger cabin throughout the flight.

By 1947 this had been modified and the stewardess was allowed in the galley to prepare baby foods. However, a month later the British Airline Pilot's Association 'expressed dissatisfaction' with the rule regarding entry into the flight crew area and asked the catering department for any 'sound reason' as to why this ruling should be maintained?

Joan Haskett (1954–57) told me that a flight deck member (who shall remain nameless) was going out with a stewardess who was on board the flight. He walked through the cabin and a voice murmured something to him in the dark. He thought it was the girlfriend, so he answered her and gave her a kiss. When he got to the back of the aircraft, he found his girlfriend sitting there. I wonder if the passenger thought it was part of the service?

## Rosters

Maureen Wade remembers being on standby and 'they were trying to find me. My landlady's son gave them my temporary phone number. On learning that I was at Captain Sharp's house, they never rostered us together again'.

Rosters at that time were not computerised and one was inclined to handle the rosters clerk with great care, especially if you were trying to organise your trip to coincide with the love of your life. The roster sheets were in the famous 221 building and you could look ahead to see where he (or she) was, make a call to the roster clerk with some innocuous excuse to see if a change could be made to your advantage. Maybe the rosters people in those days were a bunch of old romantics, because on the whole they granted your request. Conversely this building called 221 was also the centre where a callout for standby would come from.

Organising one's romantic interludes down the routes required an enormous amount of strategic planning. First the rosters for many years were compiled by women (roster clerks) whom one never had the occasion to meet, although the telephone offered some kind of relationship building. This was essential if you really wanted to organise your social life at home, which was always so difficult. To organise it down the routes with a crew member of your choice was indeed tricky.

One then had to start coming up with a story as to why you had to be in often the most undesirable places, like Toronto, on a certain date. Christmas was always a time when naturally most crews like to be at home with their families. I remember one Christmas when I saw that my favourite pilot was going to be away for Christmas. I was in the Training School at the time and as my family lived in Brisbane, it was the ideal opportunity to 'volunteer' to give someone else the chance to be in the UK. This was all agreed and I happily jumped on the Boeing 707, to the also utter delight of the person in the right-hand seat, to do the first sector to Zurich. I was in heaven and planned lots of wonderful and romantic Christmasy things to do in Zurich, where we were to be for a few days.

On arrival in Zurich, before the crew left the aircraft, as we always waited for the ongoing crew to board, the captain came up to me and said, 'Marvellous news. The flight crew and you are all going back to London for Christmas … we leave in half an hour on the BEA flight to London.'

Naturally I couldn't refuse and the rest of the cabin crew were not included. Well, as it is said, the best laid plans … so returning home feeling utterly dejected I rang my boss at the Training School to wish him Happy Christmas and he said, 'I thought you were off to Australia'. I explained about the kind gesture of BOAC to allow the flight crew and myself back for Christmas and he said, 'Just as well, I need you back…'

## Parties

This was a career that put you into a plethora of social occasions all round the world. The 'little black dress' was the first item that was packed. The stewardesses found that once arriving at a city there were Embassy functions or the Navy was in town. Endless invitations and airline PR functions were on the agenda, wherever you were in the world. As many of them said, we were exposed to social situations never dreamt about in England, and they were non stop. Passengers were also part of this, as they were suddenly taken by the particular stewardess who looked after them and invited her to meet their families, if she did not know anyone in that city. This led to lifelong friendships for both parties.

And there were the male passengers who fell in love with their stewardess – but that's another story.

The crew parties usually held in the first officer's room were de rigeur for crews. In the days when there was only one female crew member, these could become a test of stamina for all concerned. However, it was the abundance of alcohol that caused many forgettable experiences. The stewardesses were warned at the Training School never to volunteer their room for the crew party. If they did, they never did it again, as that was the room that was left littered with glasses and piles of cigarette butts to dispose of.

Even getting to a crew party could be a challenge. In a Tokyo hotel Virginia Sheehy was still in uniform but without her hat, jacket or Speedbird badge when she set off on a freezing November evening and decided to take a shortcut down the ten floors the party room via the fire staircase, armed with a bottle of gin, the glass and tonics. However, she had now shut herself out of the hotel and was on the fire escape. She then went down to the mezzanine floor and banged on a Japanese man's window. He was sitting on the bed on the telephone but opened the window. 'I stepped through, saying Japanese "thank yous", bowing and walked through still clutching my bottles. The Japanese gentleman stood there. He bowed and said a stunned goodbye.'

Apart from strip poker there were endless party games devised by crew. One captain, an ex-barrister, had a party game whereby you had to go around the party room without touching the floor. Fancy dress parties called for lots of initiative. One steward took the orange blanket from his bed, wrote destinations on it in the three-letter code and came as a 'crew label'. As one stewardess recounts:

✈  I remember being told that on my first trip I only needed two things: a dip stick (mini immersion heater to make coffee and tea) and a flask. In the early '60s as only one of two girls we felt duty bound to go to social gatherings. There were four flight deck and three stewards as the C bird was inevitably returning home. So the boys would just hammer on your door whether you wanted it or not. But mostly I enjoyed the social side. I always carried a cocktail dress, the little black dress, with me and did go to quite a few of the Embassies for meals, taking with me the latest London newspapers from the aircraft, which always went down well.

The captain always slept in another hotel. This was a hangover from the very early days but that didn't stop them socialising with the crews or enjoying all the camaraderie that became the most enjoyable feature of a trip (as well as the shopping and the sightseeing!), In the mid-'60s this changed and except for the odd place like Karachi the entire Technical Crew was put into another hotel. Various theories abounded as to why this had happened, one being that the wives had complained. Did not the wives of stewards feel the same? It was the intention, we were sure, to keep some distance between us.

## Consequences

This predictably cosy environment could produce attractiveness and lust between the most unlikely individuals. And five balmy nights in the Caribbean was a magical environment for romance. The most cynical hearts could be melted.

However, the inevitable consequences of a dangerous liaison had the horrifyingly lonely experience of an unwanted pregnancy and termination. Some sought their own solutions via the London Clinic. Others went to the BOAC Medical Centre where in the '60s there was a wonderfully understanding doctor who arranged a solution and to whom many of the stewardesses were eternally grateful. Whatever the outcome, there were many trips to Hong Kong to sort this out. One only hoped it did not go onto a personnel report for the entire airline to read. There were, of course, many married women flying. These stewardesses managed to keep their private life quite secret until of course the telltale bulge appeared and then it was time to resign.

As stewardesses were terrified of losing their jobs (and their reputation), rapes went unreported. 'Booze' was an intrinsic component of many dangerous liaisons. It fuelled continuous parties and relationships. It seemed that it was everyone's duty to get as much booze off the aircraft as possible without being caught. Empty Schweppes tonic bottles were filled with Gilbeys, and Elizabeth Arden Skin Tonic bottles also proved to a useful decoy for gin. For inexperienced twenty year olds, alcohol caused many a downfall (literally) and in many cases mammoth repercussions. Rape was a regular occurrence, which occurred under the guise of 'Let me take you back to your room' to a woman unsteady on her feet. This often led to uncalled for molestation. Then there was the 'friendly massage' and simple lust which familiarity could create. However, it is essential to state that by no means all male crews boarded the aircraft in a priapic state. The majority were officers and gentlemen, protective of their female crew members.

There were amongst the females some 'femmes fatales', gorgeous women experienced in the ways of the world. There was a very beautiful raven-haired stewardess renowned for her beauty. One stewardess recalls having hair like hers and then 'seeing the disappointment in the eyes of the flight crew when I turned round and they realised it wasn't her!'.

There were several male crew members who were renowned for aggressive approaches, especially towards stewardesses on their first flight, and as one can imagine, these young girls, inexperienced with the whole flying experience, found this both difficult and frightening to deal with. Nor did they know who to turn to, and it was particularly distressing to be away from your own environment in a foreign place and have to deal with these incidents by yourself.

Of course, it wasn't always a physical approach. There was the abundant amount of alcohol which new stewardesses often were not used to. Drinks were doctored under the guise of orange juice and tomato juice. And of course, those that took the risk of going out with a passenger in a foreign country put themselves in even more jeopardy. Bahrain was one of these places where one had to be extremely cautious.

The ultimate danger was sexually transmitted disease. Unfortunately some male crew who had unlimited access to call girls worldwide still pursued stewardesses, some of them entirely unaware of the ways of the world. The results caused immeasurable heartache and horror in many of the girls.

Many of the women who did the survey made a comment about fertility; they felt that the job, particularly after ten years 'when we were thrown out' rendered them infertile. Many married but they remained childless and felt that there was a connection with all those years in the air. Interesting as this may seem now, no studies were done about this at the time. There were, of course, a heap of studies going on about heart attacks and such with the flight crew.

Menstruation, sleep and eating patterns were affected by constant international flying and the individual's circadian rhythm was put out of kilter. This added to the anxiety of trying to lead a normal life, let alone cope with an unwanted pregnancy.

## Reputations

And so to the Mile High Club. I am yet to join. However, I have always thought a five star hotel with crisp clean sheets, mini bar and room service preferable to a very cramped aircraft loo. Some did recall funny experiences, including 'trying to join the Mile High Club in the rear loo on the ground'.

Of course there were many infamous antics in relation to the flight deck. One particular stewardess was known to say to the captain before they took off from London, 'You're my target for tonight', and then would turn to the first officer and say, 'And you're my number one alternate'.

Perhaps this is the same person who gave a party at the airport club in the late '50s to celebrate her fiftieth captain! Some did have intimate knowledge of quite a few pilots, which they willingly shared with the other stewardesses on board. One extremely beautiful, raven-haired beauty – almost a replica of Elizabeth Taylor – was a fount of knowledge. Many were fascinated by her sexual sophistication, and as the captain and first officer boarded she was known to say, 'He's not much good,' or 'That one's got a kink in it'.

This behaviour was more a fantasy and wishful thinking on the part of the males, as was the suggestion that many of the stewardesses were nymphomaniacs. However, if you were a

The Kissing Captain – and note the startled look on the stewardess! This photo was taken in 1967 on a four-night stopover of a BEA Trident crew. Stewardess Judith Farrell was certainly not quite as carried away by the romantic atmosphere of Athens as he was.

nymphomaniac this was one of the few careers which provided you with endless opportunities. In reality the Mile High Club was more a passenger fantasy than occupation.

A controversial subject which always seems to hold a tremendous fascination for the general public is the supposedly torrid sex life attributed to overnight crews. How many times have I been told, 'You can't tell me they don't get down to a few tricks down the routes!' … Well, a few!

There has always been a hint of glamour about those who earn a living in the sky. Add a smart uniform, the nuance of danger and the belief that absence makes the heart grow fonder and you have the recipe to make a person almost irresistible, especially to anyone with an ounce of romance in their soul. We attracted men from just about every walk of life, and, of course, had access to them under circumstances where we had their almost undivided attention – rugby players and cricketers, politicians, international businessmen, the Armed Forces, media and film personalities, and of course, other airline employees.

## Not all were Dangerous!

Oni Wyatt: 'The enormous fun had by the crews down the routes in their time off was legendary.' As she recalls:

✈    The difference from now, of course, was that in those earlier days there was little or no TV or radio, and with the trips often being up to three weeks away, anyone who could sing or play an instrument, tell plenty of jokes, think of silly games to play, organise crib and card games, and enjoy a game of darts was always welcome. When we got the chance to go somewhere like the haven of the Seaman's Club or The British Club, we entertained ourselves. Many people were very gifted. So we were never bored, and the room parties took on a life of their own. Meeting up with other airlines' crews was fun too. I remember terrific parties and sometimes very lively events in romantic places like Colombo and Mauritius over Christmas and New Year. Sometimes I could hardly believe

I was being PAID for all this. We worked hard on the flights but then we knew we could recuperate afterwards. I loved sport so if there was a boat to sail or a tennis racquet to swing I was off. I joined the Flying Staff Recreation Club Committee and sometimes found myself carrying things like a dinghy anchor or new windsurfer ropes in my luggage to some spot round the world where spares were needed. I remember going diving one Christmas morning in Mauritius with a mad friend of mine on the trip. We had decided we must have a 'toast' to start the day thirty down. We took down some vodka laced with blackcurrant juice (so we could see it!) in a squeezy bottle and tried to sit flopping about on the sea bed with our weights and tanks. We took off the top. Of course – silly us – we'd forgotten that the pressure would explode it all out like a squid streaking off! I laughed so much I nearly drowned. We never got a drop of the vodka.

Missing your pickup before a flight once down the routes was the greatest crime. One lived in fear of going back to sleep after the hotel wakeup call. Peggy Thorne recalls being at the hotel checkout, all the crew ready to board the transport, when it was realised one stewardess was missing. Peggy volunteered to go to her room, imagining that she had gone back to sleep. When she got to her door she heard muffled sounds, laughter and two voices. Peggy knocked and called out: 'We are all waiting for you … the transport is here,' and the reply, 'I won't be a minute, Peg. I'm just reaching the point of no return.'

There is no longer a Point of No Return today but an Equal Time Point, which means that it takes the same time from that point to return to an airfield or continue to one ahead. These days, as aircraft are so reliable, the oceans of the world are flown by mainly twin-engine jets and they conform to ETOPS rules which means that if they lose an engine they will always be within a certain time away from a diversion airfield, and this could mean flying on one engine for up to three hours. Perhaps Peggy should have declared 'Equal Time'.

Many stewardesses mentioned that this topic should have been discussed at the training school … 'the way that morals flew out the window once London Airport had disappeared'. As a trainer I admit I avoided this topic myself. This is why I feel that the more mature girls coped better. It was essential to keep your head because of all the parties and lechers.

It needs to be acknowledged that many stewardesses found the companionship of crew and the chance to travel as satisfying and enjoyable in themselves. They did not seek dangerous liaisons. However, many relationships lasted for many years. There were those that wasted their lives 'waiting' for him to eventually marry them and others who made the decision to move on and start a new life. Painful as this was, for some, even thirty years later, the love and depths of passion still linger. A poignant remark came from several of these still attractive women who admitted to ringing BA pensions 'to see if he was still alive' … 'but my husband to whom I am happily married must never know' … 'he was gorgeous and I adore him still, and the memories and love we shared for years never really fades away … and it has lasted, certainly for me … I don't know about him'. Other mentions by many commented on the 'long and lasting love undiminished by the passing years'.

Liaisons with passengers were another world altogether. My overly friendly encounter on an aircraft was in the first class cabin. Female passengers acting amorously towards stewardesses were rare, and not taken seriously. My first and only lesbian encounter was being pushed up against the galley wall with a lady's hands all over my breasts and her lips covering me in profuse kisses. This provided a great deal of amusement for the flight deck and my galley steward. I was rescued by the engineer, whom I looked at imploringly for assistance. I spent the rest of the flight in the economy cabin with the steward restraining the lady from leaving first class and wandering about looking for me.

Pat White recalls:

✈   On a charter flight an American woman pushed a $10 note down my bra and moved her fingers around. I didn't realise what was going on. I rushed back to the galley where I told the other stewardess, Ena Grogan. As I walked past her again, she said, 'Does it tickle?' I ran back to Ena, who told me to go back and say 'No it doesn't but a $50 note would'.

Refusal to communicate could also be a problem. 1A was the premier seat on any aircraft and on this occasion leaving New York a large, sullen and extremely dishevelled man was seated there. He was wearing a large weather-beaten straw hat. There was a configuration kafuffle going on and a passenger count and what amounted to a name check of all passengers had to be done. This was the late '60s and in the sensitive hijacking era. To get more than a mumble from this passenger was difficult. He kept repeating his name on the manifest in an inaudible and recalcitrant manner. Anyone who seemed uncooperative was the responsibility of the ground staff and the crew had to make a decision. Meanwhile the captain was anxious to get away on time, so the gentleman was escorted off the aircraft. What a furore this caused on our arrival at Heathrow. We had thrown off Marlon Brando and he was not pleased. As a crew member this was not easy to live down.

## Passenger Tales and Liaisons

There is an invidious feeling which comes into place at an airport. Many passengers agree they are no longer in control of their destiny. The minute you hand over your baggage you seem to lose both your identity and your personal power. Cabin crew around the world have been known to say, 'Passengers leave their brains at the airport!'

What is this transformation that takes place? To the cabin crew, the passenger is looked upon as 'self-loading freight', which is pretty apt, but how does the passenger react once he or she comes aboard? Many of today's passengers say they feel intimidated and guilty, even for getting up to use the lavatories. They spend their whole time on board pretending that they are *not* terrorists! Others get aggressive, possibly because of the fear of crashing or the fact that they can't smoke or just out of sheer frustration. 'Walking around is definitely frowned upon by the crew,' said many passengers.

There were passengers in the early '60s who, just before arriving into Heathrow from New York, would ask for a morning newspaper, and there were those who left their shoes out to be cleaned. There were several incidents of stewards and stewardesses who tripped over pairs of shoes in the aisle during a night flight. The cabin crew then had to reconcile the owners with their shoes. The passengers would say: 'Thank you, but I put them out there to be cleaned.' Cleaning passengers' shoes did happen in the 1930s on United Airlines. There must have been something about BOAC's superb cabin service that caused passengers to assume the oddest conceptions about one's duties up there at 35,000ft.

Cartoon by Oni Wyatt. Once on board, passengers seem to need exact and particular instructions for every procedure of their flight.

The Queen's Messengers always sat in first class with their diplomatic bag beside them. It was really a very boring job for them, continually having to do the same flights and having to sit through seven-course meals. However, many of them alleviated the boredom by enjoying the top French wines and brandies. Often, when they were having a post prandial snooze, crews were known to hide the diplomatic bag behind the seat. This nearly produced some heart attacks.

Passengers changed, and this is to be expected as society continually changes. A comment that occurred frequently during my research is the more frequent aggression and air rage today. One theory is that the ban on in-flight smoking, the lengthy queues and slow boarding procedures – almost stripping for the scanning devices – and claustrophobia causes the angst. The sectors are now so much longer. Cramped up together for up to fourteen hours can produce some odd behaviour.

Linda Cowe (1962–63) remembers that it was difficult to distinguish first class passengers from economy. Usually most dressed up for the occasion. 'Occasionally, we met up with passengers again, perhaps on their return journeys, and greeted them like old friends.'

The general consensus was that passengers in the '60s were usually well travelled and had a calmer air about them. Of course, we carried fewer passengers.

By the late '70s some celebrities were guilty of the 'I am so precious' syndrome. Before every flight, crews are briefed about any special requests and passenger information. You can imagine that when an iconic celebrity deeply into the mysteries of an exotic cult requests 'No eye contact', it would be hard to resist not looking her in the eye when asking: 'What would you like to drink?' Others, especially one male mega movie star, always found it difficult to reply and had their requests transmitted through a second party, usually the wife or girlfriend, when there was absolutely nothing at all wrong with their vocal chords: 'Mr So and So will have a glass of champagne.'

By the '70s passengers didn't dress as well. Isobel Proctor also recalls:

✈   I remember when they used to keep us running about during the night with drinks and everything. They seem to be more settled these days with the music and the films and they sleep a lot more now. A lot of people now, especially Americans, won't eat anything and only drink water. Sometimes even with a full first class you only open one or two bottles of wine per sector, unimaginable in the good old days. First class passengers now seem to be mainly business men and women. They immediately plug in their computers and get down to work. The media disappeared for a while but now that Concorde is not around there are a lot more celebrities on board – though many of them now go by private jet.

"Could we have your name for the Guiness Book of Records? You have now pressed the buzzer 42 times."

The big difference in today's passengers is that they don't set out to enjoy the occasion as they used to. Flying is more like catching a bus. Many stewardesses found it irritating when passengers would clap on landing. Even more annoying was their comment after a hard landing of: 'Oh, we're here, I thought we had been shot down.'

The development of passenger travel over the years has meant fewer stops, faster travelling times and more passengers per aircraft. It is not as it was in the Golden Age, when they could board in a leisurely manner, have a few drinks, move around and chat, smoke, knit, generally entertain themselves and sleep without ending up on a stranger's shoulders. Now there is the demanding 'bucket and spade' brigade who expect first class service in an economy cabin.

Economy passengers could sometimes be divided into their country of origin as far as attitude was concerned. The Americans snapped their fingers, called us waitresses, usually without any 'please' or 'thank you'. White South Africans thought we were servants. One asked me to clean their child's very dirty potty. Asian immigrants asked where to go for the free money.

'Passengers differed according to routes in the late '60s,' said Gillian Ritchie. 'Caribbean passengers were usually upper class Brits in blazers, pink shirts, straw hats and pinkie rings. New York gave us the bankers and businessmen drinking spirits with Sobranies. They started with a G&T and went steadily through the drinks trolley to liqueurs and friandises. Very different from today.'

The West Indians were charming but had no idea what they were going to – England and its cold weather. The stewards used to hold training sessions on board for them so they could work on London transport. ('Mind de doors pleas.') This was before the days of political correctness!

## Friendly Relations

The passenger service routines in the '60s gave ample time to build a passenger/crew relationship, which although not intimate was something special. Before the drink trolleys moved down the aisles, the stewardesses individually took a passenger's drink order. Thus there were many more points of contacts, taking the order, serving the drinks and then later collecting the money. In economy class when boarding, a passenger received far more attention than now and all were shown to their seats.

This time to meet and talk to passengers resulted in many marriages of stewardesses to famous cricketers, footballers and a notable porn king. And even more remarkable were the stewardesses who married Sheiks and became princesses or Sheikhas. Not all these encounters ended in marriage, with some famous passengers, like Bing Crosby, conducting long and lasting liaisons with stewardesses.

The opportunity to have a famous passenger all to yourself was a treat, especially if he couldn't sleep and wanted to chat all night. This was my memory of Rod Steiger, who had just received acclaim for his movie *The Pawnbroker*. He was off to New York to collect yet another award and couldn't settle. We spent all our time in the first class galley talking movies, drinking brandy and milk. Quite a party, as every one of the crew popped in and out for a chat and a drink all throughout the night.

The majority of the girls were not in the habit of giving their telephone numbers to passengers and airline policy was to never give out any staff phone numbers or addresses. However, one passenger had twelve dozen red roses delivered to my door. One hundred and forty-four roses were a lot to spread around my small London flat! What was even odder was that this man always seemed to know my flying schedule: there were always roses on my return. My flat mates, who eventually got to know him, never gave out my trip details. We knew very little about him, except that he went to Europe a lot. He didn't want to do the restaurant scene. He always preferred to come to our flat, doing all the odd jobs. He could fix anything. A Harrods hamper and often a dozen red roses always preceded his visit. We all dined on his hampers for eighteen months and then he suddenly disappeared. Not a word or a sign. He was truly missed by us all. I used to refer to him as MI5. Looking back I feel I was right. We never knew what he did, never met any of his friends. I missed all the roses.

I recall on the long sector between Honolulu and Tokyo we used to entertain ourselves by collecting as many business cards along our side of the passenger cabin as we could. Whoever collected the least had to buy the drinks in Tokyo. On one occasion when I was doing this a passenger asked what the other stewardess who was about eight rows ahead of me, was doing? I said she was getting a business card. 'What for?' he asked and I explained that we were having a competition. 'Hear that mate,' he said to his colleague. 'Give the little lady your card,' and turned around to fellow passengers telling them to do so. This started a ripple effect and I won by an aeronautical mile.

Jill Edmonds remembers that on a trip to Boston two elderly, genteel ladies enjoyed the flight so much that they invited all the crew to tea at their beautiful home. 'We sat chatting politely, drinking tea served from a silver Queen Anne tea service. It was a memorable occasion and one we always referred to as the "Boston Tea Party".'

Sheila Luke said, 'In my day, in the '50s, we had to treat the passengers as if we were inviting them into our own homes and act accordingly, by taking an interest in them, holding a conversation and anticipating their requests.'

Mary Patterson was flying into Detroit and one of the male passengers asked her if she had been there before. She said that she had but that she had not really liked it, and had never been out of the city. He invited her to stay with his family and said he would phone his wife when he cleared Customs. When they met up he said that he hadn't been able to get through to his wife, adding, 'No problem – off we go!' And off they went (can you imagine doing anything so foolhardy today?!). On arrival at his home, they were both greeted by a smiling wife and children, who were so excited that daddy had brought home a real live stewardess. They looked after her wonderfully and took her everywhere and then delivered her back to the airport for her return flight to London. June Blackler comments:

> ✈    The first class passengers in the '50s were so elegantly dressed; the ladies always wore hats and gloves, which we placed in the wardrobe along with fur coats, muffs and gentlemen's coats. No one carried excessive amounts of hand luggage. Flying for me, and for passengers, was more an adventure and some passengers wanted to keep in touch so I received Christmas cards for some years after I was married.

Once a tense atmosphere created by a dispute amongst the Ugandan ground staff at Kampala resulted in us being anxious to leave, and we had a tense and hurried departure. The galley steward in the rear gave a cursory check and decided all the catering and equipment was on board and that we were ready for departure. When the dinner service was about to begin we realised that we had no cutlery packs. The passengers were ravenous with the wafting aroma of the meal drifting through the cabin, getting everyone's saliva juices on the go. I made an announcement explaining about the cutlery, finishing briskly with 'and there are free wines, spirits and liquors'. We offered the trays, without the packs, and it was surprising how many passengers used their ingenuity and managed to eat the meal. Swiss army knives, penknives, pens and fruit knives all came to light as useful utensils. Naturally we had opened the bar to appease them all and this improved the situation. We told the passengers that we would lose our jobs if they complained and no one did.

A friend of mine from the '60s told me a lovely anecdote:

> ✈    Although Kerry Packer was never a passenger on one of my flights, I wish he had been as I would have made a huge fuss of him. When I first started flying I was supplementing my income as a croupier in Mayfair, no one knew and certainly not BOAC. He came in three nights running and was at my table. He won heaps. On the third night he said: 'See you tomorrow night,' and I replied, 'Sorry, I will be in Barbados,' and explained that I moonlighted at the club and did two jobs to pay my mortgage. He asked me how much I owed. '£25,000,' I replied. He passed me a whole sheaf of notes – £25,000 – and thanked me and left. Paying off that mortgage had set me up for life.

Our older passengers have given us some lovely stories: 'A little old lady passenger on board a York rang her bell and then asked the stewardess to clean the window. She took a tea towel and polished it, and the lady smiled and said: 'Thank you dear, and now the other side please.'

De Havilland Comet. The elegance of the passengers is evident in the attire. Note the beauty cases in the open hat racks.

Maureen Wade had an elderly lady in her early nineties who was visiting family in Australia for the first time. By the time they got to India, she was very tired. Having gone through several storms and a lot of lightning she rang the bell and asked, 'When are we getting there? We've gone through at least three stations and never stopped. This is the last time I travel British Rail.' Angela Froude remembers an elderly lady who insisted on keeping her hat and coat on for the whole twenty-seven-hour journey to Australia, because she had got it right in the mirror before she left home.

Andy Bennett: 'I politely asked one old ex-Raj couple on leaving Delhi if they would like afternoon tea. They replied, 'Memsahib and I will have tea and tiffin at five,' to which I politely replied, 'Is that Delhi time or English time, Sir?'

Another recollection is of an American in first class who loudly told the stewardess that he wanted a very dry martini. She mixed it traditionally – four fifths gin and one fifth dry Vermouth. He spat it out and said, 'I wanted a very dry martini'. A cockney steward overheard and said, 'I know what you want, Sir.' He filled the glass with gin and with a cork wiped the rim with Vermouth, but still the chap didn't like it. The 'camp' chief steward then swanned over, whisked away the glass, exchanged it for an 8oz tumbler, crammed it full of ice, filled it to the top with gin and whispered 'Vermouth' over the top of the glass. The passenger said, 'Now that's what I call a dry martini'.

Before the early '60s there was no in-flight entertainment apart from the stewardesses. The sectors were often long and incredibly tedious but the passengers never really made a fuss about this. One particular chief steward, a quite lovable eccentric who delighted in the absurd, used

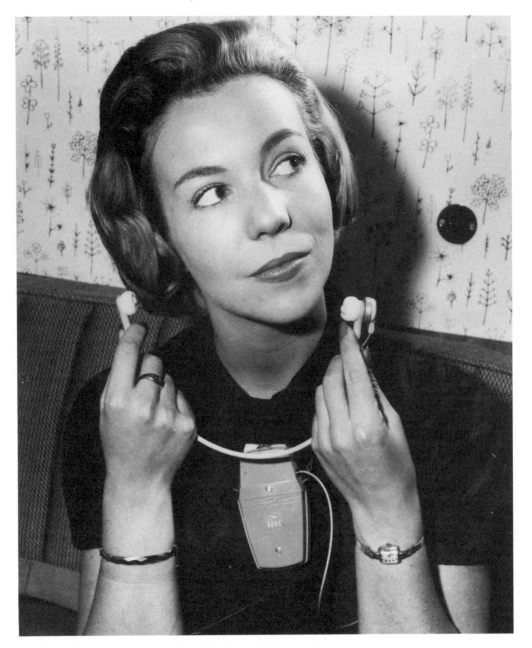

Delia Green demonstrating one of the earliest prototypes for passengers' in-flight entertainment, a concern for the airline by the late '50s.

to do a 'Passenger Alertness Test' and wander up and down the rear cabin with a stuffed olive up his nostril. He counted how many times he walked the cabin before a puzzled passenger commented on this. He then feigned absolute astonishment and had a way of wrinkling his nose to let it drop into his hand. Passengers, in those days, were far too polite to comment.

A friend of mine recalls a couple fondling under a blanket in the first class. However, the male friend was travelling in economy class, so she said 'The ITATA regulations require anyone

## VC Ten-derness ?

A COUPLE had sexual intercourse on a BOAC New York-Sydney flight in full view of other passengers, according to a report in the airline's magazine Horizon. The couple were initially sitting six rows apart. The woman threatened to sue the BOAC when the captain, after complaints from passengers said he "could not allow this sort of action on board." The couple later settled down and were "of no further bother," the report notes. No further action was taken, but a BOAC official declined to say whether this implied approval or disapproval of passengers providing their own in-flight entertainment.

travelling in economy – should **not** be in first class' and left him shame-facedly to return to his seat at the back.

Patricia White recalls that en route to Jamaica, two passengers in first class, who had not met before boarding, became extremely friendly en route and disappeared under a blanket. Another passenger complained. It was so embarrassing. The man told her to '**** off' when she tried to serve the meal. After they got off at Montego Bay, the passenger who had complained was bad tempered and accused the crew of stealing her paperback out of her seat pocket. They asked her what it was called. She replied 'The Agony and the Ecstasy'.

Shirley Swinn remembers the desperate attempt for sartorial elegance of certain passengers who flew in the early '60s:

✈     Three Nigerian gentlemen were travelling from Lagos to London, via Rome. Sitting alongside one another, they were dressed in black bowler hats, black jackets and pinstripe trousers, white shirts and black ties. Each had a furled umbrella on which they rested both hands, respectively. They were going to the City of London and they were going to be equal to the city gentlemen. On reaching Rome at approximately 3.30 a.m., all passengers had to disembark while the aircraft was cleaned, catering replenished and refuelling carried out. Passengers were escorted across the tarmac by ground staff, followed by cabin crew. Our three travellers were making their way to the terminal building. Unfortunately, no one had told them that 'city gents' wore socks and shoes. In the light of the airport we saw six black feet with white soles padding across the tarmac.

Joyce Hogge recalls all the crew being impressed by a very charming and polite passenger. 'He was a Nigerian Chief flying from Lagos to London and arrived on board in immaculate white robes and smart headgear. He asked to be woken one hour out of London and emerged from the loo in an immaculate grey suit with a waistcoat, white shirt and gold cufflinks.'

A stowaway was discovered in the freight compartment on a York out of Dakar. A young black boy had walked from Gambia to Dakar to stow away to England. He was very frightened and was only too happy to help in the galley washing up.

'I was put in charge of a 'con artist' being extradited to England from Australia,' said Phillipa Feeney:

✈     He was a very charming man in handcuffs who kept pleading with me to take them off. He tried to break the window with his fists. On a stopover in Calcutta, I took my eyes off him for a moment and he took off across the tarmac. He was caught and returned to the plane. I actually was taken in myself and quite liked him by the end of the flight. I shall never forget the look on his face coming into Heathrow when he saw two 'bobbies' standing at the bottom of the steps waiting for him, and how he thanked me when we said goodbye'.

In the early '70s, BOAC was able to supply anything that a passenger needed, from a needle and cotton to Alka-Seltzer. On one particular flight, a female passenger stopped a stewardess and asked her very quietly if she could bring back two Tampax hidden in a serviette. The man by the window seat then asked if she had something for earache. These two requests were carried out simultaneously. When the stewardess went back to deliver these items one passenger was talking to a steward in the galley and the other was nowhere to be seen and so they were left on the seat. Half an hour later, the steward wandered through the aircraft and to his astonishment saw the male passenger by the window, eyes closed with a blissful expression on his face, with a piece of white cotton hanging out of either ear. He remained that way for the remainder of the sector, oblivious to the smiles around him.

Isobel Proctor remembers a certain lord on a VC10 who went to the loo and took off all his clothes. He stood behind the steward who was serving the salad and soup course until he got to his seat. The chief grabbed a blanket and wrapped it around him and held it there till he sat down. All the other passengers carried on chatting and being terribly polite – as if nothing untoward had happened. He put his clothes back on before the end of the flight.

## *O*H NO!

Many passengers board the aircraft exhausted from the whole hassle of actually getting to the airport and on the plane. This, combined with the length of sectors, has them often nodding off within minutes of boarding. José Langrick was demonstrating the lifejacket on one trip and an old fellow, who had nodded off, woke up with a start to see the steward in the lifejacket. 'My God! What's happening?' he shouted.

The ubiquitous silver tray was the 'must have' accessory of the '50s and '60s. Andy Bennett recalls when an American passenger spilt red wine on the nasty crimplene trousers worn in those days. The steward sponged it off and put the trousers in the oven to dry. He totally forgot them and when the passenger asked for them back on landing they were a pool of plastic at the bottom of the oven. The steward scooped this grey gooey mess onto a silver tray and served it up to the passenger saying, 'Your trousers, sir.' Fortunately the passenger saw the joke and left the aircraft wearing a blanket. He thought it was very funny and said he'd live off that joke for years. The steward did too!

An unfortunate Japanese business gentleman was sitting in the economy cabin and fumbling with his hands under the blanket at crotch level. The CSD said to him, 'You can't do this on my aircraft – you dirty pig!' He pulled the blanket off him and saw the startled passenger was merely changing the film in his camera.

Jean McLaren said that on her first trip on an Argonaut, a passenger reported that a propeller had stopped. She blithely commented that it was quite normal, making vague comments about saving fuel. A few seconds later the chief steward rushed down the back, shouting, 'A duff engine! We're going back to LAP!' It took her quite a time to live that one down.

José Langrick remembers when Richard Nixon came to board the aircraft in Delhi. His car was accompanied by a fire engine because they didn't have a car in Delhi with a fire extinguisher (USA rules). Many of the passengers panicked when they saw a fire engine heading their way.

Mary Crosbie recalls:

✈　　On Constellations we did a Singapore terminator. London-bound passengers from KL had to fly to Singapore before proceeding on to the UK. At KL, I was met by a doctor and briefed about a seriously ill heart patient en route to a London hospital. I sat with her on take off, reassuring her, and I then excused myself and took cold drinks up to the crew only to be met on the flight deck by a dense fog. This, I quickly learned, was due to the undercarriage having retracted but locked in the closed position. The flight engineer then caused a certain amount of panic by taking up a trapdoor in the passenger cabin to try to wind the gear down manually. This was to no avail and we circled round and round the Malaysian rain forests dumping surplus fuel. We finally did a perfect belly landing onto a sea of foam at Singapore. There was great applause for the crew from the passengers. But the worst part for me was keeping them calm during the fuel dumping. My poor lady heart patient not only survived the ordeal but also the subsequent trip to hospital on another plane. Her surgery was successful.

Judy Farquharson Pemble said:

✈    In the late '50s in BEA and early '60s in BOAC many passengers had never been in an aeroplane before or even seen one. This was a time of mass emigration from India, Africa, and the West Indies. Some of the immigrants had never seen a loo. Keeping the loos clean was the stewardesses' job and on these flights it was a nightmare. I was often reduced to putting up an 'Out of Order' sign simply to have a loo the crew could use. Years later, a video was produced to explain the finer points of Western loos, as some nationalities were still finding them quite a puzzle to use. Night flights were the worst. If you were not in the rear galley, the odd male would pee in the ice bucket, finding that this was a far more convenient way of relieving himself!

Sheila Luke says, 'We had immigrants from India and young Greek girls going to Australia, British Army personnel who left the aircraft very untidy and Chinese seamen who left the aircraft so clean that the aircraft could be turned around without using any cleaning staff.'

✈    On a New York-bound trip, we were diverted to Washington together with every other airline in the world, because of heavy snowfalls. We were parked miles away from the terminal, with no power or facilities and inevitably, after several hours, ran out of all food and drink and got colder and colder. So I, together with a couple of passengers, hit on the idea of doing a fashion show on board, as we were carrying a delegation of the Mink Breeder's Federation. We got out all the mink coats and paraded up and down, which kept us warm and the passengers amused. We finally took the passengers to New York by train, stopping and starting mile after mile because of the adverse weather, and still with no food or drink. The entire trip from London to NY took forty-seven and a half hours!

Modern jets with pressurised cabins fly above the weather and it is rare for passengers to be sick. As late as the 1950s, however, they were often sick. Vivien Wass flew on the un-pressurised Viking and cuspidors were very much in evidence.

Sally Tibbits remembers: 'I once threw out an inebriated passenger's false teeth after she had used the cuspidor. She left the aircraft at the next stop, as I did, but reappeared on my next sector and demanded her teeth back.'

Enid Hewitt recalls her worst passenger experience:

Cartoon by Oni Wyatt.

✈     A Syrian gentleman in first class was drinking heavily and complaining all through the meal service. Later, the steward came to me in the galley and said a gentleman was asking for me. When I got into the cabin the man had literally exploded in every direction from every aperture. Needless to say all the rest of the cabin staff had disappeared and left me to clean up the mess.

Judy Farquharson Pemble remembers:

✈     We used to transport bull's sperm in the galley fridge to the States for inseminating cows. On one occasion in a rushed meal service a steward, a little worse for wear, just in the nick of time, narrowly avoided using it on the passengers' puddings thinking it was a cream or a sauce.

The passengers delighted in making up names for the airline, a favourite in the '60s was Bend Over Again Christine or British Oversexed Air Crew.

## Celebrities

Our most travelled passenger in the '60s was one who should really have set up camp on board the 707 – David Frost, now Sir David. He crossed the Atlantic twice weekly for years for his TV programme. The cabin crew saw him constantly surrounded by many pieces of paper, industriously compiling his questions for the interviews ahead. BOAC's most travelled passenger was always polite even when looking tired or stressed. North Atlantic travel at that pace must have been truly exhausting. He was definitely at that time one of the most famous of BOAC's regular transatlantic commuters.

It was generally assumed that the first class passengers could teach us a thing or two. Enid Hewitt remembers Barbara Cartland and her son Ian travelling to Delhi. They both changed into pyjamas and dressing gowns for the night flight. This was to become the fashion on board thirty years later.

One particular first class passenger, who astonished me with his request, was the late Paul Getty. All I knew about him was that he was one of the richest men in the world. Just before coming into land at London he asked me very discreetly for a set of Elizabeth Arden toiletries from the first class lavatory. This was to be a present for his wife. Naturally I complied, but oh! To be *so* mean!

Once, on leaving Rome in the early '50s, Audrey Cartmell saw a very tense and anxious Frank Sinatra join the aircraft. He was in a chronic state of anxiety for being separated from the stunningly beautiful Ava Gardner, who was remaining in Rome with Clark Gable 'and [he] was clearly upset at leaving her with another man'. On board, Audrey also had a distressed small boy, who was leaving his mother to visit his father in South Africa. She sat Sinatra with the little one and suggested that he sang the boy a song, which, surprisingly, he did. He then chatted to him until all his tears were dry.

Judy Black also won't forget Barbara Castle and her entourage on board from JFK to London. She said:

✈     The bell went constantly. 'The Minister would like a cup of tea', or 'The Minister would like a glass of water'. She fascinated me, as she seemed incapable of asking for anything for herself. After take off, the drinks trolley kept jamming, due to all the screwed up paper that her entourage kept throwing on the floor. Before the arrival in London, I asked if they would like to be woken for breakfast. Mrs Castle enquired as to how long before landing would breakfast be served. She was told three quarters of an hour. Mrs Castle replied, 'I shall need at least that to put on my face.' I resisted the obvious reply.

Pat Pearce recalls dropping two little round potatoes into Kenneth McKellar's lap. He was wearing a kilt. She had a silver spoon and fork in her hand and asked, 'Shall I retrieve those potatoes?' He replied, 'Not with that spoon and fork you don't, but you can use your hands.'

Lending an ear to a troubled passenger was a regular part of the job. Lorna Dand held hands with a nervous Queen Soraya of Persia and heard her life story, including her sad divorce from the Shah for failing to produce a son and heir. Katie Smith remembers Veronica Lake, who wanted to talk. Katie listened while she reminisced somewhat sadly about her marriages. 'She told me that she always wondered if she was married for love or because of who she was. It certainly made me think about what she said. I still remember most of it all these years later.'

Lorna Dand: 'Harry Secombe travelled with us to Bermuda. Just as the meal service started, I noticed passengers were smiling. He had taken the 'Reserved for Crew Use Only' sign from the crew seats and pinned it to my back.' Barbara Bearman also recalls Harry Secombe:

✈    He was very friendly, chatty, funny, a real joy, exactly as he came over on the Goons. He had a delightful wife and two very young and well-behaved children with him. They used to holiday in Barbados. He spent a lot of time talking to us in the cabin. The long crossings in the '50s gave us an opportunity to get to know the passengers. He asked if he could visit the flight deck as he wanted to see 'where the crew held their parties'. I am sure the flight deck crew enjoyed his company as much as we did. He drew a cartoon of Eccles on the back of a postcard of the downstairs bar of the Stratocruiser, signed it and gave it to me. I still have it.

Isobel Proctor comments:

✈    Harry Secombe was just fabulous. He was hyperactive and couldn't sit still for a minute. He was in the galley telling funny stories and having coffees with everyone. He does that Goon laugh naturally. Everybody loved him. His wife would say, 'Harry, for heaven's sake, sit down' every time he ventured into first class and his kids kept saying, 'Oh Dad' in that voice that teenagers use. They were all sweet.

Virginia Sheehy carried the late Ava Gardner, who was flying with her current boyfriend at that time, the world's greatest bullfighter Luis Miguel Dominguin. She was in first class and he was in economy. She joined him there, on three seats covered with a blanket, for the rest of the trip.

Being a superstar doesn't make you less nervous. When Rudolf Nureyev was a passenger, Sue Brown said that during a technical delay, he insisted on standing near the undercarriage to see what was happening. Rudi was also an amorous fellow, although in this instance it was Margot Fonteyn who initiated the affection, and a blanket was thrown over them. However, he had had four 'wodka' martinis.

Sue Brown recalls:

✈    During a trip to New York, we were told that we would bring a charter flight to London with the Beatles and the film crew from *A Hard Day's Night*. I was given money to have my hair done because of the Press coverage. There were thousands of fans at JFK airport, although the flight was in transit from the Bahamas and they didn't see much. The Beatles in flight were dressed in black and very chatty. Most of the crew had purchased LPs in New York to be signed on board. They were all very obliging, signing three records and a souvenir in-flight menu for me. Other passengers included Eleanor Bron and Roy Kinnear. Everyone was in a party mood. I had the opportunity to talk at length to George Harrison in the first class galley and bar area. He mentioned how difficult life had become for them because of the enormous crowds everywhere they went.

Sue remembers Beatle Paul McCartney saying how he liked to see the reassuring words Rolls-Royce on the 707 engines.

Andy Bennett's memory of the Rolling Stones was that they read comics, but her favourite pop passenger was George Melly: 'He swanned on board wearing a cloak and black hat and sat right at the back of the economy cabin saying, 'If you, darling girl, could just supply me with a bucket of ice, we won't trouble you all flight.' He then proceeded to put a bottle of champagne in it, and eat smoked salmon sandwiches he'd brought with him. He was a pussy cat!'

Caroline Chambers carried the Rolling Stones. 'They were dirty, ill mannered and foul mouthed. We put them at the back of the aircraft out of the way of the passengers.' They left a different impression with Oni Wyatt: 'Among many famous people I have looked after, I do remember being surprised at what an interesting, attractive and normal chap Mick Jagger was in the '60s. As he was on his own, in first class, he spent most of the flight chatting away with one of the stewards, who, like Mick, was crazy about cricket.'

'The best flight I ever did was to LA,' says Isobel Proctor.

✈    Part of the cast of *Frasier* were in first class, as well as Dickie Attenborough and a German woman who was supposedly his business partner. There were film directors and one called Bill Mechanic years later won an Oscar for Best Film. Jane Leeves who is Daphne in *Frasier* was there with her fiancé, who was one of the producers. After take off all the film luvvies were chatting together and it was just like a party. Dickie Attenborough is absolutely adorable. He called everyone darling, including the captain who came down to chat, and everybody loved him. He must have an iron fist in the velvet glove though because he is a very sharp businessman. They hardly sat down at all except to eat. It was great.

Oni Wyatt was amazed that during the catering strike, Paul and Linda McCartney, both vegetarians, were travelling first class. 'They were very organised and came on with their own deli bags.' They were so particular that they asked for their own bags back!

Pamela Banfill carried many VIPs in her time with BEA including a very formal and quiet Gregory Peck, an exceptionally perky David Niven, an unsmiling Gary Cooper, and a very cross Elizabeth Taylor, whose hairdresser accidentally sprayed hairspray into those beautiful violet eyes and she reacted in true Taylor style. A favourite passenger was Sir Winston Churchill and 'although very elderly, I remember him pulling himself up at the aircraft door to give his famous V sign to the crowd'. Sir Winston was the only passenger permitted to smoke cigars and we always carried a special ashtray for him.

Sue Thomas also recalls flying with Dirk Bogarde, 'He had his cigarettes initialled and some of the guys tried to get one or even just a fag end.'

Irene Tait's favourite passenger was Sir Cliff Richard: 'I had been a big fan of Sir Cliff for years and I was so excited that he was on my flight. We chatted for ages. I met him a few months later at the 'Talk of the Town' and I was very touched that he remembered me.'

Isobel Proctor recounts:

✈    I have seen the soles of Prince Philip's shoes as he had his feet up on the seat in front of him. On being asked if the Queen wished to visit the flight deck, he was reputed to have said, 'Good Lord no. She's only interested if it farts and eats hay.' The Skipper was amazed.

We carried Princess Di when she bolted off to Washington around Christmas time just after the break up. She was very beautiful. She was on her own, kept her head down, didn't eat anything and never said a word. She looked terribly upset and dashed off the aircraft when we got there.

I have carried Sarah Ferguson quite a few times. She has had some terrible press, but is the nicest and kindest person. She looked after her babies herself for most of the time and always put her own bag in the hat rack. She seemed a generally good all-round person. Her two children were also absolutely charming and well behaved. All the staff in all the airports we visited liked and respected her as well.

Liz Hurley was as thin as a stick. She was waiting for the loo just out of sight, and the galley steward said, 'Cor – Liz Hurley. If she would put on a stone then I would really give her one.' His face was a complete picture when she stuck her head round the galley. He nearly died. I had a lot of trouble persuading him into the cabin after that. However, she was lovely and just laughed.

Isobel was on the flight taking Mohamed Ali from LA to London on a DC10:

✈   He was with his brother who was dressed by Mr T. Mohamed Ali was terrified of flying and we had a bomb scare. The passengers had to go to the lounge while officials did the search. There were about forty kids all going back to school, and he chatted with them the whole time – gave his autograph, and was generally a great bloke.

When I think of memorable passengers that I carried in my early days of flying in the late '60s, I remember a very quiet and reserved passenger on a flight from New York to London, sitting in 1A. After we had bedded all the passengers down at the end of a long first class meal, he was the only passenger who couldn't seem to settle. He just gazed out of the window. I kept gently offering him drinks and tea, but he didn't seem to want anything. The night wore on, and he came into the galley in first class and said, 'I can never seem to sleep on aircraft. Do you think I could go up to the flight deck?' I asked the captain, who said that he could come up in five minutes. I then realised that I had forgotten to ask his name. I tried not to look surprised when he gave me his name. I then went back to the flight deck and told the captain that his visitor was Neil Armstrong. He raised his eyebrows and the senior first officer said, '*The* Neil Armstrong?' I said 'Yes!' He then spent several hours on the flight deck talking to the crew, drinking numerous cups of tea, and he also stayed there for the landing. After touch down, he returned to his seat and I asked him if he enjoyed his visit to the flight deck. 'Very much so,' he replied. 'It is strange. I was looking at the moon and I couldn't believe I had stepped on it.'

Delia Green operated a charter flight on a Britannia 102 with Prince Rainier, Princess Grace and Aristotle Onassis. Princess Grace was suffering from a heavy cold. The two men were trying to repair a portable record player, and Mr Onassis asked for a screwdriver. I gave a Screwdriver cocktail to Mr Onassis who asked what it was. They burst into laughter, as he had actually wanted a screwdriver to do some repairs. He had not heard of the cocktail.

In those glamorous days of the '50s it seemed the wardrobe was stuffed with mink and sable. Wyn Behenna remembers trying on Lady Docker's mink coat 'and she caught me at it'. Barbara Riordan tells a similar story of eyeing up Vivien Leigh's fur coat. While all the passengers were asleep and, with a bit of urging from the steward, she put it on. At that precise moment Lady Olivier (Vivien Leigh) put her head around the curtain to ask for a cup of tea. Barbara immediately apologised but she responded, 'It looks much better on you than it does on me, dear.'

June Blackler's greatest passenger memory was when 'Douglas Bader, the legless war hero, once flew us back across the Atlantic.'

Judy Black has fond recollections of Yehudi Menuhin:

✈   He sat in a yoga position all the way from London to JFK, probably ahead of his time re DVT. Alma Cogan, in the economy cabin, came on in a full-length mink coat and asked for it to be taken and put in the first class, which we did as she was so charming.

Diana Beresford Davis flew with Alfred Hitchcock on a flight back from Nassau:

Jeannie Lardner and Lady Olivier (Vivien Leigh).

Heather Woodcock and fellow stewardesses with a '50s film icon, Jack Hawkins.

✈ We were not particularly full, so I was able to go and sit with him and have a chat. He was wonderful, so easy to talk to and promptly gave me his autograph with a drawing of a little fat man with his name underneath. He said that once the filming had started he felt his job was done. As you know, he was always in his own films, somewhere, in the crowd or passing by, but you would really have to look. I have always felt that the bigger the star, the nicer they were.

Stephanie Parlane-Moore remembers a certain American movie star famous for his sunglasses rolling joints upstairs on the Jumbo, flying Tokyo to Anchorage where he was promoting his latest film. The captain appeared from the flight deck and oblivious to the smell of marijuana muttered, 'Roll your own, do you?' The crew was amused by the captain's naivity - or was it tact?

However, famous passengers do not always live up to our expectations. Jill Edmonds recalls:

✈ Gina Lollobrigida was just as beautiful as in her films, but very proud and a great disappointment because we didn't get a smile from her all trip. I haven't enjoyed one of her films since.

Sir Alec Douglas Hume, who was not even then the Prime Minister, could hardly open his aristocratic lips wide enough to acknowledge our existence or even say 'Thank you'.

Omar Sharif was different. We were all goggle-eyed as we saw him board the aircraft, but were very surprised to see him seated in the tourist cabin, whilst Jack Hawkins was seated in first class. He was on his way to the Middle East to begin shooting Lawrence of Arabia. I believe little was known of him in the West at that time. He was already a great hero in Egyptian films, but I believe this was his first English language film. We were all so impressed with his good looks and his extremely polite and unassuming manner.

Isobel Proctor remembers some very special passengers:

✈     We were taken out to the aircraft, which wasn't in the normal place, and told that Princess Margaret was to be on board – in economy – flying to Barbados. She got on with Colin Tennant and a couple of detectives. Norman Adams, the chief, brought down a couple of first class glasses for the Royal G&Ts. She was very pleasant in a distant sort of way. She had beautiful skin and eyes, and wore her cardigan upside down with the bottom button done up round her shoulders. Rather an odd fashion statement! Just before landing Colin Tennant dived into the back galley, stripped down to his underpants and changed into a very natty pair of white trousers, a see-through shirt and a light-coloured fedora hat. The whole ensemble was set off by a walking stick made out of the backbone of a shark. He refused point blank to sit down and crease his trousers. When we landed he was straight out onto the steps waving to his admirers. Princess Margaret stayed inside the cabin until Anthony AJ minced on board and she shot off with him. They were all quite friendly.

BOAC also carried imaginary passengers. Above the first class galley door on a certain 707 in the '60s, always on the London to New York sector, American first class passengers were amused by the caption 'We gave Kilroy a lift'.

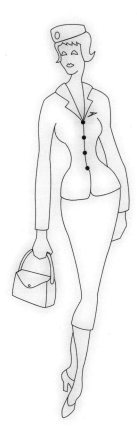

# CHAPTER 8

# The Magical Years of the Surging Seventies

American photographer Doug Wilson cleverly 'captured the outstanding impression created by the roll out of the Boeing 747. Centre is Carole Hardy and on either side are stewardesses from El Al and Air Lingus in the 9ft intake of the massive Pratt & Whitney engine.' This photograph would put any feminist in deconstruction heaven with the image of Carole Hardy and the two other stewardesses in the nacelle of, at that time, the world's largest airliner. From a semiotic point of view this famous photograph can lead to a lot of animated discussion.

The occasion was Everett in Washington State, a memorable day when 'the big beautiful world of the 747' came into being. It was the launching ceremony for the world's largest airliner in 1968. Two things need to be said about the 747 on that first day after the roll out: first was its height, and secondly it looked a very beautiful aeroplane.

BOAC's Carol Hardy of the 707 flight was the ambassadress for the airline. The 707s and VC10s were now called 'mini's'.

So the '70s saw the entry of the Boeing 747; the jumbo jet carried twice as many passengers as any previous aircraft. It was a huge leap in size for both passengers and crew. The tip of its tail was as high off the ground as a six-storey building; a tennis court could be accommodated easily on each wing. On 17 December 1903, Orville Wright made the world's first powered heavier-than-air flight, covering a distance of 120ft. Their whole flight was 90ft less than the length of the first 747!

Suddenly for passengers here was an affordable aircraft. People who had never flown before now had the opportunity. In April 1971 BOAC operated its first commercial Boeing 747 flight between Heathrow and New York. By the late '70s, mass travel had begun. Never in the history of civil aviation had there been such sweeping changes which saw a huge growth in business and tourist travel.

Cambrian Airways, started in 1935, disappeared along with Northeast, BEA and BOAC when it became part of British Airways in 1976. Two years earlier, in the March, BOAC and BEA had combined.

Everything on the 747 was done on a much larger scale. Bigger trolleys, larger galleys (wheeled on and off in one unit), more lavatories, ten passengers across in the cabin. I remember the first jumbo I worked on in the early '70s. When I looked down the cabin I couldn't see the end!

First class gradually declined. Out went elaborate seven-course gold trolley silver service where the roast was carved in front of the passengers. Under security precautions by this time the carving sets were banned on board and in came in-flight entertainment (initially film and music) and now we have the personal self-selection, multi-channel units with computer games, telephones, shopping channels, the list will continue to go on. Seats turned into beds once more and the wealthy could sleep instead of eating and drinking their way round the world.

Crew life changed forever with the new aircraft. There were now fifteen or more cabin crew and four flight deck crew. And now the term stewardess was out for good. Males and females were simply known as cabin crew or flight attendants. The larger crews found they could no longer do things together: the social life of the past became history. The almost compulsory room parties on arrival grew less frequent. This huge aircraft was divided into four sections and crew worked and stayed in their own area. Consequently with such a vast number of cabin crew one very rarely saw crew from previous trips. The camaraderie, so enjoyed by crews for over forty years and so much part of their way of life, faded away.

There was also a change in the image of the stewardess. Hair and uniform regulations were not quite as strict as in the '60s when Victoria Radcliffe described herself: 'pale blue eye shadow, pale pink lipstick, pearl pink nail varnish and pearl earrings. Hair tied up in a bun underneath navy hat and navy tights.' At least now there was less emphasis on everyone having the short off-the-collar bob hairstyle.

There was less time off with the advent of the 'big ones'. Changed also was the drinking and partying culture. It was well and truly frowned upon. With bigger crews the disparity in age meant that age groups would like to do different things and so there were splinter groups. Nowadays the younger ones like to go clubbing – so they are usually out for the count during the day.

Although the grand old trolley days were coming to an end in the first class, there was still the preparation of salads and the cooking of joints of meat, especially trying to get the beef cooked to the passengers' wishes (i.e. rare or well done), boiling eggs at altitude for breakfast, making the scrambled eggs in ovens. As Angela Froude also mentions in the Queen's Silver Jubilee Year, 'We served an Elizabethan menu and served posset from a teapot. This did cause some confusion and a lot of explanation!'

The '70s introduced the jumbo and the era of the package holiday. It is said by crews at that time that sophisticated passengers like diplomats, businessmen and movie stars (who were often in the economy cabin) were replaced by families, huge groups and lager louts. Passengers seemed to drink a lot more, dressed more casually and were far ruder.

Divisions in the cabin gave passengers more choice: there was Super Club, Business Class, World Traveller, Club Class, First Class and for a time Elizabethan Class. Originally the upper deck at the sharp end was a lounge; initially these were smoking zones and only popular with crews who smoked – non-smoking crews shunned them – but then these gave way to be filled with even more seats.

This was the era of the 'retreads', not an endearing term for the stewardesses who had left the airline, because of marriage, the ten-year contract or to try another career, and were now able to be reemployed. The correct term for these returning stewardesses was 'support cabin crew'. For those who flew 'second time around' as support cabin crew and were amongst the original batches, there was a lot of publicity as they were single mothers or divorced. This was just before married couples, and common law partners, would be able to fly and work together. Heather Bradley and Lorna Payne used to bid for the same flights and take their young children along at each half-term holiday. 'Next day at the Sheraton in Dubai, said Heather: 'we would locate the returning London crew where the children's rooms were, in case on our shuttles to Karachi or Bombay which we did at night and if we were stuck there … the children knew to go home with another crew. Our children had a wonderful time with super crews, who, as well as the hotel, spoilt them to bits. It was a charmed life.'

## BOEING 747

The Captain's view: Gerry Holland (former BA747 Captain, Rtd 1981)

Our first jumbo arriving at LHR, Boeing 747–136.

I grew up in the Second World War admiring the huge Lancaster and B17 bombers of the time, fervently wishing that one day I could fly something that big.

Some thirty years later, sitting up in the front seat of a 'jumbo' and looking the 35-odd-foot drop from the cockpit to the ground I had 'arrived' – I tingled all over!

Although this aeroplane had many brand new technical advances, the 747 of the mid-'70s (known today as the 'classics') was a different bird from the new 747-400 series of the mid-'90s. We sported a flight-deck crew of three (two pilots and a flight engineer); well over two-thirds of our landings were done 'by hand' and the many electronic goodies available to the two-pilot crew of today were simply not around. Nevertheless, the Boeing 747 was – and is – to me a remarkable aircraft; the very idea of such a large machine to be used commercially and make a healthy profit for its operators was in itself daring and innovative. The 747 genre will go on until at least the 2030s, with an unrivalled sixty-year dynasty which will be hard to follow.

On flying it, one develops a 'size awareness' of the aircraft's 200ft span and length making it surprisingly easy to operate. On the ground, the 360 tonnes are easily manoeuvrable with one hand on a 'tiller' utilizing steering with the main landing-gear as well as the nose-wheel.

Once in the air it is light on the controls and can be flown with one hand – the pilot flying the aircraft needs the other hand to control the power of the four huge engines. Because it's so big, it has no problem staying in whatever flight condition you put it – Newton's immutable law of 'it'll go where it's going' was never truer! It is also, incidentally, one of the fastest airliners in the sky today, useful if Air Traffic Control wants to nudge you up a bit!

The cockpit is big and comfortable and outside visibility is good, as befits one of today's largest commercial aircraft.

Safety-wise it can sustain flight with only two of its four engines operating and has four independent systems for just about everything – it can, and has, sustained incredible damage and still kept flying.

To me the 747 is one of the first genuine liners of the sky, on a par with the *QE2* and *Canberra*. Amazingly, it can take over three times the number of passengers and baggage to and from New York and the UK than the ten-day round trip taken by a large passenger liner! And all this utilising less than 100 crew members.

One of the most impressive things I have found on the 747 technical course was that, whereas on other aircraft before this one, one of the dreariest tasks was to learn by rote the capacities of the fuel tanks. The answer for the Boeing 747 was simply, 'Enough!' And in the ten years of flying the thing, I found they were right!

## ENTEBBE

Celia Penney remembers when Idi Amin, the head of Uganda's army, staged a coup in 1971 and seized power from President Milton Obote while he was away at a Commonwealth Conference in Singapore. She said:

✈ Nobody could then have foreseen the carnage that Sandhurst-trained Amin was to unleash on his country.

We had flown into Uganda and were staying in the Apollo Hotel in Kampala. I was really tired, having been called out on standby the night before, and gone to bed.

I was woken from a deep sleep by what I thought were very loud fireworks. I could hear loud explosions and the spit of fire crackers and assumed locals were enjoying a noisy firework display. I looked out of my hotel window, expecting to see the night sky lit up by a dazzling display. Instead I saw jeeps surrounding the hotel, troops running around with weapons, and explosives, not fireworks, lighting up the sky. I phoned the hotel operator and asked her if we were in the middle of a war and she put me through to reception and I was told that we were in the middle of a coup.

Deciding that it really was not my problem, and still very tired, I fell back into a deep and untroubled sleep to be woken again by the frantic ringing of the phone. On the other end was an equally frantic captain, who told me that in coups, one of the first things they did was to rape the stewardesses. He said I had to go to his room.

Being only in my twenties, I felt totally invincible. I ignored the captain's offer of protection and decided to go back to sleep. Half an hour later, there was a hammering on my door and a very angry captain demanded that I went to his room.

I arrived there to find the whole crew assembled with a siege mentality. They had put mattresses against the balcony walls, but had left spy holes, so that they could view the battle in style, drinking the obligatory G&Ts. The noise outside was deafening. Windows were being shattered and it seemed as though they were targeting our hotel. Around 5 a.m. there was an enormous explosion in the grounds, which rocked the hotel. We were quite a few floors up, so thinking we were going to be blown into the sky we scuttled down to the lobby, scared out of our wits.

Chaos reigned for a few hours. The large explosion had been the police commissioner's house being blown up. Looking back, I can only assume the whole family had been killed. Most of the hotel staff had fled. They were a different tribe from Amin's lot and obviously knew what was in store for them.

Somehow, our captain was in communication with the BA staff, in downtown Kampala. We were advised to go back to our rooms. The hotel was surrounded and more troops were marching from Entebbe to Kampala – a distance of about thirty miles. The runway at Entebbe Airport had been blown up. The troops had then broken into the bonded stores and got extremely drunk. They had fired at and killed some unfortunate passengers stranded at the airport and had then gone on the rampage in the hotel at Entebbe, where other crews were staying. They had attacked the crew and staff and some of the Sabena stewardesses were also hurt. We were told they had been raped, so our captain had been correct. And they were coming our way!

I waited in my room for quite a few hours. I can't remember feeling afraid. Suddenly, there was a loud knocking at my door and some very smelly and angry troops stormed in. They were hungry, having just marched thirty miles, and fortunately too exhausted to rape, but not too tired to pillage! They asked for money and jewellery, which I gave them without a fight. They also searched my room. The manager of the hotel had been hiding one of Obote's cabinet ministers. He had been discovered and had been shot.

During the next few days, I can remember Amin's jubilant tribes coming in from the bush and wandering through our hotel, saying, 'Big House!' Idi Amin came in for a swim. The troops and tribes were storming the town and we were advised to stay in the hotel. Because the hotel was called The Apollo (Obote's second name) every window bearing the name of the hotel was smashed, as were the outside signs.

The bar staff had fled. I can't remember how we ate but I can remember how we drank! We had a kitty at night for the drinks and just helped ourselves, giving the money to someone. We used to drink with some American tourists, who were also stranded like ourselves, as the runway at Entebbe was unusable. They asked us what we were collecting for and one of our more cheeky stewards said that we were collecting for the Bantu orphans. Obote belonged to the Bantu tribe and they were now being killed. The steward was just joking, but the Americans took him seriously. We were unaware that he had told them this until after the Americans had left, and now we understood why our kitty grew and grew!

After a few days, the tourists escaped by going overland to Nairobi in the middle of the night. They hugged and thanked us for keeping up their morale and seemed to think that they were leaving us to a terrible fate. After their departure, our kitty diminished, and we had to pay for our own drinks. We suddenly realised who had been our benefactors.

Eventually we were smuggled out at 3 a.m. and, like the tourists, went overland to Nairobi. We arrived at Heathrow where waiting newspaper reporters interviewed us. A few weeks later, I was embarrassed to receive a letter of thanks from BA. The American tourists had written to them and their letter had been published in the British Airways News. They praised us for keeping up their spirits and also for our compassion and generosity in collecting for the Bantu orphans. We never did confess.

Andy Bennett remembers that when she landed in Uganda, Amin had just taken over:

✈    6ft 6ins black guys with no IDs and machine guns just swept on to the aircraft. Idi Amin had seized power and expelled thousands of resident Indians. Entebbe soon ceased to be a crew change and all flights to Uganda were terminated. The country's economy was in tatters.

As Oni Wyatt says:

✈    My memory of the takeover was bizarre. We knew that Uganda's regime was brutal and all the flights were overbooked by foreigners desperate to get out. The airport swarmed with frightened and angry people fleeing the country. Our stopover – normally a delightful place – had been scary, with troops on the streets. We were relieved to be back on our plane and to be closing the doors for London. A young Asian duty officer was supervising the last of the paperwork on the steps when suddenly there was a scuffle.

'What's going on?' said the chief steward in alarm. Our BOAC-uniformed duty officer was pushed through the aircraft door into the cabin by two heavies in army uniform. 'They have taken my watch and chain! They have taken my house! All my papers,' gasped the duty officer. 'They will attack me again if we stay here any longer! Please take me with you!' He was in tears. 'We don't want you! Get out!' shouted the army guys. The first officer was watching with growing alarm from the flight deck door. We had been expecting trouble but this was the last thing we had expected. The captain said, 'We go!' The door was slammed, and we found a seat for our poor evacuee.

On the flight back we learned the full story. One minute he had been supervising the passengers. Next he was a hunted man. Luckily he was single. All he had was the uniform he stood up in. 'Surely BOAC will give you a job in London?' I asked. He told us that he had been born and recruited in Uganda. So he would have to apply again for a job if he was allowed to stay in the UK. The last we saw of him was him being led away by immigration, since he had no passport and was a sort of stowaway. Of course this was the start of so many tales of political refugees like this. But it was a highly dramatic moment for a flight, before the days of security had really made us think in a totally different way. Now we would, sadly, have had to probably leave the man to his fate. So ended for many years any more flights to Kampala.

## Retreads

### By Wendy Field

With the introduction of the big jets and at that time having a very young female workforce there was the opportunity to go back. I was actually out of the airline business for ten years and had very little idea of how things had changed. I was terribly nervous on the first day of training, now only six weeks long. I was certainly the oldest at nearly forty. I had no idea that with the equality of the sexes, girls now took an equal part on the aircraft, running galleys, bars and duty free trolleys and, of course, girls could now become pursers and cabin service directors. We were always referred to as 'retreads' but we could also work our way up to purser and beyond. The training was pretty much the same as yesteryear, and before long we were all kitted out, had the official photograph taken en masse and were assigned to our 747 fleets.

On one of my first trips, I had just signed in and was walking up the stairs, when I walked into a steward I had known in the past. 'Hello Wend, haven't seen you for a bit. Have you been on holiday?' It was as though I had never gone. Except that now I was running a bar trolley in the back end of a 747! Believe me, that was a huge shock! Off we went again to the lovely destinations not, however, with the long stopovers.

Now the old system of rostering stewardess as A, B or C was finished. Everything ran on seniority. The crew of up to fifteen arrived at the briefing room and the jobs on board were bid for on seniority. Wendy said:

As the junior I would get the last choice, usually the back end bar, meaning that quarter of the economy cabin was my domain for drinks, duty free and all the meal service. I was considerably slower than my younger workmates and it was very hard work. I was not sure I liked this way of life this time around, although everyone was very nice and helpful to me – never any nastiness at one being older. Later I went onto the TriStar fleet. The TriStar had an underfloor galley and I loved running that. You were in charge of your own little world, running it the best way you saw fit.

TriStars did many Eastern trips and so gained the expression 'no jackets required'. Destinations were Khartoum, Dacca, Cairo, Bangladesh – all the hot places. It was a small fleet and just 'one big mad party'. The TriStars took the place of the VC10s in the late '70s, so another 'mini' like the 707 was phased out.

Debbie Speller, another retread, began flying when she was twenty and rejoined at thirty-five. She recalls: 'It was very difficult and I felt like a middle-aged mother in uniform.'

In 1972 BOAC recruited 300 crew and there were only about 2,000 cabin crew at that time. When the 747s started in service, many were of the opinion that they had to lower their standards, and the Equal Opportunity Act which came in the mid-'70s then meant that the old contract could be torn up. Stewardesses did not have to leave after ten years. The Equal Opportunity Act also meant the 'height/weight requirement could not be imposed' and allowed partners to travel and work together on the same aircraft. As a result more gays and lesbians within the organisation 'came out' with the new legislation.

The uniform worn since the swinging sixties had to go. The Hardy Amies uniform originally issued to BEA staff, which was well underway before the amalgamation of BOAC and BEA, became the uniform up until 1979. It was then the turn of Baccarat Weatheral to design the first uniform for British Airways. Roz Hanby (on the back cover) is wearing the navy felt hat with a brim and leather hat band with the smart red trim.

## 12 September 1970

VC10 G-ASGN hijacking to Dawsons's Field, Jordan.

The '70s saw the beginning of hijacking and terrorism with aircraft and passengers being used as hostages. One day a BOAC VC10, a TWA 707 and a Swissair DC-8 were all hijacked. The perpetrators were called The Popular Front for the Liberation of Palestine (PFLP). The three aircraft were taken to Dawson's Field, an abandoned wartime RAF airfield near Amman in Jordan. They were blown up on 12 September. This day was known as 'Black September'. The following extract is from Archie Jackson's *Can Anyone See Bermuda?*:

> BOAC flights through the Middle East were flown by VC10s. In September the terrorists hijacked a VC10, a TWA 707 and a Swissair DC-8, forced their pilots to fly to a landing ground in Jordan, and waited long enough for the television reporters to arrive on the scene, then released the passengers and blew up the aircraft. Captain Cyril Goulborn and his crew were held captive in a part of Amman controlled by the Palestinians. The stewardesses on this flight were Francis Duck, Mandy Thomas and Nirmala Subba. When King Hussein was no longer prepared to tolerate the existence of an armed force within his kingdom, independent of his own rule, he sent his troops to quell them. The captors fled as the soldiers approached. A British major, also held captive with the crew, suggested hanging

something white from a window so that the soldiers did not throw a grenade into the building where the crew were held prisoners and several weeks of captivity were ended. 'I remember being told later on a different flight by one of the stewards involved that he and the co-pilot had been ordered to dig their own graves'.

In Christopher Dobson and Ronald Paynes' book *The Carlos Complex*, it is clear that the BOAC aircraft was hijacked to secure the release of Leila Khaled, who 'was captured and handed over – reluctantly, because the Israelis wanted to take her back to Tel Aviv to the British authorities.' Her capture was the result of a mid-air gun battle on board an El Al Boeing 707 over the Thames Estuary on 6 September. Dobson and Payne continue:

> There they (the PFLP) remained with 425 hostages sweltering under a merciless sun until eventually the Governments concerned – except Israel – agreed to the PFLP's demands. Leila Khaled and a number of other imprisoned terrorists were released and all except forty of the hostages were set free. The unlucky forty were imprisoned in a refugee camp while the airliners were blown up.

Another hijacking involving a VC10 happened during a transit stop at Dubai:

> The aircraft was rushed by hijackers who made their intentions clear by shooting and wounding a receptionist and loader. Some passengers had left the aircraft and were shopping in the duty free shop while others remained on board. Captain Jim Ritcher was in the duty room checking his flight plan for the next sector. When the hijackers realised that they did not have the captain as a hostage they said that they would kill passengers if he did not come forward. Although urged by the airport's security officer to keep out of sight, the captain refused and promptly walked out to his aircraft. Mounting the steps to the VC10, he was confronted by a hijacker holding a pistol to the head of a young New Zealander. The crew were ordered to fly to Tunis. The hijackers demanded the release of some of their supporters held in gaols in Cairo and The Hague. But before the Egyptian authorities agreed to release and send prisoners to Tunis, the hijackers shot a passenger and threw his body out of the aircraft. A girl became hysterical and, losing his temper for the first and only time, Captain Ritcher shouted at the terrorist leader to allow the women and children to leave the aircraft. To his surprise he agreed, and the nightmare finally ended when the Dutch government sent their detainees to Tunis and the prisoners of the Egyptians arrived from Cairo.

A third VC10 was hijacked over the Mediterranean when two armed men burst into the cockpit. The co-pilot, 'Bunny' Warren, was at the controls, the captain being on the point of visiting the passenger cabin. A grenade was held at Bunny's throat and he recalls that glancing down he could make out the words 'Made in Czechoslovakia' embossed on the metal. The hijackers took the captain into the passenger cabin and ordered the co-pilot to fly to Amsterdam. After landing, all the passengers were allowed to escape using the emergency chutes while the hijackers set the VC10 ablaze, hurling passengers' bottles of duty-free spirits into the fire.

Although the 747 was stealing the limelight, there were still incidents and adventures occurring in other parts of the world. Security was paramount and safety briefs were given before the crew boarded, by the cabin service director. The crews were then literally sealed off for security (with a tape across the door of the transport) and driven to the aircraft, forty-five minutes before take off. Crews didn't feel that they had the 'freedom' as they knew in the previous aircraft. One didn't go to the first class without a very good reason; besides there was a telephone that could do the leg work for you. Economy crews were not encouraged to go to the sharp end for a chat and a drink.

What was new and a tremendous boon to stewardesses and stewards was the designated rest area. At long last the days of sleeping in a hat rack, on the floor behind the last row of seats, on a cold steel food box or the jump seat resting your head against a freezing door, were over.

Andy Bennett began her flying career in the early '70s and flew for twenty-six years. She was one of those well-rounded personalities, very slim, with legs that went on forever, and is a Trustee for the Dhaka Orphanage. She contributed articles to the cabin crew magazine *Contact* about her affection for India and the Himalayas, and became known as 'Sherpa Bennett' as the Himalayas were her favourite spot. Andy managed to avoid flying the 747s for many years: 'too big and too isolated. I got used to being able to pop up and see the flight deck and I loved sitting on the flight deck for take off ... never got over that feeling of exhilaration at "Vee 1".'

Her first thoughts on joining were: 'the freedom, glamour, and gorgeous-looking men – especially the gays! I felt privileged to stay at five-star hotels and rest houses, seeing places no ordinary person went to: Khartoum, Fiji, Darasalaam, Kilimanjaro, Abu Dhabi, Muscat, Peru, Hong Kong, and Bombay ... the laughter, the fun and the champagne!'

The meal service would never be the same again. It was the era of the microwave oven and this revolutionised the heating of meals. There was great excitement when the microwave ovens were introduced. Sarah Forsyth says: 'We were afraid that if we stood in front of them, when they were on, that we might be sterilised.' The first class now offered a choice of seven main meals from the freeze box and the microwave would do the rest.

Gloria Morrison: 'Different themed menus were introduced – new Polar Route menu featuring reindeer meat and Elizabethan service featuring honeymoon meals' and she recalls a meal service best summed up as 'an octopus on roller skates shaped like Racquel Welch in her heyday!' This was before the huge trolleys!

Pat Pearce also discusses how:

✈ Today's aircraft, with the huge economy classes, meant we had lost quite a lot of the individual service just by the sheer numbers and the long flights we now do and the requirement for the crew – rest. We used to carve joints of meat in front of the passengers in the first class then with the 747s and the arrival of microwave ovens in the first class today it is like TV dinners!

She continues: 'In the '70s, the era of the 747, there was an increased use of trolleys in the economy cabin. No longer the silver tray for drinks. We had to have larger equipment for larger aircraft and plastic glasses replaced the glass ones in economy.'

What had not changed was the popularity of a career as a stewardess. Celia Penney recalls, 'it was very competitive then. There were fewer exciting jobs for well-educated women. At the interview I was told I probably would not get the job as it was so popular. Asked what I would do if they turned me down, I replied that I would go to Australia as there was no other airline worth working for (creep)!'

Pat Pearce had a long and fulfilling career in BOAC and then British Airways. She joined in 1965 and resigned in 2004 having flown on nine different aircraft from DC3s to 747 and 777s. However, she will never forget the two months she spent on the Royal Flight at the beginning of 1974. She said:

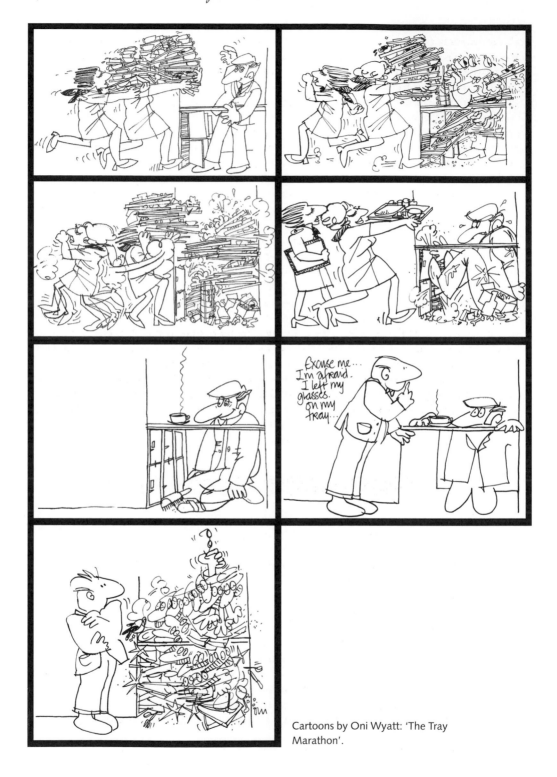

Cartoons by Oni Wyatt: 'The Tray Marathon'.

I can remember standing on the tarmac in Honolulu as the Queen's VC10 taxied towards us with the Royal Standard flying. We all felt really proud as we stood to attention. During our two months we took the Queen from Honolulu to Raratonga, from Singapore to Dubai, from Dubai back to Singapore and finally from Djakarta to Singapore.

The aircraft had been completely refitted inside. There was a small conference area, a sitting room and dining area and five bedrooms, for the Queen, Prince Phillip, Princess Anne and her then husband (Mark Phillips), and for the late Lord Mountbatten. There were dressing rooms with tables and full-length mirrors. The rest of the aircraft had first class seats fitted for the entourage. The galleys and toilets had all been carpeted. The special galley equipment included an electric frying pan and cut glass decanters. The Queen is extremely easy to please and eats quite simply. She carries her own bottled water with her.

When we arrived in Raratonga the Royal Party were carried away from the aircraft on platforms lifted by local people all wearing banana leaf skirts. As we stood on the aircraft steps after she had left it was quite exciting to see as she was being carried towards the thousands of cheering people. That night we were invited to an evening event which involved Princess Anne opening a new school and banquet.

The next day the Queen left on an Air New Zealand aircraft to fly to Christchurch. We followed with the rest of her entourage.

For me it was a doubly exciting trip as Gordon Franklin was one of the Queen's entourage and I had known him since my Youth Club days. On our very last evening in Djakarta, Gordon had invited me and the rest of the crew to go on board the Royal Yacht *Britannia*. What great excitement that was. The three of us girls were in long dresses and felt so exhilarated as we went up the gangplank. We were given a guided tour of most of the ship and were surprised how small it really was. The dining room was quite a lot smaller than we had all imagined it to be. The engine room was absolutely spotless. I have to say that those two months were the most exciting part of my thirty-nine-year flying career.

## Dreamflight

What is Dreamflight? Patricia Pearce, MBE explains:

> The original idea of Dreamflight was to do one trip to prove that it could be done. The first was in 1987 and we have completed one a year ever since. Our aim is to give incurably ill, sick and disabled children their holiday of a lifetime visiting the Theme Parks in Orlando, Florida. It is an action-packed ten days and we do not take parents with us. An army of volunteers, including fourteen doctors, fifty nurses and thirteen physiotherapists and other non-medical helpers to look after the children, who usually total about 192 each trip.
>
> Wonderful friendships are made by the children during the week and some come back saying they have seen other children who are far worse off than they are. It makes them feel better. It also gives the parents a break from continually caring for their sick child and if they have other children it gives them the chance to take them off on a holiday.
>
> Many of these children attend normal schools and they feel they are the 'odd one out' in their class. On Dreamflight there is something wrong with all the children, so there is no 'odd one out'. I am always so impressed at how knowledgeable they are about their handicaps and illnesses. They will discuss the pills they are on, just as other children might talk about sweets. When a child comes up to you

Patricia Pearce MBE, 1965–2004.

on a trip and puts their arms around you and says, 'Pat, I have just had the best day of my life', that is what Dreamflight means to me. It's not the location that makes the holidays so special. Anyone, if they have enough money, can go to America. As one child told me: 'It was the knowledge that I was not alone, that there were other people in similar situations who knew what I was going through. Because I am used to the pain of everyday life, the frequent stays in hospital and the side effects of chemotherapy treatment have become normal to me and I tend to dismiss these problems as minor inconveniences. Instead of trying to forget and deny my illness, Dreamflight showed me how to face up to it and be proud of who I am and what I have to offer.'

Pat recalls a young girl aged twelve who had a condition that meant that the last layer of skin would not stay on her body:

She had to be bandaged from head to foot every morning, which took about two hours. She was determined to be ready to go with the rest of the group at 9 a.m. each day and she was never late. She had never worn shoes before, but we managed to bring her home wearing a small pair of trainers. Sadly, she died some six months later, just before her thirteenth birthday. At her funeral the priest said that whenever he mentioned Dreamflight to her it always brought a smile to her face. Her family all wore Disney ties and tried to make her funeral a happy occasion. They said that Dreamflight had given her something that they as a family could not have given her.

The '70s saw many changes. The Common Market and close ties with Europe and new legislation allowed many cabin crew from Europe to join British Airways. In one of the first batches was a German girl with impeccable English – well almost. Bridgita was serving the tea and coffee where the two girls split the cabin in two, her half was from the front of the cabin to the middle. The other stewardess worked from the rear to the centre. She finished at the halfway mark and the passenger in the next row said, 'What about me?' to which she replied: 'The other stewardess will be serving coffee Sir, from her bottom.'

In the opinion of Vicky Radcliffe, the passengers and male crew members made a play for young girls which was always very difficult and sometimes unpleasant, especially when male crew members would not take 'no' for an answer. There was no 'politically correct policy', at the time, so there was no sensible way to make a complaint. Conversely, Celia Penney previously a Bunny Girl at the Bunny Club, thought that BOAC was simply an extension of that industry.

'I thought the early days of the '70s were really fun,' said Isobel Proctor, who flew for thirty years with BA.

✈    It was very chauvinistic though. I remember my first trip to Singapore; the crew took me to Bugi Street, where all the pretty girls were really men. Bugi Street doesn't exist anymore.

The cockroaches in our rooms were enormous, especially the inner rooms.

In Australia, I was amazed that women couldn't go into bars without a man and everything closed at 7.30 (Canada too!). The beer glasses were like thimbles and the wine was like paint stripper. I was amazed when I saw Bondi Beach. I was expecting miles of beach – and it is only about two miles long. We used to stay at the Whitehall Hotel, where the lads from the Vietnam War were doing R&R – but we didn't see much of them as they were all down at Kings Cross.

Carol McIntyre flew for twenty-eight years. She joined in 1973:

✈     The navy Speedbird on the silver bird, what a beautiful sight. Passengers changed: initially 'toffs', then ordinary business people whose firms paid for them to travel and thenpop groups who thought throwing food was funny, and the economy passengers. Well, most sat in their seats and hardly spoke but on the JFK flights I had passengers who were rude, demanding, getting in the way of trolleys, standing in the aisles when it was quite obvious we were trying to do a meal or cocktail service. Passengers changed so much over the years being in the beginning polite, less demanding and showing far more common sense. They did not 'create' over circumstances beyond human control.

A bad moment for me was when due to a fireman's strike at the airport I missed my flight to LHR and was late to report. I was suspended without pay for one month.

The challenges came with the change of position of where you worked on the aircraft. Integration with British Caledonian was difficult as they all came with chips on their shoulders.

Carol was:

✈ … in Beirut when the war started, under curfew in the then Seychelles, in an earthquake in Tokyo and I was in Tehran when the revolution started. I remember that on a three-week trip to Hong Kong I lived on tea and toast provided free by the hotel because I had saved all my allowances to buy a diamond ring.

## ON WOMEN IN MANAGEMENT

There was no career structure for stewardesses for many years. It was only when the Equal Opportunity Act came into existence that changes had to be made. In the past, several stewardesses became flight stewardesses for their particular fleets and a select few had postings overseas to be in charge of national stewardesses in Calcutta, Hong Kong and South America. Seniority for many was getting to ten years – and then out. Seniority also had a few perks such as inaugural flights and to be a route check stewardess. In fact, some of the route stewardesses mentioned that they felt this position was offered as a panacea for the more career-minded stewardess. Management, as such, could be construed as being in the training school or in charge of a certain number of stewardesses from a grooming, disciplinary and personnel perspective. Some senior stewardesses were on the recruitment and interview panel.

Delia Green decided while she was still at school that she wanted to be an air stewardess. She achieved that ambition in 1957 when she joined BOAC. After nearly a year as a Comet flight stewardess, petite, blonde Delia went to Hong Kong to become the flight stewardess in charge of Japanese and Chinese stewardesses. Cynthia Arpthorp-White was the first woman to take charge in Hong Kong when BOAC became the first international airline to employ them. She was followed by Tess Curtin and then Delia Green: 'We had such a high reputation, that many families told me that they viewed our airline as a finishing school for their daughters.' As well as the same requirements as the British girls, the Chinese girls were required to speak fluent Mandarin as well as Cantonese and Japanese girls had to have fluent English. This meant that we were usually recruiting graduates. The uniform was cheongsams, white for summer and navy blue for winter, with two-toned navy and white court shoes.

After thirteen years as a stewardess, Peggy Thorne went to Calcutta early in 1964 to replace her colleague, Joy Henderson, who was to become the first and only chief stewardess appointed by the airline. Joy was a BOAC stewardess for more than ten years with experience of most of the airline's routes and Royal Flights and spent two years in Calcutta, where she was in charge of the Indian and Pakistani girls.

Tess Curtin, perhaps seen by some as a martinet, in truth was not. She was known for her qualities of fairness, strength, a rigid adherence to rules and a courteous and caring attitude toward the girls. Part foster mother part sergeant major was how the flight stewardesses were seen to be. A former Wren, she joined in 1950. A former supervisor of the Asian stewardesses, Tess became a VC10 flight stewardess in 1964 with her duties being the 'well-being, deportment and efficiency of stewardesses for the flight'. In the latter part of her career in BOAC, in the mid-'60s, Tess moved into personnel. She became the first stewardess personnel officer. Rene Benson, Penny Casson, Sue Graham, Aileen Aitken and Audrey Vidler were all flight stewardesses and the pioneers of women in management.

Joy's role when appointed in February 1964 was to supervise the airline's flight stewardesses of the fleets and areas, advising on the recruitment, selection, training, working conditions, deportment and appearances of its stewardesses the world over. This position did not remain for long. When she left the position was not filled, although there were many capable and experienced women who could have done so. It seemed that BOAC Cabin Crew Management in the early' 60s was not ready for a Queen Bee.

Delia Green followed her flying career with BOAC to Hong Kong, where she was in charge of Asian stewardesses until 1970.

## Equal Opportunity at Last

At last, the Equal Opportunity Act 1975 put an end to discrimination and gave stewardesses the opportunity to rise through the ranks as equals of male cabin crew. Previously promotion was only open to men and based on seniority. Stewardesses were now given courses through the ranks of steward, senior steward and purser. This was followed by the new rank of cabin service officer with the 747 flight. Many made the transition in five years with much depending on when the courses could be fitted in. This rapid promotion did not always go down too well with their male colleagues. Stewardesses who had more than served their time as the humble 'A' lady in first class, were now more than ready for more demanding positions and responsibility. The old rule that stewardesses could only fly for ten years or until they were thirty-five was gone. All those secret marriages could stop, married women could fly as married women and mothers. The 'reasonable ratio between height and weight' of old didn't seem to matter so much anymore, although a person couldn't be so large as to not be able to get through an over wing exit. The recruitment age went up to forty-nine and retirement age became fifty-five.

The first female cabin crew training manager was Jill Parker, who joined British Airways as a stewardess on VC10s in 1966, having graduated in Chemistry ('the most expensive cookery course available') from Nottingham University. She had an accelerated career through fleet planning, marketing research and at the same time studied for a diploma in management studies leading to her appointment as hotel marketing and service manager. She then returned to Cabin Services to take up this appointment in 1976.

Jill Parker took over from Len Smee, who was the chief steward who took off into the desert to rescue the crew and passengers of the Hermes flight. He was my old boss. In 2005, I valued the opportunity to thank him for being such a kind and considerate person to work for.

Now BA were getting prepared for the many women in British Airways who were keen to take on management roles and deemed it their right to use their skills in an equal opportunity workplace. Indicative of the push for greater credibility and promotional structure in civil aviation was the International Chief Hostess conferences started in 1969.

In 1976, Jill Parker chaired the Seventh International Chief Hostess conference and she stressed the fact that '75 per cent of cabin crew are female and this should be reflected in management structure'. She also confirmed that 'the wastage rate of cabin crew was dropping drastically, and that women were looking for longer careers with the airline and jobs in management.'

## TRUE EQUALITY WAS RUNNING YOUR OWN AIRCRAFT

Josie Watson had flown for nearly thirty-nine years by the time she left BA in 2004 – quite a record.

Flight stewardess officers (better known as 'the girls from the office' and recognised in person as Christine Gadd, Brenda Muir, Eileen Billings and myself) undertook a flight training programme as part of a progression to the grade of senior cabin service officers, to which we were promoted on 1 January 1977. This entailed operating a required number of trips in all grades on both the 747 and integrated flights. Here are a few of the highlights and problems of a 'woman in charge' as experienced by Josie:

> ✈    Anticipation is probably the worst problem of all when thinking about your crew. They are no doubt all speculating as to what you are going to be like and you are wondering how they are going to work for a woman. The briefing at London and the first sector were the times I felt on trial. However, the crew soon realised it was not my intention to stalk the cabin with horns protruding from my head, flames preceding my every utterance. We all settled down to become what after all makes for happy passengers – a happy crew. To give us plenty of

experience, one of our CSO trips was the long trek to Australia via all points east. In addition to encountering the inevitable problems of catering deficiencies and double bookings the trip did provide lots of laughs.

On landing in Perth, the duty officer leaped up the aircraft steps with the words: 'Is it true there's a Sheila in charge?' On confirming this he burst into fits of laughter. There was a quick crossfire about Australian Male Chauvinist Pigs and we parted the best of friends, having persuaded him (using social skills best known to females) to sort out the double bookings and seats for five passengers left strap hanging to Singapore.

Hotels found it especially difficult to accept a Mrs as a CSO. Two incidents make me chuckle. Being phoned for call time in Singapore and answering in my palest voice, the operator asked if I was Mr Watson. I replied, 'Yes, but it is Mrs.' Silence ensued followed by fits of giggling and the receiver was replaced. Bombay called me at four o'clock one morning and when I answered the phone there was a moment's silence and a calm voice said: 'Would you be kind enough to tell Mr Watson it is his call time.' On a more serious note one of the more aggravating sides of the job is the lack of identity and the continuous repetition of 'Yes, I am the CSO'. While the star system of rank marking means something to cabin crew (and the jokes about being a four star general are a bit tired now), it is not sufficient when travelling public and overseas ground staffs are only tuned into gold braid. Not that I am in favour of making the retrograde step to gold braid for females. Passenger reactions were varied but on the whole favourable and sometimes quite amusing. Difficult passengers, when insisting to see the 'man in charge', were invariably deflated on being told that I was that person and tended to become less demanding. Many of our regular businessmen passengers have commented and shown interest; it has amazed me just how much they appear to know about our cabin service structure.

Before embarking on the set number of trips as CSO, one might have expected to find a certain amount of hostility among some of the male cabin crew. I feel sure we were all apprehensive about this. However, I can claim that everyone, especially the pursers, could not have been more helpful and co-operative. All crew members have understood the status of the 'girls from the office'; they have been willing and given every support. I hope they enjoy flying with female CSOs as much as I enjoyed the experience and challenge.

## Women of Persistence & Vision

### Pat Kerr, MBE

The sorry plight of orphaned children in Cambodia, India, Somalia and Bangladesh led to a courageous British Airways stewardess launching a project to help some of them. BA crews slipped for three or four days in Bangladesh and Pat Kerr, who was there in 1981, and who had begun flying with BOAC in 1974, worked as a part-time volunteer in the children's home there between flights. In 1982 Pat took unpaid leave for five months to work there full-time. From then on crew involvement increased and it was at this time that the establishment became overcrowded.

BA Chairman Lord King in 1984 agreed to a staff project to raise funds for a new orphanage. The following year Pat and BA colleague Gerry Devereux established the British Airways Staff Dhaka Orphanage project.

In 1986, the project trustees completed the purchase of a new site, Sreepur. In 1987, building began and the fundraising continued. In 1988, 600 children moved into Sreepur. Pat had planned a new children's village, which was officially opened in 1989, but needed someone to run it: Pat. Some forty miles outside Dhaka, Sreepur is a 13-acre village where 600 children eat well, sleep safely, and go to school. The fact that they do so is Pat's magnificent achievement.

This remarkable woman had inspired other crew members and BA management to get involved in this project. Pat began this quest by taking five months unpaid leave from BA and she then went to live with the children at the orphanage to get to know the system and what went into the day-to-day running of the orphanage. Whilst she was living there, crews who were passing through also got involved in the orphanage and the problems the orphanage was facing, the main one being the outrageous rent the landlord was charging, because it was on a prime piece of real estate.

Pat's dedication, passion and persistence caught the attention of the BBC and *Blue Peter* featured the orphanage in their documentary about *A Day in the Life of a Stewardess*. In 1983, the Queen visited Bangladesh as part of her tour of the sub-continent. She heard about the BA crew involvement in the project and several of her household visited the orphanage. In 1984, Princess Anne visited Dhaka as President of the Save the Children Fund, and in response to a letter from Pat, visited the orphanage. What began simply as a visit to help care for the orphans became an incredible story of hope, faith and charity.

Pat was featured on *This is Your Life* and wrote her story with Susan Hill entitled *Down to Earth*. In 1989, Pat left BA to run the orphanage full time. Under her guidance and leadership the orphanage is almost self-sufficient. Having their own well gives the children fresh water. Fruit trees have been planted, vegetable gardens are run by the boys, chickens are fed with the vegetable peelings and chicken manure is used for algae growth in the fish farm. 'Whenever possible, we now take in destitute women whose husbands have died or deserted them with their children,' says Pat:

> ✈ These women work as ayahs looking after the children. We are running courses in literacy, health and hygiene and training them in skills such as weaving, in the hope that they will learn enough to become independent. I feel that this project has been a very special expression of the caring nature of people throughout the world – especially British Airways people.

What a legacy to leave.

## Concorde – The Magical Years – The Symbol of British and French Engineering Excellence

The BAC/Aerospatiale Concorde, the aircraft that brought excitement and vibrancy to the world of aviation, the aeroplane that even today, years after it ceased flying, still represents the absolute pinnacle of transport technology. Nothing else comes close; nor is anything likely to challenge its impressive list of records in the foreseeable future. Concorde was designed as an 'all first class' aircraft and speed came at a price.

A total of twenty Concorde airframes were built. Of those, two were prototypes and two pre-productions aircraft, leaving sixteen to be operated commercially by BOAC (later British Airways) and Air France, the major airline companies of the United Kingdom and France where Concorde was designed and built.

Technically Concorde was impressive. It was very fast, cruising at twice the speed of sound, faster than a bullet fired from a rifle, so fast that the outside of the aeroplane became as hot as a pan frying eggs. It cruised very high, up to 60,000ft or eleven miles, where the air is so thin that an unprotected human could live no longer than a second or two. And it carried its hundred-plus passengers in pampered luxury, their only worry being if their champagne was a little too warm or their coffee too cold. How we all take for granted the wonders engineers give us.

The statistics make interesting reading. The aeroplane weighed about 65 tons empty, could carry up to 95 tons of fuel and up to about 30 tons of payload. On take off the engines were developing about 70 tons of thrust and burnt about 1 ton of its precious fuel just rolling down the runway to take off. If it continued to burn fuel at that rate after taking off from Heathrow it would be lucky to reach the Bristol Channel, let alone New York. It had to climb to a high altitude as quickly as possible so that it could become much more efficient. Without air traffic delays and restrictions on supersonic flight over land it could reach its initial cruising level and Mach 2 (twice the speed of sound) in thirty minutes. Then the engines would be sipping fuel at only approximately 20 tons an hour.

### Concorde Facts & Figures:

- There were seven altogether in the A fleet and the average age was twenty-five years
- It had a range of 4,200 miles with each of its four Rolls-Royce/SNEC MA Olympus 593 engines producing 38,000lb of thrust with reheat
- Take off speed was 250mph
- It landed at 187mph

The Concorde, almost 204ft long, stretched between 6-10in during flight due to the heating of the airframe. She was painted in a specially developed white paint that adjusted to these changes and dissipated the heat generated by supersonic flight. A typical London to New York crossing took a little less than three and a half hours as opposed to nearly eight for subsonic flight. The five-hour time difference meant Concorde effectively arrived before it had taken off because she travelled faster than the sun. As she burned fuel and became lighter she was able to climb up to 10,000ft higher into less dense air where she could operate even more efficiently, while carrying her passengers over ten miles in the time it took to fill a champagne glass. Even though the time to fly from London to New York was halved, she was almost always on or ahead of time. The wonder woman of the air! Talking about the Concorde sends shivers up my spine; what a tremendous experience it was for all those who flew her and the cabin crew who were so proud to be Concorde crew.

## First Flights

The British Concorde GH-BOAA made its maiden flight from Heathrow to Bahrain on 21 January 1976. This first commercial flight was in fact to New York via Bahrain. Passengers had to change planes in the Middle East as American aviation authorities refused to allow Concorde to land because of concerns over noise. Its departure was linked with the take off of Air France's Concorde to Rio.

The cabin crew on our first flight were Sue Graham, Francine Carville, David Brackley, Ken Taylor, John Hitchcock and Jack Hawkins. Captain Norman Watson was in command, Captain Brian Calvert second in command, and SEO John Lidiard was the flight engineer.

The passenger list was impressive. Among those on board included HRH the Duke of Kent, the Duchess of Argyll and Lord Boyd-Carpenter. Some passengers were Americans who had saved for months to be part of the occasion. During the flight, television cameras watched every move of the cabin crew service of cocktails and lunch. Vintage champagne was served in crystal glasses and there were tons of caviar!

For the first flights there were special crews, all of whom had the same rank. There was also a special uniform designed by Sir Hardy Amies for these four initial stewardesses – two colours: light blue and navy blue, with coordinating skirts and jackets. The blouses were navy, the whole uniform was of a high-quality French material, very easy to wear. The jacket (a safari style) had a tie belt which was tied around the waist and the accessory was the BA scarf. At that time the union would not agree to salary rates for working this new aircraft so a small band of Cabin Service Directors (CSD) were 'permanent' until that was resolved. Sue Graham was for five months one of this select band. After the agreement the BA uniform at that time became the Concorde uniform as well.

# CONCORDE

## Captain John Hutchinson, Rtd, British Airways

[The Concorde © (Adrian Meredith)]

Concorde was once described as a piece of twentieth-century sculpture. That is a very apt description; she was truly a fusion of art and technology. She was an aeroplane that commanded attention, an aeroplane that one felt compelled to look at and admire for her beauty and grace. She transcended mere technology, inspiring a fierce loyalty and pride amongst all who were privileged to work with her. Concorde was not only beautiful to look at, she was also beautiful to fly. Concorde really was an aircraft that lived up to the adage that 'if she looks right, she will fly right'.

It is worth remembering that this is an aeroplane whose design technology goes back to the late 1950s and 1960s. The aerodynamicists and engineers who created her were a remarkable group of people who were far ahead of their time. It is eloquent testimony to their genius in overcoming the problems of supersonic flight that we are now in the twenty-first century and there is still no sign of a second generation supersonic transport anywhere on the horizon. I am sure that it will come but we are probably going to have to wait for another twenty to thirty years.

I spent fifteen years flying Concorde and, out of all the seventy-plus types I have flown, I rate her as the most outstanding. She was a powerful and extremely responsive thoroughbred that could be flown with finger and thumb. Her handling qualities were superb throughout the whole speed range. From landing speeds of around 160 knots to cruising at Mach 2, twice the speed of sound, she was a sheer delight to fly and she did it effortlessly. The only clue when going through the sound barrier was the Mach meter going from 0.99 to 1.01 Mach and a fluctuation of the rate of climb indicator as the shock wave attached on the nose.

It is impossible to convey in words the sensation of supersonic flight but I will try. When cruising at 50,000ft up to her ceiling of 60,000ft one was above all the jet streams and thunderstorms. In that calm and tranquil environment on the edge of space one had no impression of speed. It felt as though one was hanging suspended in space waiting for Mother Earth to spin around and for the destination to appear below. The curvature of the earth was clearly visible at those heights and the colour of the sky took on a deep midnight blue. Only when flying over subsonic aircraft 20,000ft below did one get any feeling of speed; the subsonics would appear to be going backwards as Concorde overtook them, flying some 800mph faster!

The tragic crash at Paris left an unjustified blemish on her reputation and was the catalyst that led to the premature grounding of this truly special aircraft. If that tragedy had not occurred, she would still have been flying today and continuing to grace the skies until around 2020. Sadly, there is no turning back of clocks and it will be several decades before air passengers can enjoy the great benefits of supersonic flight again.

In summary, Concorde was an aviation icon; the supreme achievement of passenger flight. People never talked about 'the' Concorde or 'a' Concorde. She was simply Concorde; the ultimate flying experience.

Sue Graham, a State Registered Nurse, had an illustrious career in BOAC and BA and was on that first flight. She had received the Queen's Commendation in 1970 for her skill and courage in saving the life of a passenger on a Boeing 707 on a flight from Chicago to Montreal. A woman became unconscious and Sue massaged her heart, gave oxygen and mouth to mouth resuscitation during that flight. The passenger 'died' three times. Each time the kiss of life brought her around. The passenger recovered later in hospital. Apart from this Sue held many management roles. In 1964 she was a deputy flight stewardess. Later she became a flight stewardess and was my flight stewardess when I started in BOAC. I held her in high esteem. Her progression continued until the CSD role. I asked her to tell me about Concorde:

✈      There was huge excitement that had built up over the months before we took off. There was an extraordinary feeling of anticipation, almost palpable. So much preparation had gone into every single aspect of this flight. There was a brass band playing and hundreds of photographers and thousands of sightseers were at Heathrow to watch us take off. Such a wonderful party atmosphere.

The Concorde was described by Londoners near Heathrow as 'a sleek white dart blasting into the heavens … with an unmistakable sound, a powerful roar distinctly different from all the other airliners filling the skies…'

*In the BA cabin crew newsletter of February 1976, Concorde was called 'The Most Exciting Piece of Airline Hardware for Years'. In November 1977 Concorde began the JFK (New York) and Heathrow (London) service.*

Sue Graham 1958–88.

## On Board

The flight began in the Concorde lounge. Your coat was taken and one was cosseted to extremes and made to feel a most privileged person. Certainly the fare was indicative of a most privileged bank account. It was the symbol of the flying rich, the elitist aeroplane. The only criticisms were from passengers who were size challenged. The seats were on the narrow side. Many regular travellers of the Concorde used to say that this aircraft was like a state-of-the-art sports car and the seating was secondary to the magnificent and unique technical feature of being able to travel at twenty miles a minute, well over twice the speed of the next fastest passenger aeroplane in existence.

Jeannette Hartley crossed the Atlantic 740 times supersonically and some Concorde captains crossed 2,000 times in twenty years. In a career of twenty-seven years Jeannette totalled over 1,000 Atlantic crossings. She joined BA in April 1971 and flew for twenty-nine years, twenty years of that time being on Concorde. In conversations with her about Concorde she said:

✈    On Concorde the meal service procedures were very ordered. The galleys were small like the Comet; in fact you stood in the galley aisle to work rather than in the actual galley. We had a hundred first class passengers to serve in three hours and *just* got it done before arrival in JFK or LHR.

In fact the transatlantic record was 2 hours, 52 minutes and 59 seconds, on 7 February 1996 under the command of Captain Les Scott. It was from JFK to LHR.

Concorde was an all first class cabin service. There was no economy cabin. Because we were rather limited for space and time we were unable to offer the wide choice of menu that passengers get in first class on the subsonic fleet, so we made up for this by offering the best possible standard of cuisine. Immediately after take off Concorde passengers were offered a glass of Dom Perignon champagne in crystal glasses or a cocktail if they preferred, together with a small dish of canapés – they could be pastry boats of caviar, rolls of smoked salmon on toast garnished with aspic or pate maison. Lunch would be hors d'oeuvres of cold lobster and the chefs would do it beautifully, garnishing the fish with the head and tail of the lobster. There was a choice of main course: steak, Dover sole in a white wine sauce, venison or game pie, or lobster thermidor. This was followed by a choice of cheeses: stilton, cheddar or camembert. The sweet, which could be sorbet of some kind, strawberries in cream sauce, pineapple rings in Grand Marnier. And then we came through the cabin with coffee or tea, liqueurs, Jamaican cigars, and a little Concorde giveaway for each passenger. All the food was served on special Royal Doulton Concorde crockery with a smart blue band and little gold Concordes all around.

It was the best of food and the best of wine:

**Silver Jubilee 77 cocktail**
1oz Sloe Gin in a 6oz glass
Fill with iced champagne
Decorate with slice of orange and maraschino cherry. Stir.

As well as the Dom Perignon champagne others were offered, for example Dom Ruinart 1973, Heidsieck Dry Monole 1975 and Mumm Cordon Rouge 1975. The white wines in the early '70s were a Bordeaux Chateau Brane Cantenac 1970 or Chateau Cantermerle 1973 or a Burgundy such as Chablis-Laroche et Fils 1975 or Chateau Leoville Las Cases 1971 and Chablis Grand Cu Blanchot 1974. Initially in the early '70s cigars were offered, Jamaica Macanudo cigars, which caused some consternation in the cabin. And a problem it was when people like Robert Maxwell used to stub his out on the carpet. When smoking was banned on all aircraft this solved the problems.

Jeannette continues:

✈    Our first class passengers, particularly on the Concorde, included the 'old school' type, English gentry, and so courteous and charming. This contrasts with the cut and thrust no nonsense business people, brisk, where speed is of the essence. Never mind the delectable food and wines, just get me to New York at breakneck speed. Short and sharp.

Jeannette was totally dedicated to the aircraft and had the honour to be selected to carry the Queen and the Duke of Edinburgh on a flight to the Arabian Gulf in February 1979.

To most of the passengers Concorde was an elite club and there were many regular passengers including Sir Paul McCartney, Sir Elton John, Joan Collins and Sir David Frost. Jeannette particularly remembers Julie Andrews, whom she carried twice on Concorde, as 'such a perfect lady' and Sir Richard Attenborough, 'such a perfect gentleman'. However, on the winter Barbados flights she remembers that there were some extremely demanding passengers. Cabin crew 'were frequently abused and some refused to operate on these flights'.

Some of the passengers could get quite bemused by the Cabin Mach Meter. 'What does M 2.00 mean?' 'Oh so it means we are travelling at 200mph are we?' 'No sir, 1,200mph!' I would reply.

Amanda Pepper had the honour of being the first chief to work on Concorde and later was successful in being promoted to Fleet Director when the role was originally established. By now, in the late '70s, equality was making its mark.

My flight stewardess when I was training was Sue Graham, who flew on the first Concorde. Julia van den Bosch, whom I trained, brought in the last. Julia, a tall, elegant blonde, was a former model and was the longest-serving Concorde cabin crew member. She joined the Concorde fleet in 1976. She says:

✈    I've flown Concorde about 1,400 times, which probably means I've been supersonic more times than anyone else in the world. I can honestly say that each time has been as thrilling as the first. In the early days, when we came into Heathrow you'd see the roads blocked with cars for miles around. People would just pull over and stare. I loved telling first-time passengers to look up and see the sky, which was dark because we're on the edge of space, or pointing out the curvature of the Earth. One of our pilots used to welcome people on board by telling them that NASA says anyone who flies at more than 55,000ft is an astronaut. 'Welcome aboard fellow astronauts,' he'd say.

The celebrity passengers were great; sometimes we'd be invited to first nights or concerts. I remember getting tickets from violinist Yehudi Mehuin and chatting to Placido Domingo.

One day we were due to fly to Barbados, and a group of really scruffy passengers got on. They looked as if they had been up all night. It turned out they had won the lottery and had been wondering what to do to celebrate when somebody said 'let's fly Concorde to Barbados.' And that is exactly what they did.

And I'll always remember the blind man who said he just wanted to experience flying supersonic. I sat beside him, telling him what the different noises represented as we reached full speed.

'As the more regular passengers – and particularly the business passenger – used the Concorde, there was less interest in the food or wine,' says Scarlett Raymond. 'The business passenger was more interested in the Perrier. He just wants to get from A to B in the quickest time.'

## Charters

This aircraft epitomised for both passengers and crew the mystique, elegance and excitement that was flying. Concorde was an aircraft of dreams for people who saved and saved, and charter flights gave a lot of ordinary people a chance to fly supersonic. Jeannette Hartley, who dearly loved Concorde, organised the first charters.

✈    These were on July 18 and 19, 1981. I organised these because several friends, curious of me flying on it every week, nagged me into organising a ride for them. We had just discontinued the Singapore route and I knew BA wanted to increase the supersonic charter work as only very few charters had taken place. So I rang the Concorde Charter Officer and knocked him down to a bargain price – £175 per pax. Thanks to some publicity in the National Press I filled two Concordes and could easily have filled a third. After that, the supersonic charters really took off.

Jeannette really made a huge contribution to revenue here and Concorde's success. I personally regard her contribution to BA's coffers as significant. As she told me, 'We went supersonic around the Bay of Biscay and went right up to Concorde's normal cruising speed of just over twice the speed of sound, 1,350mph. It was a super weekend and a great time was had by all.'

Jeannette Hartley's enthusiasm and love for Concorde initiated many successful charters. She hired Concorde for £17,000 for 20 supersonic minutes. The trip was from London Heathrow Airport over the Bay of Biscay and cost £175 a head.

Josie Watson was the first woman in charge of a Royal Flight for Cabin Services:

✈    It was a huge honour to be asked to head up the Queen's Concorde trip on her State visit to Eastern Arabia in 1979. We had only flown from Bahrain (to Riyadh) that morning, 268 miles – not far in Concorde. However, as everything is done to precision schedules, one hour and ten minutes was allocated so that we wouldn't arrive before the red carpet was rolled out into position to where the Concorde would stop exactly on the markers for the steps – such is the detail for these occasions and it always works!

She continues: 'On this occasion all her Ladies in Waiting and female members of the Royal Household had to disembark wearing long skirts in deference to Saudi customs. We were counted as Honorary Men so kept our normal uniforms.'

## And the Passengers Were:

Concorde BA News of 28 October 2003 had this to say: 'The exclusivity of supersonic travel meant that when you flew on Concorde you joined an elite band of travellers. Over the years Concorde has carried legendary movie stars, world leaders and the fabulously wealthy. Concorde used to be the last word in glamour, the choice of royalty, the aristocracy, rock stars and top businessmen. And from the impromptu songs by ex-Beatles to record-breaking golf stunts, anything can happen on board.

To fly Concorde was to add your name to passenger lists oozing glamour and wealth. On the same blue leather seats might have reposed the bottoms of the Queen, Sir Sean Connery, Sir David Frost, Henry Kissinger, Robert Redford, Jack Nicholson, Mick Jagger, Rupert Murdoch, Gwyneth Paltrow, Joan Collins, Barbra Streisand, Sir Elton John, Sir Paul McCartney or Luciano Pavarotti (who acknowledged his proportions by booking two seats).

But it is still Sir David Frost who can claim to be the best-known regular user (although the most travelled Concorde passenger is in fact oil tycoon Fred Finn who clocked up his 700th flight in 1992).

It is generally agreed that the front of the aircraft is the place to be. On the New York run, for example, regulars used to vie for Window Seat 1D. But Sir David, in a smooth act of reverse snobbism, favoured row 23. There with a bit of luck he would find fewer passengers and thus more space for him to enjoy a supersonic snooze.

Concorde flew the flag and dominated the skies from 1969 when two first flights, one from Toulouse 001 (2 March) and the other from Filton 002 (9 April), made history. That same year man first walked on the moon. For nearly three decades, it remained the ultimate form of transport for the rich and famous.

Sir Paul McCartney used to like to take his favourite guitar as hand luggage and has been known, when given enough encouragement by other passengers, to start strumming some of his favourite songs mid-air.

In 1985 pop star Phil Collins hopped on Concorde to perform at Live Aid in London and Philadelphia on the same day.

### Crew who make history with these last flights of Concorde

BA organised a special occasion to mark the end of Concorde. On 24 October 2003 three Concordes landed at Heathrow within minutes of each other, one from Edinburgh, one from the Bay of Biscay and the last from New York. Chief Executive Rod Eddington said of Concorde's final day: 'It was a ceremony to mark the end of an era, the end of a global career, the end of an icon, an emotional occasion.'

Alpha Echo, Concorde from Edinburgh, carried one hundred BA staff who had won their seats in a draw. It touched down at 4.01 p.m. The cabin crew were CSD Jerry Smith, Purser Sue Berry and crew members Linda Martin, Craig McCormick, Joanne Van Gaver, Sam Kingdon and Iona Ferguson.

Concorde Cabin Service Director Sue Berry, a purser on the day, said one of the best moments of the final flight coming in from Edinburgh was the landing at Heathrow:

> ✈   As we came around to the hangars all the engineers outside saluted the aircraft. It was a real tear-jerking moment. The flight itself was very intimate. I've only been working on Concorde for a year, but as a team you become such a close family. You know everyone and we're just so grateful that we could share these last moments together.

The Heathrow to Heathrow flight of Alpha Foxtrot, with invited guests and VIPs on board, looped the Atlantic to the Bay of Biscay and back to Heathrow, landing at 4.03 p.m. The cabin crew were CSD Lorraine Longden, Pursers Louise Brown and Karen Robb, and crew members Zoe-Ann Corfield, Joanne Lewsley, Jason Smith and Tarnia Gadd. Louise Brown, one of the longest-serving Concorde crew, said her final fight around the Bay of Biscay was extremely emotional: 'Today has been a celebration of a magical, super aircraft, although it has also been very sad.'

New York JFK to Heathrow G-BOAG Concorde touched down at 4.06 p.m. The cabin crew were: Cabin Service Directors Tracey Percy and Clare Sullivan, Purser Julia van den Bosch and crew members Sabre Moate, Andrew Hayden, Heather Ellis and John Middleton.

As the historic final flight from JFK taxied slowly from the runway to the hangars, Captain Mike Bannister and First Officer Jonathon Napier saluted the waiting crowds of staff and media by waving huge Union Jack flags out of the cockpit windows.

The stars added sparkle to this final flight. First off the celebrity-packed flight was British Airways Chairman Lord Marshall, followed by actress Joan Collins, looking every inch the Hollywood star, accompanied by husband Percy Gibson.

Sir David Frost was next to walk the specially laid red carpet. As one of the supersonic aircraft's most frequent flyers, Sir David was happy to acknowledge the service of BA's Concorde staff. 'They looked after me superbly on the flight and I am looking forward to seeing them on the slow ones.' Also on the flight was designer Sir Terence Conran, who had redesigned the interior of the aircraft and the lounges only two years earlier. He said, 'I feel very sad. We did some of our best work on Concorde and now it is gone.'

As Christine Rolka said in her Concorde special report: 'To cheers, applause and tears, Concorde touched down at Heathrow for the final time last Friday, marking the end of an era for supersonic flights.' Her aircraft's famous nose dipped for the crowds as the British Airways flagship, an icon in the aviation industry and a symbol of national pride, bowed out from the world stage with her last commercial flight, which arrived from New York's John F. Kennedy Airport at 4.06 p.m.

At the helm, Captain Mike Bannister summed up the mood when he told his passengers: 'Concorde was a fabulous legend born from dreams, built from vision, operated with pride by a family that loved her.'

Despite the bitterly cold weather, the warmth and affection for Concorde shone through. BA engineers saluted the aircraft as she taxied to a halt. Up to 6,000 spectators lined the airport perimeter cheering and waving flags, and in the packed concourses at Heathrow's terminals business people, holidaymakers and Concorde fans from all over Britain burst out in spontaneous applause as the jets landed.

Tens of thousands more also watched the landings from vantage points under Concorde's flight path. The crew gave their all to ensure the aircraft's last passengers had an enjoyable experience that would live with them forever.

Chairman Lord Marshall admitted it was a day of mixed emotions. 'Everyone has enormous pride in all she has achieved but there is inevitable sadness that we have to say farewell.' Since starting commercial service she had carried more than 2.5 million passengers.

She was the most photographed aircraft in the world – a true superstar. The camera loved her. Former BA photographer Adrian Meredith added: 'From underneath she looks like a rocket and if you look down she's like a swan.'

So it was as the *BA News Concorde Special* said it was: 'Cheers and Tears for 27 *Great* Years.'

### Farewell to Concorde

Arrow of grace
You took your place
In history.

To leave the air
Without an heir
Your destiny.

Throughout the world
Your flights unfurled
Your supremacy.

Our love and pride
Will long provide
Your legacy.

– Sylvia Poole, BOAC Stewardess 1956

## Signing Off

The Golden Age for an air stewardess is over. Carol McIntyre wishes that she 'could turn the clock back and do it all again!' Throughout the four decades of this Golden Age, hundreds of stewardesses agreed it was the most wonderful time of their lives and wished that they could live again those glamorous and halcyon days. The persistent theme from the surveys was the camaraderie and the value of the experience, an experience which combined a sense of belonging, teamwork, leadership and professionalism.

Many women in the early days had shared camaraderie in the defence forces. Stewardesses from the '40s onwards highlighted this one aspect which had truly enriched their lives. Added to this was the continual persiflage, which enlivened both their experience and certainly that of the passengers.

Today the sky is the limit for women in aviation. They may be found in the aircraft cabin, on the flight deck, in all levels of management, in the boardrooms of airlines, and in space. This great adventure of flying, which began so humbly in 1930 when Ellen Church and seven other nurses were hired as the world's first air stewardesses, has continued to attract generations of women. It would be difficult to surmise that this first group of flying nurses would have known that their new career would reach the iconic status and historic and enviable mystique which evolved from those initial arduous flights. The mystique will carry on. It is a love story with no ending.

# Appendix I

## Disasters – The Price of Progress

Despite the tag of Golden Age there were also tragedies: crew and passengers losing their lives in incidents, disasters and tragic circumstances. Inevitably, over the years accidents have occurred and flights came to grief, but from every accident a lesson has been learned.

In those early years there were several fatal accidents; as Harald Penrose writes in his *Wings Across the World*: 'Perhaps it was memory of huge wartime losses that made this total seem acceptable in relation to the enormous mileage the three Corporations were flying.'

Listed below are some of the incidents. All the aircraft beginning with 'Star' are British South American Airways:

### 1946
30 August:   The Lancastrian G-AGWJ 'Star Glow' crashed at Bathurst, Gambia. The aircraft was written off. No casualties.

### 1946
7 September:   A York of BSAA, G-AHEW 'Star Leader', en route to Buenos Aires, crashed soon after take off from Bathurst, Gambia killing nineteen passengers and four crew members.

### 1947
A BOAC Dakota G-AGJX crash landed on 11 January at Stowting, near Lympne, Kent. The captain, three cockpit crew and four passengers died. The steward and seven other passengers survived. The aircraft ran out of fuel having been unable to land due to fog both in France and the south of England.

### 1947
13 April:   The York G-AHEZ crashed at Dakar after attempting to land in poor visibility. This was a BSAA aircraft, 'Star Speed'; six of the nine passengers on board died, with the remaining six passengers and and crew suffering injuries.

2 August:   The BSSA Lancastrian G-AGWH, 'Star Dust', was lost without a trace in the Andes, with pieces of the wreckage miraculously found fifty-three years later on the slopes of the Tupungato by two Argentinean mountaineers.

28 August:   The Sandringham G-AHZB: three crew and seven passengers were killed in a heavy water landing after crashing in Bahrain. The captain misjudged the approach and allowed the aircraft to touchdown heavily short of the flare path, then failed to maintain control during the bounce and the aircraft took a nose down attitude and sank.

5 September:   The Lancastrian G-AGWK 'Star Trail' crashed at Bermuda during a storm – the aircraft hit the radio mast during approach. There were no casualties.

23 October:   Lancaster 1 Freighter G-AGUL 'Star Watch' crashed at London Airport and fortunately there were no casualties.

13 November:   Lancastrian G-AGWG 'Starlight' crashed at Bermuda at night. Fortunately, again, there were no casualties.

## 1948
30 January:   The BSSA Tudor G-AHNP 'Star Tiger' disappeared between the Azores and Bermuda.

6 January:   A BEA Viking G-AHPK crashed, with the death of the pilot and injuries to the other eight occupants. This was caused by an incorrect barometric setting and then a visual landing. The pilot hit a row of trees and crashed into a ploughed field at Northolt.

5 April:   A BEA Vickers 610 Viking 1B G-AIVP collided head-on with a Russian Air Force Yakovlev 3 fighter performing aerobatics. The Viking spiralled slowly without control. Four crew and ten passengers died near Berlin-Gatow. The fighter pilot was also killed. The collision was caused by the action of the Yak which disregarded the accepted rules of flying and in particular, quadripartite flying rules to which Soviet authorities were parties.

## 1949
5 January:   The Avro York G-AHEX, 'Star Venture', came to an unfortunate end 400 miles north of Rio, killing three of the nine passengers. G-AHEX crash-landed at Caravelas Bay, Brazil, an hour after take off due to a fire on board.

17 January:   Within a fortnight the Avro Tudor G-AGRE, 'Star Ariel', vanished without a trace between Bermuda and Jamaica with thirteen passengers and seven crew on board. As a consequence, all Tudor IVb operations were suspended pending further investigation.

## 1950
13 April:   A BEA Vickers Viking bound for Paris experienced an explosion at the rear end of the fuselage. Captain Ian Harvey turned the aircraft and landed safely at Northolt Airport. There were no casualties. The stewardess was severely injured. The details for this accident are on page 96.

17 October:   Another BEA aircraft, a DC3, crashed with the loss of twenty-eight lives after a starboard engine failed while climbing away from Northolt Airport near London in foggy weather. The pilot tried to turn back but hit beech trees on Millhill.

## 1952

26 May:   The Handley Page Hermes aircraft, GALDN, crash-landed in the desert on a flight from Tripoli to Kano in West Africa. It crash-landed short of fuel after an eleven-hour flight as it was on a too westerly course due to a navigational error. Only one life was lost in this incident, the first officer who died from exhaustion five days later. This story is detailed in Chapter 6.

## 1953

2 May: Comet 1 G-ALYV went down near Calcutta with forty-three passengers and crew on board.

## 1954

*Comet disasters*

The de Havilland Comet 1 came into service in BOAC, providing the world's first commercial jet operation. The Comet was fast and quiet. However, three accidents, which happened in quick succession during 1953 and 1954 swiftly obliterated passenger confidence in this aircraft. In two of the Comets, the cabin became suddenly depressurised and the aircraft exploded:

10 January: G-ALYP blew up near Elba. Thirty-five people lost their lives.

8 April: G-ALYY blew up in the Naples area. Twenty-five people lost their lives.

The reason for these crashes was metal fatigue, a consequence of the initial design of the squared-off windows, which put undue stress on the corners. Once the oval window was introduced the problem disappeared. However, world confidence in jet aircraft shifted to the Boeing 707s. The pressurisation problem was sorted out and BOAC and BEA continued to operate the much safer Comet 4 well into the '60s.

26 October: A Comet 1 flight to Johannesburg from London was taking off from Rome. The pilot lifted the nose too high. He thought he was losing power on a left engine and attempted an immediate landing on soft ground beyond the runway. The aircraft was damaged and the fuel tanks punctured but there was no fire and the passengers and crew escaped unharmed.

*Other disasters*

13 March: BOAC ConstellationG-ALAM landed short at Kallang, Singapore. Two crew survived and thirty-one passengers were killed. The under-carriage snagged a raised concrete step at the end of the runway and although the concrete step was almost impossible to see from the air, the accident was 'crew error'. The crew had been on duty for twenty-four hours. The incident was instrumental in the changes to flight time regulations.

25 December: BOAC Stratocruiser G-ALSA approaching Prestwick Airport from London going to New York on Christmas morning undershot the runway. The port undercarriage collapsed, fuel lines severed in the wings and the aircraft turned over and caught fire. Twenty-seven people lost their lives and seven survived.

## 1955

16 January: A BEA Viscount mistook the end of a disused runway for the correct one and struck a steel girder barrier which tore off part of the undercarriage and the two port engines. Only the captain and one passenger were injured.

Also in the mid-'50s, two BOAC Argonauts were destroyed in Africa. In both incidents, weather was deemed the cause. Tripoli Airport in Libya at this time badly needed an upgrade and had only one radio beacon. The airport was in the midst of a dust storm on the night of 21 September 1955 when the pilot of G-ALHL tried unsuccessfully to land. In this incident the steward, stewardess and thirteen of the forty passengers were killed and seventeen injured.

## 1956

24 June: Another Argonaut, G-ALHE, crashed at Kano in Northern Nigeria. Immediately after take off the aircraft encountered a sudden wind reversal, which in turn produced a

thunderstorm in its path. There were forty-five people on board; thirty-two died and eleven were seriously injured. If the airport had installed a weather radar system this may have been prevented. The Argonauts were phased out and weather radar systems were not installed as it was seen as not economically viable.

## 1957

14 March:   A BEA Viscount struck houses on the approach to Ringway Airport, Manchester. All the crew and passengers lost their lives. The cause was metal fatigue of the bolts on the starboard flap.

28 September:   BEA DH Heron G-AOFY used for air ambulance work in the highlands of Scotland crashed while attempting to land in bad weather. None of the crew survived.

23 October:   BEA Viscount G-AOJA crashed on the approach to Belfast when it struck the ground in low cloud and rain. The crew of five and two passengers died.

## 1958

6 February:   BEA Ambassador G-ALZU crashed in Munich while attempting to take off for the third time on a snow-covered runway and failed to get airborne before the end of the runway. The aircraft was carrying Manchester United's legendary 'Busby Babes', one of the most famous football teams in the world, returning from a match against Red Star Belgrade. Many of the team perished. One of the cabin staff lost his life. He had swapped his roster to be on the prestigious flight. After this, many cabin crew resolved never to swap rosters no matter what the circumstances might be. Of the forty-four on board twenty-three were killed. The cause of the accident was eventually established as slush on the runway, which prevented the aircraft accelerating to the correct speed for take off. The fact that the aircraft had not been de-iced during its transit stop may have been a contributory factor.

There were a few instances of stewardesses who did fly in someone else's place or didn't for some reason or other. Anne Fullagher (1956–59) recalls:

> ✈    My strangest experience was returning from Lagos to Kano, just a day's work … being asked by the chief steward who was taking the aircraft on to Tripoli whether I would carry on with the flight as his stewardess was not well with sinus trouble. However, the stewardess did not want to stay in Kano and wanted to do the flight. She said to me: 'I am not going to stay in this bloody place, Kano, any longer than I have to so I will do the flight'. So she took over and about an hour later I had a knock on my door at the Central Hotel in Kano. It was my first officer with a grave face bringing me the news that the aircraft had crashed just after take off and the stewardess and second steward had been killed. I could hardly believe it … it might have been me. From that day on I became a fatalist – my number was not yet up. The next day we took the flight to London. Another Argonaut had been flown out and we had some of the surviving passengers on board, one of whom was a man whose wife had been killed and he was flying home to the UK to tell his children at boarding school that their mother was dead. Awesome the whole thing!

22 October:   To make matters worse for BEA there was a mid-air collision between a Viscount and an Italian Air Force fighter. It was a fatal result for passengers and crew. However, the pilot of the fighter managed to escape by parachute.

24 December: A BOAC Britannia 312 G-AOVD from Heathrow crashed at Christchurch, Hampshire. It was a foggy day and the aeroplane flew into the ground because of the misleading nature of the three-pointer altimeter. Nine of the twelve passengers on board, who were all BOAC employees, lost their lives.

## 1961

Four days before Christmas a BEA Comet crashed a few seconds after take off at Ankara. Fire started immediately the aircraft hit the ground. The flight crew and cabin crew lost their lives. Of the thirty-four on board twenty-seven were killed. It was then discovered that the director horizon indicator was faulty.

## 1964

James Nightingale was the first officer on a Comet IV airliner with sixty-two passengers aboard which touched down in a Nairobi Game Reserve, nine miles from the runway the pilot was aiming for. However, some pretty quick thinking on the part of the pilot meant that the passengers felt only a jolt as he took the plane up into the air again. The Aviation Ministry and BOAC officials at the time flew to Africa to investigate what was being called the most fantastic air escape for years. There were many theories about the cause of this Comet touching down in the Nairobi Game Park, one being that the aircraft was lower than it should have been on its approach because of a misreading of an altimeter. The Comet had two altimeters, one showing the height above sea level and another which had to be set according to the height of the runway being used.

## 1965

A Vanguard GAPEE from Edinburgh to London on 27 October crashed 2,600ft along runway 28R at Heathrow. It was a third attempt to land in fog. Following a climb to 400ft the control column was pushed forward. No attempt was made to reverse the long pushover until two seconds before impact. Reason? Significant lag in air-driven instruments. The aircraft stalled trying to climb out again and aboard all were killed. (*Safety in the Air*, Maurice Allward Abelard-Schuman, 1967)

## 1966

5 March: BOAC Boeing 707-436 shortly after leaving Tokyo Airport for Hong Kong disintegrated with pieces falling over a wide area around Mount Fujiyama. No one survived. As with the Comet this was metal fatigue failure. Inspections of other 707s revealed hairline cracks in the structure. This was caused by severe turbulence due to extremely strong winds across the top of Mount Fuji, the presence of which was not relayed to the crew. None of the 113 passengers and eleven crew survived.

## 1967

21 November: There was another incident involving a BOAC 707 aircraft at Honolulu. On this occasion the engine caught fire when the aircraft reached 100 knots and was about to take off for Tokyo. The take off was stopped and the aircraft never left the ground. The fifty-nine passengers escaped the burning aircraft but during the evacuation four passengers suffered slight injuries and one woman a broken ankle. The aircraft was under the command of Captain Kenneth Emmott. Captain Emmott's crew included stewardesses Jan Harding, Christine Ferris, Angela Wong and Fujiko Yasa.

12 October: BEA Comet G-ARCO, in flight out of Athens, exploded with the loss of all on board. It is believed there was a bomb on board; speculation abounded that there was a passenger who looked like Archbishop Makarios.

## 1968

8 April:   BOAC Boeing 707 G-ARWE Flight 712, taking off for a flight to Zurich, made a forced landing at Heathrow one and a half minutes after take off. No.2 engine broke away from its mounting. Captain Cliff Taylor landed the aircraft; the cabin crew had the doors open and passengers used the chutes while the aircraft began exploding, the port wing fell off and fire engulfed the airport. There were 126 people on board and 121 survived. Five, including the stewardess, lost their lives. The details on this incredible incident are on page 123.

## 1970

12 September:   A BOAC VC10, a TWA 707 and a Swissair DC-8 were hijacked. The passengers were released and the aircraft later blown up at Dawson's Field in Jordan. This heralded a spate of hijackings. One ocurred during a transit stop at Dubai, when a passenger was shot by the hijackers who wanted a flight to Tunis. Then a third VC10 was hijacked over the Mediterranean. The captain was ordered to fly to Amsterdam. The pasengers were allowed to escape using the emergency chutes. Once again the VC10 was set on fire. The details on this incident are on page 176.

## 1971

2 October:   Over Belgium, Vanguard G-APEC, flying from Heathrow to Salzburg, suffered an explosive decompression due to corrosion in the pressure bulkhead. The eight crew and fifty-five passengers were killed.

## 1972

18 June:   BEA Trident 'Papa India' crashed near Heathrow, killing 118 people. The cause was that the aircraft stalled. The leading edge droop slots had started to retract, which caused the aircraft to enter a stall condition and, due its very high nose-up attitude, was unrecoverable.

After this incident, a statement issued by Captain George Stone and signed by forty-five other pilots set out what they believed were the root causes of the deteriorating safety record. His report stated two fundamental problems: the pilots' hours of duties were too long and the number of young inexperienced pilots requiring supervision by the captain were too high.

## 1974

3 March:   Another hijacking of a British Airways VC 10 flight from Beirut to London. In this instance two Arab terrorists forced the aircraft to land at Amsterdam. The ninety-two passengers and the crew of ten were released before they blew the aircraft up.

## 1976

10 September:   British Airways Trident carrying a crew of nine and fifty-eight passengers was in a mid-air collision with a DC9 over Zagreb. Air Traffic Control at Zagreb was at fault. There were no survivors.


Air safety has improved considerably over the years. The legacy of the crews who lost their lives are the discoveries and modifications that have furthered the safety of Civil Aviation. Flying is still the safest form of travel and the safety record of the airlines has never been better.

Following the terrible events of 9/11 in New York, flight deck doors are now kept securely locked. Consequently the close liaison between the flight crew and cabin crew now relies on verbal communication.

Cabin crew have a vitally important role to play in aviation today ensuring the safety of the huge numbers of people flying around the world and it is a credit to the airlines and regulatory authorities that their training is conducted to such a high standard.

# Appendix II

## Phonetic Alphabet

The phonetic alphabet is used in various occupations (including flying, the police, etc.) so that letters and words can be passed over the radio clearly and without risk of their being misheard. On an aircraft it is used mostly by the pilots when talking to air traffic control, but there are some occasions when it is used by cabin crew too. The idea was to make each word totally distinctive. For example, if you are flying on an aircraft with the registration letters G-BHST, this aircraft will be abbreviated to Sierra Tango.

The following is the full phonetic alphabet. The old alphabet (below left) was used by the RAF from 1943–56.

| OLD PHONETIC ALPHABET | | NEW PHONETIC ALPHABET | |
|---|---|---|---|
| A | Able/Affirm | A | Alpha |
| B | Baker | B | Bravo |
| C | Charlie | C | Charlie |
| D | Dog | D | Delta |
| E | Easy | E | Echo |
| F | Fox | F | Foxtrot |
| G | George | G | Golf |
| H | How | H | Hotel |
| I | Item/Interrogatory | I | India |
| J | Jig/Johnny | J | Juliet |
| K | King | K | Kilo |
| L | Love | L | Lima |
| M | Mother | M | Mike |
| N | Nab/Negat | N | November |
| O | Oboe | O | Oscar |
| P | Peter/Prep | P | Papa |
| Q | Queen | Q | Quebec |
| R | Roger | R | Romeo |
| S | Sugar | S | Sierra |
| T | Tare | T | Tango |
| U | Uncle | U | Uniform |
| V | Victor | V | Victor |
| W | William | W | Whiskey |
| X | X-ray | X | X-ray |
| Y | Yoke | Y | Yankee |
| Z | Zebra | Z | Zulu |

# Appendix III

## Background History and Timeline

In August 1919 the world's first international scheduled flight left London for Paris. The flight took three and a half hours. The airline, Airline Transport & Travel Ltd, was formed in 1916 and was one of the ancestors of today's British Airways.

After early difficulties, four small British companies were merged in 1924 to form **Imperial Airways** Ltd – a company with its mind firmly fixed on the future of civil aviation as a link between Britain and the Empire. During the next fifteen years considerable results were achieved in pioneering the air routes to South Africa, India and beyond to Australia.

During the inter-war years development had also continued in routes from England to the Continent, and routes within the United Kingdom. A merger of three major airline companies was made in 1936 to form the **first British Airways**.

During the early months of the Second World War (1940) Imperial Airways and British Airways were amalgamated to form the **British Overseas Airways Corporation**.

In 1946 BOAC relinquished control of its European routes and two new corporations were formed, **British European Airways**, responsible for development of routes within Europe, and **British South American Airways**, responsible for development of routes in Central and South America. The latter was soon to be merged again with BOAC in 1949.

The post-war years saw great development in civil aviation by both BOAC and BEA. The commercial era had begun. In March 1950 the Handley Page Hermes began services from London to Accra. The Stratocruisers continued with great success on the North Atlantic route. In fact BOAC in 1950 earned for the first time in history £2 million in one month from all its services.

Further expansion in the '50s saw the development of more services with gas turbine and then jet aircraft providing shorter and more comfortable journeys for travellers.

Financially, the recession in the '60s almost had BOAC on its knees. The older aircraft had to go. In fact what got BOAC out of the mire was the increasingly successful freight and cargo industry, particularly on the North Atlantic run. By 1964 all round increases in load and traffic resulted in a significant improvement in revenue. Although this change in financial circumstances augured well for the future, it was not good enough for the government. Unprofitable routes like Washington and the South American services were scrapped. Sir Giles Guthrie was appointed Chairman and under his stewardship BOAC in 1965 was able to announce a profit of £7 million. However, interest payments had grown to such a size that a lot of money was written-off under the Air Corporations Act – £130 million no less. By 1970 BOAC had completed six years of record profit making and was able to wipe the slate clean financially as far as the government was concerned.

The wide-bodied generation of aircraft was appearing and 1970 saw the jumbos take to the skies. Meanwhile the Anglo-French Concorde was undergoing trials. The supersonic age was just round the corner.

In 1968 a committee recommended to the British Parliament the merger of BEA and BOAC. In 1971 the Civil Aviation Act provided for the formation of the British Airways Board to take over BOAC, BEA and any of their subsidiaries. Under the Air Corporation Dissolution Order of 1973, BOAC and BEA ceased to exist. In 1974 **British Airways** had arrived.

Like its predecessors, it had its eyes on the future. Already in its early years it had introduced and developed the world's first supersonic airline service.

In a world that has seen a six-fold increase in normal aircraft speeds (thirteen and a half for supersonic travel) and a seven-fold increase in aircraft size, BOAC and BEA had each been leaders and pioneers of aircraft development in their respective spheres of long and short haul travel. Their expertise continues in the British Airways of today.


## SIGNIFICANT YEARS

**1940**      1 April, the first day of BOAC operations.

**1941**      BOEING 314 flew the rugged North Atlantic route for five years, braving difficult wartime conditions, the Ferry Service.

During the war BOAC flew over hostile territory to Sweden with Allied personnel, returning with sets of important ball bearings.

**1943**      The first BOAC air hostess, Rosamond Gilmour. She flew in a 200mph Frobisher from Whitchurch in Somerset to Rineanna Airport, Shannon. This was a shuttle service connecting with the BOAC flying-boat operations from nearby Foynes.

**1945**      England–Australia route was re-opened using Lancastrians (modified Lancaster bombers) to give a weekly service. The aircraft cruised at 174mph taking three days from London to Sydney and carrying up to nine passengers.

Hiltons (ex-Halifax bombers) went to Cairo and West Africa, Avro Yorks (military transports) to India and South Africa and the Hythe flying-boats (Sunderland 3s) to Australia. Avro Yorks carried twenty-one passengers or twelve if sleeping berths were required.

**1946**      Operations began in February 1946 when BOAC's No.1 Line, DC 3 Dakotas based at Whitchurch, started regular services for the BEA Division from Northolt to Paris, Amsterdam, Brussels, Madrid, Lisbon, Stockholm and Helsinki. The network was later extended to Oslo, Copenhagen, Gibraltar, Rome and Athens. This remained unchanged until the creation of BEA in August 1946. Additional routes to Prague, Berlin, Vienna, Zurich and Ankara were implemented.

In its first year of operation the BEA fleet consisted of DH 89s, Avro 19s (Ansons) and DC 3s. Expansion into Europe was made with the Viking, an aircraft developed from the Wellington bomber of the Second World War. The Viking was faster than the DC 3 Dakota and was the main aircraft throughout Europe. The first version had twenty-one seats and began on the London-Copenhagen route in 1946. The Viking suffered from icing problems and was withdrawn, only to re-emerge in a Mark 2 version in 1947 called the Admiral Class Viking and carrying thirty-eight people.

British South American Airways made its first flight to South America, Buenos Aires-Santiago-Lima. BSAA at first used Yorks and Lancastrians.

Lockheed Constellation 049s, fondly called 'Connies', took over the London-New York from the Boeing 314s carrying up to thirty-eight passengers on a nineteen and a half-hour journey, thus establishing the first British commercial air service between London and New York.

**1947**    BEA Helicopter Unit operated a service between Heathrow and Waterloo Heliport using the Westland-Sikorsky WS 55. This service was still operating in 1956.

**1948**    BEA supervised the civil aircraft, which took part in the Berlin Airlift (see Chapter 7).

The first BOAC Lockheed Constellation 749 service left London Airport on 1 December for the 24,000-mile journey to Australia and return. This service was operated in conjunction with its partner Qantas Empire Airways. The journey took three days. By July 1956 Constellation had done 1,000 flights, the 049 carrying thirty-eight passengers, and the 749, sixty passengers.

The BOAC Flying-Boat Base was transferred from Poole to Southampton and Solent flying-boats entered service carrying up to thirty passengers to Africa.

**1949**    The Airways Corporation Act became law, merging BSAA with BOAC.

BOAC introduced the Argonaut, powered with Rolls-Royce Merlin piston engines. This aircraft was one of the most successful post-war designs. It had wide vision windows and chairs amply spaced for legroom. The broad central aisle connected the cabins and there was a six-seat Cocktail Lounge at the rear. The Argonauts did the long Eastern run, London-Tokyo.

Boeing 377 Stratocruisers began flying London–New York in nineteen and a half hours, carrying eighty-one passengers. Special features of the twin-decked aircraft were the large bar lounge and the full-length sleeping berths.

**1950**    First BEA scheduled service operated from London Airport. This was a London to Paris Viking service. The world's first gas turbine powered service was inaugurated by a BEA flight from Northolt to Le Bourget in a Vickers V630 Viscount prototype.

**1951**    The Comet 1 prototype flights began. When scheduled service began later, the Comet cruised at 490mph with smoothness and ease. In flight the absence of any sign of propellers, the quietness and freedom from vibration gave one the illusion of being fixed in, rather than travelling through space. Comet 1s took over the long Eastern route, the 10,400-mile London-Tokyo route, reducing by fifty hours the Argonaut time (eighty-six hours from London on the Argonaut, thirty-three hours fifteen on the Comet).

**1952**    BOAC introduced the world's first pure jet scheduled passenger service with Comets, carrying between thirty-six and forty-four passengers London to Johannesburg.

BEA began Elizabethan flights using the De Havilland Ambassador. Each aircraft took the name of a prominent Elizabethan and carried up to forty-seven passengers. BEA's first Royal Flight took HRH the Duke of Edinburgh to Malta in an Elizabethan.

Tourist fares were introduced on the Atlantic route.

**1953** BEA routes in Europe introduced Tourist fares.

The Viscount 701 Turbo-Propeller, carrying up to forty-seven passengers for BEA, cruised at 316mph over a range of 1,000 miles and began the world's first fully sustained turbo powered service in April.

**1954** After two Comet 1 disasters (Elba and Naples) Comets were withdrawn from service. The Hermes 4 (forty passengers) was recommissioned for the Eastern route. Stratocruisers, Constellations and Argonauts continued to earn their keep. Delays in the delivery of Bristol Britannia 102s Propeller-Turbines meant BOAC ordered the Douglas DC7C (92 passengers) as a stop-gap on the lucrative London–New York route

**1955** BEA moved its main base from Northolt to Heathrow.

**1956** By this time BEA was using larger Viscounts, the 802 and 806. The first Douglas DC7C was handed over to BOAC, who also signed a contract for fifteen Rolls-Royce Conway powered Boeing 707 Pure-Jet airliners, the first of the long-range, high-capacity jet generation.

**1957** BOAC introduced the world's first gas-turbine service to the North Atlantic route, the Bristol Britannia 312 almost halving the nearly twenty hours of the Stratocruisers.

**1958** A redesigned and strengthened Comet 4 ushered in the world's first transatlantic pure jet commercial service.

BOAC ordered the standard Vickers VC10 jet airliner.

BEA ordered six De Havilland Comet 4Bs.

**1959** BOAC began the first Round the World Service.

**1960** BOAC re-opened the South American route with the Comet 4s.

To meet competition in the European market, BEA used a short haul version of the Comet 4 (B) while waiting for the specially designed Trijet, the DH121, called Trident by BEA.

BOAC began transatlantic services with the Boeing 707s and signed a contract with BAC for ten Super VC 10s. The Comet 4s were retired from this service.

The jet age of mass travel had arrived and the older aircraft, such as the Argonauts, the Connies and the Stratocruisers and even the Comets, were phased out.

**1962** BOAC booked delivery positions for the Supersonic BAC – AeroSpatiale Concorde (see Chapter 11).

**1964** Trident's first BEA passenger flight was from London to Copenhagen. It began to dominate the European skies with its three jet engines at the rear, a large passenger cabin, and a cruising speed of 600mph and a range of 1,000 miles.

**1965** Super VC10s, carrying 139 passengers, began service across the Atlantic.

**1966** BOAC ordered six Boeing 747s 'jumbo jet' airliners, which carried up to 365 passengers cruising at about 600mph (the 707s had carried 146).

BOAC became the first airline to operate two distinct around the world routes. The South Pacific service opened for BOAC when a Boeing 707 left London for Sydney via New York, San Francisco, Honolulu and Fiji, linking passengers to the Sydney–London service. The author, one of the few Australian stewardesses with BOAC at that time, was one of the crew and felt that round the world runs were the crème de la crème of one's flying career.

By now BEA was developing the tourist market. British Air Services incorporated the smaller UK air services to provide a feeder service into the European network.

**1968**    BEA took delivery of fifteen Trident 2s and the first BAC Super 1-11 aircraft, which carried more than ninety passengers each. The later Trident 3 accommodated 135.

**1969**    The London-Anchorage-Tokyo polar route was inaugurated with a Boeing 707 – 336c.

**1970**    BEA received the Queen's Award to Industry for pioneering automatic landing for civil aircraft.

BEA Air Tours' first commercial flight from Gatwick to Palma. It was set up to develop group travel and package deals linked to car hire and hotels etc.

The Boeing 707 Trans-Siberian route, London–Moscow–Tokyo, was opened.

**1971**    First commercial flight of Trident 3 was made from London to Paris.

The Boeing 747 was introduced by BOAC on the North Atlantic routes.

**1972**    Steps were taken towards the merger of BOAC and BEA to form British Airways.

A BEA Trident landing at Heathrow in Category III A weather conditions became the first aircraft in the world on an international scheduled flight to do so was a first in international travel.

BEA and BOAC dissolved under the Air Corporations (Dissolution) Order.

British Airways.

**1975**    BA introduced the Lockheed TriStar on the European routes. London–Malaga, Brussels Palma, Paris run.

BA and Air New Zealand initiated a joint DC10 London–Los Angeles–Auckland service

**1976**    The world's first supersonic flights were made by Concorde, for British Airways on the London to Bahrain run, for Air France, from Paris to Rio de Janeiro.

BA's first supersonic transatlantic service was by Concorde from London to Washington.

The Concorde service London–New York began as well as London to Singapore in association with Singapore Airlines. The latter service was suspended after three flights because of political difficulties. (1977)

**1980**    Deliveries began of a fleet of new Boeing 737-236s for use on British Airway's European and UK domestic services and by Gatwick-based British Air Tours.

## NOTES:

The Austrian physicist Ernest Mach gave his name to a measurement of speed, called a Mach number. Mach 1 is the speed of sound under the conditions the aircraft is flying. The speed of sound at sea level is 760mph, and at greater altitudes it is 660mph. The Boeing 707 is .81, the Boeing 747 normally flies at about Mach .85. The Concorde is twice the speed of sound at 2.2.

Passenger configurations for the above aircraft, particularly from the late '50s, were a moveable feature. For example numbers of first class affected totals. Some aircraft had a number of variants with different carrying abilities.

(Source: *Highways in the Air*, the Story of British Airways pub. by BA Public Relations. Pine & Co. Twickenham, 1979)

# Bibliography

## BOOKS

Barry, Kathleen M., *Femininity in Flight* (Duke University Press Durham & London, 2007)

Beaty, D., *The Water Jump - The Story of Atlantic Flight* (Secker & Warburg, 1976)

Bray, W., *The History of BOAC (1939–1974)* (Wessex Press, Camberley, 1975)

Brimson, S., *The World's Great Airlines* (Golden Press Bullion Books, Australia, 1989)

Cooper, B. (ed), *BOAC Book of Flight* (Parish, 1959)

Dobson, C. & Payne, R., *The Carlos Complex: A Pattern of Violence* (Hodder & Stoughton, London, 1977)

Fellows, J., *Snobs* (Weidenfield & Nicholson, London, 2004)

Frater, A., *Beyond the Blue Horizon* (William Heinemann, London, 1986)

Gallon, Roger C.C., *Tales of a Thousand and One Flights* (Personal Memoir)

Gallop, A., *Time Flies: Heathrow at 60* (Sutton Publishing, Gloucestershire, 2005)

Greenwood, J. (ed), *Milestones of Aviation: Smithsonian Institution National Air & Spec Museum* (Macmillan Publishing, New York, 1989)

Gwynn-Jones, T., *The Air Races* (Lansdowne Press, Sydney, 1983)

Hudson, K. & Pettifer, J., *Diamonds in the Sky* (Bodley Head & the British Broadcasting Corporation, London, 1979)

Iliffe, A., *From Little Ships to Comets* (Biddles of Guilford, Suffolk, 2001)

Jackson, A., *Can Anyone See Bermuda* (Cirrus Associates, Dorset, 1997)

Jackson, A., *Both Feet in the Air: An Airline Pilot's Story* (Terence Dalton Ltd, Suffolk, 1977)

Jackson, A., *Pathfinder Bennett Airman-Extraordinary* (Terrence Dalton Ltd, Suffolk, 1991)

Kerr, P., *Down to Earth* (Ebury Press, London, 1992)

Lovegrove, K., *Airline Identity, Design & Culture* (Laurence King Publishing, London, 2000)

Mackworth-Praed, B., *Aviation: The Pioneer Years* (Studio Editions, London, 1990)

Mc Robbie, a *Lifestyles* Signature, 1980

McRobbie, M., *Walking the Skies: The First 50 Years of Air Hostessing in Australia* (Published by Author, Victoria, 1986)

Milburn, Irene, *Runways to Adventure* (Robert Hale Ltd, London, 1960)

Morris, J. (intro), *Riding the Skies* (Bloomsbury Publishing, London, 1989)

Munson, K., *Pictorial History of BOAC and Imperial Airways* Ian Allan, 1970)

Omella Johanna & Waldock Michael, *Come Fly With Us* (Collectors Press Inc., Portland, Oregon, 2006)

Orlebar, C., *The Concorde Story* (Osprey Publishing, Oxford, 1986)

Ottoway, Susan & Ian, *Fly with the Stars* (Sutton Publishing, Stroud, 2007)

Ottoway, Susan, *Fire Over Heathrow* (Pen & Sword South Yorkshire, 2008)

Penrose, H., *Wings Across the World* (Cassell Ltd, London, 1980)

Quinn, T., *Wings Over the World: Tales from the Golden Age of Travel* (Aurum Press Ltd, London, 2003)

Raynor, J., *Star Dust Falling* (Transworld Publishing Doubleday, 2002)

Stackhouse, J., *The Longest Hop* (Focus Publishing, Edgecliffe, NSW, 1997)

Thomas, G. & Forbes-Smith, C., *British Airways Flight Paths* (Aerospace Technical Publications International Pty Ltd, Western Australia, 2004)

Tickell, J. (ed), *Wings on My Suitcase* (Allan Wingate, London, 1958)

Wall, R., *Airliners* (Quantam Publishing, London, 2003)

Wall, R., *Airlines A Stunning Visual History of Air Travel* (Quantum Books, London, 2003)

Witcomb, N., *Up Here and Down There (*Pub by author, printed by Gillingham Printers, Adelaide, 1986

Woods, Eric (Timber) *From Flying Boats to Flying Jets* (Airlife Publishing Ltd, Shrewsbury, 1997)

*Highways in the Air. The Story of British Airways* (British Airways Publication, 1979)

## OTHER SOURCES

March *Aeroplane* 2001

*Clipped Wings* Quarterly, summer 2004

Air Transport and Travel Industry Training Board

*BOAC Review*, April 1964; November 1966; July 1956; 1958

*BOAC News*, December 1967; October 1968; 6 November 1970

*British Airways News*, October 1976 No.146; 1976 No.149; 1977 No.175; March 1974; August 1984; December 1989; January 1993; 1999; August 2000; Concorde Special October 2003; March 1981

*Esso Air World*, November 1972

*Touchdown*, autumn 2003; summer 2004

A Look at BOAC Pub. BOAC Air Terminal London

BEA Stewardess Grooming Handbook, 1966

*Daily Sketch*, February 1964

*The Honolulu Advertiser*, 22 November 1967

*The Times*, 9 April 1968

*Daily Mail*, 9 April 1968; September 1975; 13 March 1981; April 1987; 15 February 1997; 24 October 2003

*Daily Mail* weekend magazine, August 1996

*Daily Mirror*, 9 May 1955

*The Observer*, 18 June 1967

*Telegraph Magazine*, 1985

*Evening Standard*, 20 November 1952

*The Mail on Sunday*, July 1999

*YOU*, July 2002

*USA Today*, 7 November 1983

*Manchester Evening News*, 1958

*The Scotsman*, Wednesday 22 January 1986

*The Sunday Telegraph*, April 1994; 16 November 1980

*The Sunday Telegraph* magazine, 28 April 1996

*The Daily Telegraph*, 24 January 2005

*The Weekend Australian*, 3-4 April 2004

Three BBC Tapes, BBC, London

*The Independent*, 21 May 2005

*Joan Patricia Nourse Air Hostess Number 1 Charles Reid World Digest*, July 52

*Jungle Telegraph* Vol.1 No.5 1951

*Incentive* April 1968 Pub BOAC Air Terminal Victoria

*BOAC Cabin Crew Bulletin* Nos 31 summer 1972, No.19 March 1969. No.20 June 1969, No.30 1972, Year 32 72/73

Princess Tina, February 1970
*Speedbird*: The staff magazine for BOAC April 1974
British Airways Overseas Division Cabin Crew Newsletter February 1976
British Airways Cabin Crew Newsletter February 1977
Airline,Ship&Catering ONBOARD SERVICES May 1989
BOAC BRATS October 2001 Newsletter

The author has tried her best to establish the source of the material used in this book and would happily redress any omission that subsequently comes to light for future editions. Every effort has been made to contact copyright holders. If there are any errors or omissions we apologise to those concerned, and ask that they contact her via the publisher so that we can correct such oversights as soon as possible.

# Index

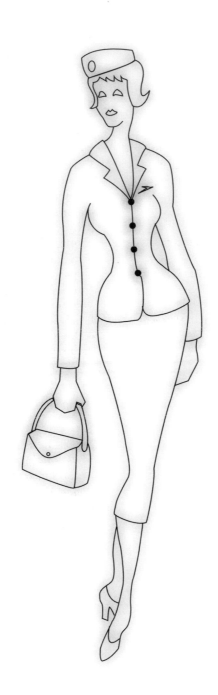